	a	u	o
ky	きゃ kya	きゅ kyu	きょ kyo
sh	しゃ sha	しゅ shu	しょ sho
ch	ちゃ cha	ちゅ chu	ちょ cho
ny	にゃ nya	にゅ nyu	にょ nyo
hy	ひゃ hya	ひゅ hyu	ひょ hyo
my	みゃ mya	みゅ myu	みょ myo
ry	りゃ rya	りゅ ryu	りょ ryo
gy	ぎゃ gya	ぎゅ gyu	ぎょ gyo
j	じゃ ja	じゅ ju	じょ jo
by	びゃ bya	びゅ byu	びょ byo
py	ぴゃ pya	ぴゅ pyu	ぴょ pyo

初級日本語

〔げんき〕

AN INTEGRATED COURSE IN
ELEMENTARY JAPANESE

GENKI

SECOND EDITION

げんき

〔第2版〕

I

Eri Banno　坂野永理
Yoko Ikeda　池田庸子
Yutaka Ohno　大野裕
Chikako Shinagawa　品川恭子
Kyoko Tokashiki　渡嘉敷恭子

the japan times

付属ディスクについて
付属のディスクには、MP3 形式のデジタル音声ファイルが収録されています。
コンピューターやデジタルオーディオ機器で再生してください。
CD プレーヤーでは再生できませんので、ご注意ください。

Note on the accompanying disk
The disk that comes with this book contains digital audio files in MP3 format.
The files can be played on computers or digital audio players, but not on CD players.

初級日本語 げんき I
1999 年 5 月 20 日　初版発行
2011 年 3 月 20 日　第 2 版発行
2019 年 1 月 20 日　第 57 刷発行
著　　者：坂野永理・池田庸子・大野裕・品川恭子・渡嘉敷恭子
発行者：堤丈晴
発行所：株式会社 ジャパンタイムズ
　　　　〒 102-0082 東京都千代田区一番町 2-2
　　　　一番町第二 TG ビル 2F
　　　　電話　(050)3646-9500（出版営業部）
ISBN978-4-7890-1440-3

First edition: May 1999
Second edition: March 2011
57th printing: January 2019

Illustrations: Noriko Udagawa and Reiko Maruyama
English translations and copyreading: 4M Associates, Inc., and Umes Corp.
Narrators: Miho Nagahori, Yumiko Muro, Tomoki Kusumi, Tsuyoshi Yokoyama,
　　　　　and Kit Pancoast Nagamura
Recordings: TBS Service, Inc.
Typesetting: guild
Cover art and editorial design: Nakayama Design Office
　　　　　　　　　　　Gin-o Nakayama and Akihito Kaneko
Printing: Nikkei Printing Inc.

Published by The Japan Times, Ltd.
2F Ichibancho Daini TG Bldg., 2-2 Ichibancho, Chiyoda-ku, Tokyo 102-0082, Japan
Phone: 050-3646-9500
Website: https://bookclub.japantimes.co.jp/
Genki-Online: http://genki.japantimes.co.jp/

ISBN978-4-7890-1440-3

Printed in Japan

はじめに

　本書は 1999 年に刊行された『初級日本語 げんき』の改訂版です。初版以来、多くの先生方や学習者の方々に使用していただき、増刷を重ねてきましたが、この度、改訂版を刊行することとなりました。

　『げんき』は 1999 年、日本語教師にとって「教えやすい」、学習者にとって「学びやすい」教科書を目指して、学習者のニーズ調査をもとに作成し、何度も試用しながら細部にわたる改訂を重ねた末に出版しました。もともと日本で日本語を学習する留学生を対象に作成した教材でしたが、その後、日本だけでなく海外でも広く使用されるようになりました。それに伴い、「もっと文化情報がほしい」「教科書に音声教材をつけてほしい」など、いろいろなご意見、ご要望が寄せられるようになりました。また、初版刊行から 10 年以上が経ち、語彙等にも改訂の必要が出てきていました。

　この改訂版では、『げんき』の特長である「教えやすさ」はそのままに、私たちの経験や皆様の声を反映させて、新しい内容の追加、改訂を行いました。改訂作業には 2 年の歳月を要しましたが、今までよりもさらに教えやすく学びやすい教材になったと自負しています。

　改訂版の作成にあたっては、『げんき』を使用してくださっている多くの先生方や学習者の方々の貴重なご意見が、大きな原動力となりました。心より感謝いたします。また、今や『げんき』のトレードマークになっているイラストを描いてくださった宇田川のり子さん、ジャパンタイムズの皆様、そしてだれよりも、初版作成時からずっと労を注いでくださったジャパンタイムズ出版局の関戸千明さんに、著者一同心より感謝いたします。

　この新しい『げんき』で、いっそう楽しく日本語を学んでいただけることを願っています。

2011 年 1 月　著者一同

Preface

This is a revised edition of the textbook *GENKI: An Integrated Course in Elementary Japanese*, which was published in 1999. Since it first came out, *GENKI* has become widely used by teachers and students of Japanese and has gone through numerous reprintings. Such wide acceptance led to the decision to publish this revised edition.

In 1999, our aim was to develop a textbook that teachers would find convenient and helpful, and one that students could easily use. We thus wrote the book based on a survey of students' needs and refined it through many test-teaching situations. Originally meant as a text for foreign students studying in Japan, *GENKI* gained popularity among those studying in other countries as well. As use increased, we began to hear from those who wanted "more information on culture" and "audio aids appended to the text." It's also been more than ten years since *GENKI* was originally published, and the passage of time has required revisions to vocabulary and expressions.

While retaining the ease-of-use quality for teachers, we have added new content and revisions that reflect our experiences and the voices of those who have used the text. The task of revision took two years to complete. We believe that this effort has resulted in a book that instructors and students will find even easier to use and learn from.

The opinions of the teachers and students who have used *GENKI* have been a major driving force in the preparation of this revised edition. We are truly grateful to those who have provided this input. The authors would also like to express their sincere appreciation to the following: Noriko Udagawa, our illustrator, whose work has become a *GENKI* trademark; the staff of The Japan Times; and particularly to Chiaki Sekido of the Publications Department of The Japan Times, who has worked tirelessly with us on this project since its inception.

It is our hope that students of the language will find additional pleasure in learning Japanese by using this new edition of *GENKI*.

The Authors
January 2011

初級日本語 ［げんき］ I

もくじ

会話・文法編
かい わ　ぶん ぽう へん

巻 末
　かん まつ

本書について

Ⅰ 対象とねらい

『初級日本語 げんき』は初めて日本語を学ぶ人のための教科書です。第Ⅰ巻・第Ⅱ巻の2冊、全23課で初級日本語の学習を修了します。大学生はもとより、高校生や社会人、日本語を独習しようとしている人も、効果的に日本語が習得できます。文法の説明などは英語で書いてあるので、英語がある程度わかることを前提としています。

『初級日本語 げんき』は総合教材として、日本語の四技能（聞く・話す・読む・書く）を伸ばし、総合的な日本語の能力を高めていくことを目標としています。正確に文を作ることができても流暢さがなかったり、流暢ではあっても簡単なことしか言えないということがないように、言語の習得の目標とすべき「正確さ」「流暢さ」「複雑さ」がバランスよく高められるように配慮してあります。

Ⅱ 改訂版について

今回の改訂版では、以下の点を中心に改訂を加えました。

1. Culture Noteの追加

学習者が日本に関する知識を得られるように、「会話・文法編」の各課に「Culture Note」という項目を新しく設け、日本文化や生活についての情報を提供しました。

2. 音声をテキスト・ワークブックそれぞれに付属

これまで別売としていた音声教材をMP3形式でテキストに付けるとともに、ワークブックで使用する「聞く練習」の音声はワークブックに付け、より使いやすくしました。また、テキスト「読み書き編」各課の読み教材も、今回新たに収録しました。

3. 語彙・表現の見直し

語彙や表現を細かく見直し、「カセットテープ」「LL」などあまり使われなくなったものは削除して、より使用頻度の高いものを入れました。

4. 文法・練習・読み物の改訂

「文法」では、各課で扱う文法項目に変更はありません。その中で、よりわかりやすくなるよう、細部にわたり加筆・修正しています。

また、形容詞・名詞文の否定形「～くありません／～じゃありません」と「～なくちゃいけ

ません」の2つの表現は、日常の場面でより使用されている「〜くないです／〜じゃないです」「〜なければいけません／〜なきゃいけません」に変更しました。

「練習」は、各文法項目に対して十分な練習ができるように、会話形式などのコミュニカティブな練習をさらに増やしました。また、読み書き編の読み物についても、内容が古くなった部分には変更を加え、日本の現状に合わせました。

Ⅲ テキストの構成

テキストは大きく「会話・文法編」「読み書き編」「巻末」から構成されています。以下、順番に説明します。

A▶会話・文法編

「会話・文法編」では、基本的な文法を学び、語彙を増やしながら、「話すこと」「聞くこと」について学習します。「会話・文法編」の各課は以下の部分から構成されています。

●会話

「会話」は、日本に来た留学生とその友人・家族を中心に展開し、学習者が日常生活で経験しそうなさまざまな場面から成っています。会話文を通して、学習者は「あいづち」などを含めた自然なやりとりに触れ、会話の中で文と文がどのようにつながっていくか、どのような部分が省略されたりするかなどを学ぶことができます。「会話」には、その課で学ぶ新しい学習項目が多く含まれているため、課の初めに学習者がこれを読むと非常に難しいと感じるかもしれません。これらの項目は練習を通して定着が図られるので、初めは難しくてもあまり心配しないようにしてください。

また、「会話」は付属の音声教材（MP3形式）で聞くことができます。学習者には、音声教材を聞いて、発音やイントネーションなどに気をつけながら、くり返して言う練習をすることを勧めます。

●単語

「単語」には、その課の「会話」と「練習」に出てくる新しい単語がまとめてあります。この中で、「会話」に出てくる単語には＊印が付けてあります。第1課と第2課では機能別に単語を提示し、第3課からは品詞別に提示してあります。また、巻末には全課の単語を収録した「さくいん」があります。

「単語」の中の言葉はその後の課でもくり返し出てきますから、学習者は毎日少しずつ覚えるようにしたほうがいいでしょう。付属の音声教材には単語とその英語訳が入っていますか

ら、それを聞きながら覚えることもできます。第3課から、単語には漢字を併記してあります
が、この漢字は覚える必要はありません。

　なお、このテキストでは語のアクセント（拍の高低）を示していません。日本語のアクセン
トは地域差や個人差（世代間の差など）が激しい上に、語形変化や単語の連結などによる変化
も複雑です。ですから、単語のアクセントにはあまり神経質になる必要はありません。

●文法

　文法説明は、独習している人も容易に理解できるように、説明の平易さを心がけました。ま
た、教室で学んでいる学習者はあらかじめ文法説明を読んでから授業に臨んでください。

　後の「練習」で取りあげられている項目はすべて「文法」の中で説明してあります。練習は
しないが説明が必要な文法や語彙については、「文法」の最後の「表現ノート」に随時まとめ
てあります。

●練習

　「練習」は、各学習項目に関して基本練習から応用練習へと段階的に配列してあり、学習者
がこれらの練習を順番にこなしていくことによって、無理なく日本語が習得できるように配慮
してあります。

　答えが一つに決められるような基本練習は付属の音声教材にも録音されており、 🔊 の印が
ついています。音声教材には解答も録音されていますから、学習者は各自で自習することが可
能です。

　また、「練習」の最後には「まとめの練習」があります。これは複数の学習項目を組み合わ
せた練習や「会話」を応用して別の会話を作る練習など、その課の仕上げとなる練習です。

●Culture Note

　各課に「Culture Note」というコラムを設け、日本の文化や生活習慣などについて説明して
います。「家族の呼び方」など言語に密接に関連した事項から、「日本の気候」など生活に密着
した情報まで、幅広い分野が扱われています。学習者は、この説明を出発点にして、インター
ネットで情報収集をしたり、身近な日本人と話したりして、理解を深めていくことが期待され
ます。

●Useful Expressions

　課の最後に必要に応じて、テーマごとに単語や表現を集めた「Useful Expressions」を設け
てあります。ここには、第1課の「じかん・とし」のようにその課のトピックに関連した表現や、
第10課の「駅で」のように場面ごとに使われる表現をまとめました。これらの単語も、巻末の
「さくいん」に載せてあります。

B ▶ 読み書き編

「読み書き編」では、日本語の文字を学び、文章を読んだり書いたりすることによって、読解力と書く力を伸ばします。第1課でひらがな、第2課でカタカナを学習した後、第3課以降で漢字を学習します。第3課以降の各課は、以下のような構成です。

● 漢字表

漢字表には、その課で学ぶ新出漢字が掲載されています。各課で約15の漢字を学びますが、一度に覚えるには無理があるので、毎日少しずつ覚えていくようにしてください。漢字表は以下のようになっています。

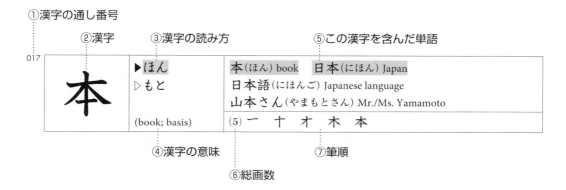

③に示された漢字の読み方で、▶は「音読み」、つまり昔の中国語の発音を輸入したものであることを示します。▷は「訓読み」、つまり日本語古来の読みです。音読みも訓読みも、単語の中で使われた時、音が変化する場合があります。（たとえば、「学」という漢字は「ガク」と読みますが、「学校」という単語の中では「ガッ」と読みます。）そのような派生的な読み方もこの部分に表記されています。

なお、漢字の中には多くの読み方を持っているものもありますが、漢字表には、初級レベルにふさわしい読みを中心に挙げています。

③と⑤で　　　の中に入っている読み方や単語は、その課で覚えるべきものです。一方、　　以外のものは参考として挙げたもので、覚えなくてもかまいません。

それぞれの漢字は、ワークブックの読み書き編の中に練習シートがありますので、テキストの漢字表に示された筆順を見ながら何度も練習してください。

● 練習

『げんきⅠ』には、漢字の練習、読解本文と内容についての質問、そして書く練習があります。漢字の練習は、漢字を分解してできる部品から漢字を再構築する問題や漢字から単語を作る問題など、さまざまな練習を通じて漢字に慣れていくことを目標としています。読解本文は、短

く、親しみやすいものを中心に構成しています。それまでに「会話・文法編」で学んだ文法や単語の知識が前提とされており、新出単語はその都度、単語表を掲載しています。練習の最後には、書く練習としての作文トピックが提示されています。

『げんきⅡ』には、読解本文と内容についての質問、そして書く練習があります。読解本文は、手紙、物語、エッセイ、広告など、さまざまな分野の日本語を取り上げています。その課までに学んだ単語や文法、漢字の知識が前提とされており、課を追うごとに、長さや難易度などが増していきます。新出単語も本文での出現順に掲載されています。練習の最後には、作文トピックが提示されています。

なお、今回の改訂版では、第Ⅰ巻・第Ⅱ巻とも、新たに読解本文も音声教材に収録しました。 🔊 のついているものは、付属の音声教材（MP3形式）で聞くことができます。

C▶巻末

第Ⅰ巻・第Ⅱ巻それぞれの巻末に「さくいん」を準備しました。一つは和英さくいんで、各課の単語表や Useful Expressions に掲載されている単語を五十音順に再録しました（「Culture Note」の語彙は含みません）。単語に付された数字は、その単語が導入された課の番号を示しています。英和さくいんでは、各課の単語が訳語のアルファベット順に再録されています。今回の改訂版では、各動詞に [ru] [u] [irr.] の記号を表示して、どのグループに属する動詞かわかるようにしました。

その他に、全県名リスト付きの日本地図、および数字と助数詞の音の変化をまとめた表と動詞の活用表を掲載しました。

Ⅳ 表記と書体について

本文は基本的に、漢字仮名交じりで表記しています。漢字表記は、基本的に常用漢字表に従いましたが、常用漢字に含まれている漢字でも、初級の学習者には無縁であるようなものは、ひらがな表記にしてあります。

また、「会話・文法編」のみを学習することも可能なように、「会話・文法編」では漢字にはすべてふりがなが振ってあります。

ただし、「会話・文法編」冒頭の「あいさつ」と第1課、第2課は、学習者の負担を軽減し自習を容易にするため、ひらがな・カタカナ表記とし、ローマ字を併記しました。このローマ字併記はあくまでも補助的なものですから、最初から頼りすぎないように心がけてください。ひらがなは「読み書き編」の第1課で、カタカナは第2課で、それぞれ学習します。

なお、「読み書き編」では、漢字を第3課以降に学習していきますが、学習の定着が図れるよう、既習の漢字にはふりがなが振ってありません。

　本文の日本語は、ほとんどが「教科書体」の書体で組まれています。教科書体は手書き文字に近い書体ですから、学習者は自分が書く文字のモデルとすることができます。ただし、実際に印刷された日本語文では、さまざまな書体を見ることがあります。文字によっては、書体によってかなり形が異なります。特に離れた二つの線が筆づかいによって一つにつながる場合があるので、注意が必要です。

例：	教科書体	明朝体	ゴシック体	手書き文字
	さ	さ	さ	さ
	き	き	き	き
	り	り	り	り
	ら	ら	ら	ら
	こ	こ	こ	こ
	や	や	や	や

||| Introduction

Aim and purpose

GENKI: An Integrated Course in Elementary Japanese is a textbook for beginners in the study of the Japanese language. Students can complete the elementary-level study of Japanese in the 23 lessons of this text, which is divided into two volumes. The book is designed mainly for use in university courses, but is also effective for high school students and adults who are beginning to learn Japanese either at school or on their own. Hopefully, students will have at least a basic knowledge of English, because grammar explanations are given in English.

GENKI: An Integrated Course in Elementary Japanese is a comprehensive approach to developing the four basic language skills (listening, speaking, reading, and writing), which aims to cultivate overall Japanese-language ability. Emphasis has been placed on balancing accuracy, fluency, and complexity so that students using the material will not end up speaking accurately yet in a stilted manner, or fluently but employing only simple grammatical structures.

II Revised edition

The revised edition features changes in four major areas.

1. Addition of Culture Notes
Each lesson now contains a "Culture Note," which is designed to enhance students' knowledge of Japan through information on Japanese culture and daily life.

2. Audio material bundled with text and workbook
Audio aids, which had previously been sold separately, have now been added to the textbook and workbook in MP3 format. The addition of audio material for the workbook's "Listening Comprehension" exercises is especially convenient. We have also recorded the readings from the Reading and Writing section of the book.

3. Vocabulary and expressions
We rigorously reviewed the vocabulary and expressions to replace words, such as "cassette

tape" and "LL" that are no longer in common use, with words and phrases that students will encounter more frequently.

4. Grammar, practice and readings

While no changes were made to the grammatical topics introduced in each lesson, we supplemented the text and/or made the necessary corrections to make the material even easier to understand.

In the revised edition, we have replaced the negative forms of adjective and noun phrases *-ku arimasen/-ja arimasen* and *-nakucha ikemasen*, meaning "must," with the *-ku nai desu/ -ja nai desu* and *-nakereba ikemasen/-nakya ikemasen* forms, which are more commonly used in everyday life.

We also increased communicative practice material—mainly dialogues—so that students would be given sufficient opportunity to practice the grammar that they learn. Moreover, we have updated the readings in the Reading and Writing section to make them more relevant to the Japan of today.

Ⅲ Structure of the textbook

This textbook basically consists of three sections: Conversation and Grammar, Reading and Writing, and the Appendix. A detailed explanation of each part follows.

A ▶ Conversation and Grammar

The Conversation and Grammar section aims at improving students' speaking and listening abilities by having them learn basic grammar and by increasing their vocabulary. The Conversation and Grammar section of each lesson is organized as follows:

● Dialogue

The dialogues revolve around the lives of foreign students living in Japan and their friends and families, presenting various scenes that students are likely to face in their daily lives. By practicing natural expressions and *aizuchi* (responses that make conversations go smoothly), students are able to understand how sentences are connected and how some phrases are shortened in daily conversation. Because the Dialogue section of each lesson covers a lot of new grammar and vocabulary, students may feel it is too difficult to understand at first. Don't be overly concerned, however, because the grammar and vocabulary will gradually take root with practice.

Students can listen to dialogues on the accompanying audio aids (in MP3 format). Students are encouraged to practice regularly by listening to the audio and carefully noting pronunciation and intonation.

● Vocabulary

The Vocabulary section presents all the new words encountered in both the Dialogue and Practice sections of each lesson. Words that appear in the Dialogue are marked with an asterisk (*). Words are listed according to their function in Lessons 1 and 2, and by parts of speech in Lesson 3 and all subsequent lessons. In addition, all words presented in the text are also found in the Index at the end of each volume.

Words found in the Vocabulary section of each lesson appear frequently in subsequent lessons, thus encouraging students to learn little by little each day. The new words, along with their English translations, also appear in the audio material, which enables students to absorb through listening. Starting with Lesson 3, the Vocabulary section also gives the kanji rendering, but students are not required to memorize the kanji orthography.

This textbook does not indicate a word's accents. The accent of a Japanese word varies considerably, depending on region, the speaker's age (including the generation gap between speakers), the word's inflections, and its connection with other words in the sentence. Therefore, there is no need to be overly concerned about accent, but try to imitate as closely as possible the intonation heard on the accompanying audio aids.

● Grammar

Easy-to-understand grammar explanations are provided so that even those studying on their own can easily follow. Students at school should read the explanations before each class.

All grammar items covered in the lesson's Practice section are explained in the Grammar section. Grammar and vocabulary that require explanation but are not practiced are summarized in the Expression Notes section at the end of each Grammar section.

● Practice

For each grammar point covered, Practice sections provide drills that advance in stages from basic practice to application. The intent is to enable students to gain a grasp of Japanese naturally by completing the drills in the order presented.

Basic exercises that call for a single predetermined answer are marked with a and recorded with their answers on the audio aids, thus allowing students to practice and learn on their own.

The last part of the Practice section contains Review Exercises that help summarize what has been learned. For example, some exercises combine various topics covered in the lesson, while others require students to create dialogues by applying what was learned in the Dialogue section.

● Culture Note

We have integrated a Culture Note section into each lesson, where we explain aspects of the culture and everyday life of Japan. These notes cover a wide variety of topics, ranging from matters closely linked to language, such as kinship terms, to information deeply ingrained in daily life, such as the Japanese climate. Our hope is that these comments will serve as a springboard for students to deepen their understanding of Japanese culture even further by taking steps of their own, such as by gathering information from the Internet or by discussing the topics with their Japanese friends.

● Useful Expressions

When necessary, we include sections on Useful Expressions at the end of the lessons in order to present supplementary vocabulary and phrases. These sections list expressions that are related to the lesson's topic (as in "Time and Age" in Lesson 1) or to particular situations (as in "At the Station" in Lesson 10). The vocabulary introduced in Useful Expressions is also listed in the index of each volume.

B ▸ Reading and Writing

The Reading and Writing section aims to foster comprehension and writing ability through the study of Japanese characters and through practice in both reading and writing. After learning *hiragana* in Lesson 1 and *katakana* in Lesson 2, students begin studying kanji in Lesson 3. Each lesson after Lesson 3 is organized as follows:

● Kanji list

The list contains the new kanji introduced in each lesson. Students are exposed to about 15 new characters in each lesson. Since it is probably not feasible to learn all of these at once, we encourage students to tackle a few each day. We have formatted each kanji list as follows.

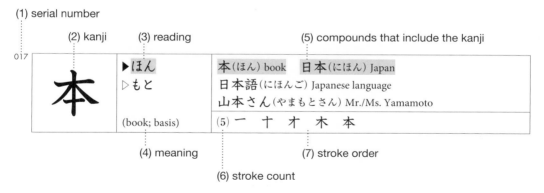

The ▶ mark appearing next to readings in item (3) indicates the *on-yomi*, or the reading of the character that was imported from China. The ▷ mark indicates the *kun-yomi*, or the native Japanese reading. The sound of *on-yomi* and *kun-yomi* may change when the kanji is used in certain words. For example, the ordinary pronunciation of 学 is *gaku*, but this becomes *gak* when the kanji is used in the word 学校 (*gakkoo*). Such derivative readings are also included in the readings section.

Although some kanji have many readings, we include principally those readings that are appropriate for an elementary level course.

Readings and words that are shaded should be memorized. The others are for reference, so students don't need to memorize them. The Reading and Writing section of the workbook includes practice sheets for the kanji learned in each lesson. Students should practice writing the kanji repeatedly, following the stroke order shown on the kanji list in the textbook.

● **Practice**

GENKI I consists of kanji practice, readings for comprehension, questions about the content of the readings, and writing practice. Kanji practice is aimed at getting students accustomed to kanji through practice in various forms, such as reconstructing kanji from their component parts or making new words by combining kanji. Readings for comprehension are generally short and deal with subjects familiar to the students. They assume knowledge of the vocabulary and grammar that the student has learned in the Conversation and Grammar section. New words that appear in the readings are listed. At the end of each Practice section, we suggest topics for students to write on.

GENKI II contains readings for comprehension, questions about the content of the readings, and writing practice. The readings introduce Japanese as it is used in a variety of areas, ranging from letters and fables to essays and advertisements. They assume knowledge of the vocabulary and grammar that the student has encountered in the lesson so far, and with each lesson the readings become longer and more difficult. New words in the readings are listed in the order in which they appear. At the end of each Practice section, we suggest topics for students to write on.

We provide recordings of these readings in both Volumes I and II of the revised edition. These are denoted by a 🔊 mark. Students can listen to them through the accompanying audio aids (in MP3 format).

C ▶ Appendix

The Appendix of Volumes I and II contains an Index. The Japanese-English Index, in *hiragana* order, lists words and expressions from the Vocabulary and Useful Expression sections of each lesson (the index does not contain the vocabulary used in Culture Notes). The number next to a word indicates the lesson in which the word was introduced. In the English-Japanese Index, English equivalents to Japanese words are arranged in alphabetical order. In both indexes of this revised edition, verbs are indicated with [ru] [u] [irr.], to show which verb group they belong to.

Also included in the Appendix are a map of Japan with the names of all the prefectures, a table of changes in the sounds of numbers and counters, and a table of verb conjugations.

Ⅳ Orthography and font

The basic text is written in kanji and *hiragana*. In the case of kanji, we follow the official Joyo Kanji list. However, *hiragana* is used instead when the Joyo Kanji equivalent is deemed unnecessary for beginning students of Japanese.

The pronunciation of every kanji in the Conversation and Grammar section is indicated in *hiragana* so that this section can be studied alone. To lessen the burden on the students and allow them to study on their own, however, the "Greetings" unit and Lessons 1 and 2 are written in *hiragana* and *katakana*, alongside which the same statement is presented in romanization. The romanizations are purely for supplemental purposes and students should avoid relying on them too much. Students study *hiragana* and *katakana* in Lessons 1 and 2, respectively, of the Reading and Writing section.

Students begin studying kanji in Lesson 3 of the Reading and Writing section. To encourage students to maintain a firm grasp of the kanji they have learned, the Reading and Writing section does not provide *hiragana* readings for kanji that have already been introduced.

The Japanese in the basic text is set mainly in the Textbook font, which resembles handwriting and serves as a good model for students. Students will encounter a variety of fonts used for Japanese materials, however, and should be aware that the shape of some characters differs considerably, depending on the font used. Note especially that in certain fonts two separate strokes may merge into a single stroke because they mimic the characters produced by a writing brush.

Example:	Textbook font	Mincho font	Gothic font	Handwriting
	さ	さ	さ	さ
	き	き	き	き
	り	り	り	り
	ら	ら	ら	ら
	こ	こ	こ	こ
	や	や	や	や

Japanese Writing System

There are three kinds of characters in Japanese: *hiragana*, *katakana*, and kanji.[1] All three characters can be seen in a single sentence.

テ レ ビ を 見 ま す。   *I watch television.*
katakana   *kanji*   *hiragana*

Hiragana and *katakana*, like the alphabet, represent sounds. As you can see in the above example, *hiragana* has a roundish shape and is used for conjugation endings, function words, and native Japanese words not covered by kanji. *Katakana*, which has rather straight lines, is normally used for writing loanwords and foreign names. For example, the Japanese word for "television" is written in *katakana* as テ レ ビ (*terebi*). Kanji, or Chinese characters, represent not just sounds but also meanings. Mostly, kanji are used for nouns and the stems of verbs and adjectives.

① Hiragana

1. Basic *Hiragana* Syllables

There are forty-six basic *hiragana* syllables, which are listed below. Once you memorize this chart, you will have the skill to transcribe all of the Japanese sounds.

あ *a*	い *i*	う *u*	え *e*	お *o*
か *ka*	き *ki*	く *ku*	け *ke*	こ *ko*
さ *sa*	し **shi*	す *su*	せ *se*	そ *so*
た *ta*	ち **chi*	つ **tsu*	て *te*	と *to*
な *na*	に *ni*	ぬ *nu*	ね *ne*	の *no*
は *ha*	ひ *hi*	ふ *fu*	へ *he*	ほ *ho*

---

[1] There is another writing system called *rōmaji* (Roman letters) which is used for station names, signs, and so on.

ま *ma*	み *mi*	む *mu*	め *me*	も *mo*
や *ya*		ゆ *yu*		よ *yo*
ら *ra*	り *ri*	る *ru*	れ *re*	ろ *ro*
わ *wa*				を ****o*
ん *n*				

* The syllables し, ち, つ, and ふ are romanized as *shi*, *chi*, *tsu*, and *fu*, respectively, to closely resemble English pronunciation.
** を is also pronounced as "*wo*."

The romanization is given for general pronunciation reference.

2. *Hiragana* with Diacritical Marks

You can transcribe 23 additional sounds by adding diacritic marks. With a pair of short diagonal strokes (˝), the unvoiced consonants *k*, *s*, *t*, and *h* become voiced consonants *g*, *z*, *d*, and *b*, respectively. The consonant *h* changes to *p* with the addition of a small circle (˚).

が *ga*	ぎ *gi*	ぐ *gu*	げ *ge*	ご *go*
ざ *za*	じ *ji*	ず *zu*	ぜ *ze*	ぞ *zo*
だ *da*	*ぢ *ji*	*づ *zu*	で *de*	ど *do*
ば *ba*	び *bi*	ぶ *bu*	べ *be*	ぼ *bo*
ぱ *pa*	ぴ *pi*	ぷ *pu*	ぺ *pe*	ぽ *po*

* ぢ (*ji*) and づ (*zu*) are pronounced the same as じ (*ji*) and ず (*zu*), respectively, and have limited use.

3. Transcribing Contracted Sounds

Small や, ゆ, and よ follow after letters in the second column (*i*-vowel *hiragana*, except い) and are used to transcribe contracted sounds. The contracted sound represents a single syllable.

きゃ *kya*	きゅ *kyu*	きょ *kyo*
しゃ *sha*	しゅ *shu*	しょ *sho*
ちゃ *cha*	ちゅ *chu*	ちょ *cho*
にゃ *nya*	にゅ *nyu*	にょ *nyo*
ひゃ *hya*	ひゅ *hyu*	ひょ *hyo*
みゃ *mya*	みゅ *myu*	みょ *myo*
りゃ *rya*	りゅ *ryu*	りょ *ryo*

ぎゃ *gya*	ぎゅ *gyu*	ぎょ *gyo*
じゃ *ja*	じゅ *ju*	じょ *jo*

びゃ *bya*	びゅ *byu*	びょ *byo*
ぴゃ *pya*	ぴゅ *pyu*	ぴょ *pyo*

4. Transcribing Double Consonants

There is another small letter, っ, which is used when transcribing double consonants such as *tt* and *pp*.

Examples:　かった　*katta*　(won)　　cf. かた　*kata*　(shoulder)
　　　　　さっか　*sakka*　(writer)
　　　　　はっぱ　*happa*　(leaf)
　　　　　ざっし　*zasshi*　(magazine)

Note double consonant *n*'s as in *sannen* (three years) are written with ん + a *hiragana* with an initial *n* sound (な, に, ぬ, ね, a s nd の).

Examples:　さんねん　*sannen*　(three years)
　　　　　あんない　*annai*　(guide)

5. Other Issues Relating to Transcription and Pronunciation

A. Long Vowels

When the same vowel is placed one right after the other, the pronunciation of the vowel becomes about twice as long as the single vowel. Be sure to hold the sound long enough, because the length of the vowel can change one word to another.

aa	おばあさん	*obaasan*	(grandmother)	cf. おばさん	*obasan*	(aunt)
ii	おじいさん	*ojiisan*	(grandfather)	cf. おじさん	*ojisan*	(uncle)
uu	すうじ	*suuji*	(number)			

ee   The long *ee* sound is usually transcribed by adding an い to an *e*-vowel *hiragana*. There are a few words, however, in which え is used instead of い.

    えいが　　*eega*　　(movie)
    おねえさん　*oneesan*　(big sister)

oo   The long *oo* sound is in most cases transcribed by adding an う to an *o*-vowel *hiragana*. There are, however, words in which the long vowel is transcribed with an お, for historical reasons.

    ほうりつ　　*hooritsu*　(law)
    とお　　　　*too*　　　(ten)

B. Pronunciation of ん

ん "*n*" is treated like a full syllable, in terms of length. Its pronunciation varies, however, depending on the sound that follows it. Japanese speakers are normally not aware of the different sound values of ん. Therefore, you do not need to worry too much about its pronunciation.[2]

C. Vowels to Be Dropped

The vowels *i* and *u* are sometimes dropped when placed between voiceless consonants (*k*, *s*, *t*, *p*, and *h*), or at the end of an utterance preceded by voiceless consonants.

Example:　すきです　*s(u)kides(u)*　(I like it.)

D. Accent in the Japanese Language

Japanese has pitch accent: all syllables are pronounced basically either in high or low pitch. Unlike English stress accent in which stressed syllables tend to be pronounced longer and louder, in Japanese each syllable is pronounced approximately in equal length and stress. The pitch patterns in Japanese vary greatly, depending on the region of the country.

---

[2] One variety of the ん pronunciation merits discussing here. When it is followed by a vowel or at the end of an utterance, ん indicates that the preceding vowel is long and nasalized. (Nasalized vowels are shown here with a tilde above vowel letters. You hear nasalized vowels in French words such as "bon," or the English interjection "uh-uh," as in "no.")
    ex. れんあい　*rēai* (romance)　　ほん　*hõ* (book)
Followed by *n*, *t*, *d*, *s*, and *z* sounds, ん is pronounced as "n."　ex. おんな　*onna*　(woman)
Followed by *m*, *p*, and *b* sounds, ん is pronounced as "m."　ex. さんぽ　*sampo*　(stroll)
Followed by *k* and *g* sounds, ん is pronounced as "ng" as in "song."　ex. まんが　*maṇga*　(comics)

Examples: あさ $\underset{sa}{\overset{a}{\dotsb}}$ (morning)

なまえ $\underset{na}{\overset{ma\ e}{\dotsb}}$ (name)

たかい $\underset{ta\quad i}{\overset{ka}{\dotsb}}$ (high)

Ⅱ **K a t a k a n a**

ア *a*	イ *i*	ウ *u*	エ *e*	オ *o*
カ *ka*	キ *ki*	ク *ku*	ケ *ke*	コ *ko*
サ *sa*	シ **shi*	ス *su*	セ *se*	ソ *so*
タ *ta*	チ **chi*	ツ **tsu*	テ *te*	ト *to*
ナ *na*	ニ *ni*	ヌ *nu*	ネ *ne*	ノ *no*
ハ *ha*	ヒ *hi*	フ *fu*	ヘ *he*	ホ *ho*
マ *ma*	ミ *mi*	ム *mu*	メ *me*	モ *mo*
ヤ *ya*		ユ *yu*		ヨ *yo*
ラ *ra*	リ *ri*	ル *ru*	レ *re*	ロ *ro*
ワ *wa*				ヲ *o*

ン *n*				

*The syllables シ, チ, ツ, and フ are romanized as *shi*, *chi*, *tsu*, and *fu*, respectively, to closely resemble English pronunciation.

ガ *ga*	ギ *gi*	グ *gu*	ゲ *ge*	ゴ *go*
ザ *za*	ジ *ji*	ズ *zu*	ゼ *ze*	ゾ *zo*

ダ *da*	*チ *ji*	*ヅ *zu*	デ *de*	ド *do*
バ *ba*	ビ *bi*	ブ *bu*	ベ *be*	ボ *bo*
パ *pa*	ピ *pi*	プ *pu*	ペ *pe*	ポ *po*

*チ (*ji*) and ヅ (*zu*) are pronounced the same as ジ (*ji*) and ズ (*zu*), respectively, and have limited use.

キャ *kya*	キュ *kyu*	キョ *kyo*
シャ *sha*	シュ *shu*	ショ *sho*
チャ *cha*	チュ *chu*	チョ *cho*
ニャ *nya*	ニュ *nyu*	ニョ *nyo*
ヒャ *hya*	ヒュ *hyu*	ヒョ *hyo*
ミャ *mya*	ミュ *myu*	ミョ *myo*
リャ *rya*	リュ *ryu*	リョ *ryo*

ギャ *gya*	ギュ *gyu*	ギョ *gyo*
ジャ *ja*	ジュ *ju*	ジョ *jo*

ビャ *bya*	ビュ *byu*	ビョ *byo*
ピャ *pya*	ピュ *pyu*	ピョ *pyo*

The pronunciation of *katakana* and its combinations are the same as those of *hiragana*, except for the following points.

(1) The long vowels are written with ー .

Examples:　カー　　*kaa*　　(car)　　　　ケーキ　*keeki*　(cake)
　　　　　　スキー　*sukii*　　(ski)　　　　　ボール　*booru*　(ball)
　　　　　　スーツ　*suutsu*　(suit)

When you write vertically, the ー mark needs to be written vertically also.

Example:　　　　　　　　ボ
　　　ボール　→　　　｜
　　　　　　　　　　　ル

(2) Additional combinations with small vowel letters are used to transcribe foreign sounds which originally did not exist in Japanese.

Examples:	ウィ	ハロウィーン	*harowiin*	(Halloween)
	ウェ	ハイウェイ	*haiwee*	(highway)
	ウォ	ミネラルウォーター	*mineraruwootaa*	(mineral water)
	シェ	シェフ	*shefu*	(chef)
	ジェ	ジェームス	*jeemusu*	(James)
	チェ	チェック	*chekku*	(check)
	ファ	ファッション	*fasshon*	(fashion)
	フィ	フィリピン	*firipin*	(Philippine)
	フェ	カフェ	*kafe*	(cafe)
	フォ	フォーク	*fooku*	(fork)
	ティ	パーティー	*paatii*	(party)
	ディ	ディズニーランド	*Dizuniirando*	(Disneyland)
	デュ	デュエット	*dyuetto*	(duet)

(3) The sound "v" is sometimes written with ヴ. For example, the word "Venus" is sometimes written as ビーナス or ヴィーナス.

ⅢＫａｎｊｉ

Kanji are Chinese characters which were introduced to Japan more than 1,500 years ago when the Japanese language did not have a writing system. *Hiragana* and *katakana* evolved later in Japan based on the simplified Chinese characters.

Kanji represents both meanings and sounds. Most kanji possess multiple readings, which are divided into two types: *on-yomi* (Chinese readings) and *kun-yomi* (Japanese readings). *On-yomi* is derived from the pronunciations used in China. Some kanji have more than one *on-yomi* due to temporal and regional variances in the Chinese pronunciation. *Kun-yomi* are Japanese readings. When people started to use kanji to write native Japanese words, Japanese readings (*kun-yomi*) were added to kanji.

By the time of high school graduation, Japanese are expected to know 2,136 kanji (called Joyo kanji), which are designated by the Ministry of Education as commonly used kanji. A total of 1,006 kanji are taught at the elementary school level, and most of the remainder are taught in junior high school.

There are roughly four types of kanji based on their formation.

(1) Pictograms

Some kanji are made from pictures:

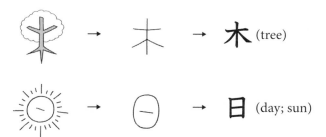

木 (tree)

日 (day; sun)

(2) Simple ideograms

Some kanji are made of dots and lines to represent numbers or abstract concepts.

三 → 三 (three)　　　•́ → 上 (up)

(3) Compound ideograms

Some kanji are made from the combination of two or more kanji.

日 (day; sun) + 月 (moon) → 明 (bright)

人 (person) + 木 (tree) → 休 (to rest)

(4) Phonetic-ideographic characters

Some kanji are made up of a meaning element and a sound element.

Meaning element	Sound element	On-yomi
氵 (water) +	青 *sei* (blue) →	清 *sei* (clean)
日 (day; sun) +	青 *sei* (blue) →	晴 *sei* (clear sky)

会話・文法編
かい　　わ　　ぶん　ぽう　へん
Conversation and Grammar Section

あいさつ

Greetings

おはよう。	Ohayoo.	Good morning.
おはよう ございます。	Ohayoo gozaimasu.	Good morning. (polite)
こんにちは。	Konnichiwa.	Good afternoon.
こんばんは。	Konbanwa.	Good evening.
さようなら。	Sayoonara.	Good-bye.
おやすみ (なさい)。	Oyasumi(nasai).	Good night.
ありがとう。	Arigatoo.	Thank you.
ありがとう ございます。	Arigatoo gozaimasu.	Thank you. (polite)
すみません。	Sumimasen.	Excuse me.; I'm sorry.
いいえ。	Iie.	No.; Not at all.
いってきます。	Ittekimasu.	I'll go and come back.
いってらっしゃい。	Itterasshai.	Please go and come back.
ただいま。	Tadaima.	I'm home.
おかえり (なさい)。	Okaeri(nasai).	Welcome home.
いただきます。	Itadakimasu.	Thank you for the meal. (before eating)
ごちそうさま (でした)。	Gochisoosama(deshita).	Thank you for the meal. (after eating)
はじめまして。	Hajimemashite.	How do you do?
よろしく おねがいします。	Yoroshiku onegaishimasu.	Nice to meet you.

表現ノート………1
ひょう げん

おはよう/ありがとう ▶ *Ohayoo* is used between friends and family members, while *ohayoo gozaimasu* is used between less intimate acquaintances, similarly with *arigatoo* and *arigatoo gozaimasu*. The rule of thumb is: if you are on the first-name basis with someone, go for the shorter versions. If you would address someone as Mr. or Ms., use the longer versions.

Ohayoo is the greeting used before noon, but some people use it in casual settings in the afternoon or even at night when they see their classmates or co-workers for the first time that day.

さようなら ▶ There are several good-bye expressions in Japanese, the choice among which depends on the degree of separation. *Sayoonara* indicates that the speaker does not expect to see the person spoken to before she "turns a page in her life"; not until a new day arrives, or until fate brings the two together again. It sounds dramatic and ritualistic, and its daily use is largely restricted to school children taking leave of their teachers.

じゃあ、また。　　Jaa, mata.
(between friends, expecting to see each other again fairly soon)

しつれいします。　　Shitsureeshimasu.
(taking leave from a professor's office, for example)

すみません ▶ *Sumimasen* means (1) "Excuse me," to get another person's atten-tion, (2) "I'm sorry," to apologize for the trouble you have caused, or (3) "Thank you," to show appreciation for what someone has done for you.

いいえ ▶ *Iie* is primarily "No," a negative reply to a question. In the dialogue, it is used to express the English phrase "Don't mention it," or "You're welcome," with which you point out that one is not required to feel obliged for what you have done for them.

いってらっしゃい/いってきます/ただいま/おかえりなさい ▶ *Ittekimasu* and *itterasshai* is a common exchange used at home when a family member leaves. The person who leaves says *ittekimasu*, which literally means "I will go and come back." And the family members respond with *itterasshai*, which means "Please go and come back."

Tadaima and *okaeri* are used when a person comes home. The person who ar-rives home says *tadaima* (I am home right now) to the family members, and they respond with *okaerinasai* (Welcome home).

れんしゅう Practice

Act out the following situations with your classmates.

1. You meet your host family for the first time. Greet them.

2. It is one o'clock in the afternoon. You see your neighbor Mr. Yamada.

3. You come to class in the morning. Greet your teacher. Greet your friends.

4. On a crowded train, you stepped on someone's foot.

5. You dropped your book. Someone picked it up for you.

6. It is eight o'clock at night. You happen to meet your teacher at the convenience store.

7. You are watching TV with your host family. It is time to go to sleep.

8. You are leaving home.

9. You have come back home.

10. You are going to start eating.

11. You have finished eating.

Culture Note

あいさつと おじぎ Greetings and Bowing
Aisatsu to ojigi

Japanese people greet each other by bowing, which has many other functions, such as expressing respect, gratitude, or apologies. There are different ways of bowing, ranging from a small nod of the head to a 45-degree bend at the waist. Generally, the longer and the deeper you bow, the more formal and respectful it appears to others.

Many Japanese tend to feel uncomfortable with physical contact, although handshaking is becoming quite common in business situations, especially those involving foreigners.

When meeting someone in a business situation for the first time, it is customary to exchange *meeshi* (business cards) with a small bow. Etiquette guides list a vast number of rules and pointers, but just remember that the important thing is to clearly show your respect when exchanging *meeshi*.

第1課 だい いっ か　L E S S O N ·················1

あたらしいともだち New Friends

かいわ D i a l o g u e

Mary, an international student who just arrived in Japan, talks to a Japanese student.

Ⅰ  K01-01/02

1　メアリー：　すみません。いま なんじ ですか。
　　Mearii　　　Sumimasen.　　Ima　 nanji desu ka.

2　たけし：　じゅうにじはんです。
　　Takeshi　　Juuniji han desu.

3　メアリー：　ありがとう ございます。
　　Mearii　　　Arigatoo　　 gozaimasu.

4　たけし：　いいえ。
　　Takeshi　　Iie.

 K01-03/04

1 たけし ： あの、 りゅうがくせいですか。
　Takeshi　　　　Ano,　　ryuugakusee desu ka.

2 メアリー ： ええ、 アリゾナだいがくの がくせいです。
　Mearii　　　　Ee,　　Arizona daigaku no　　gakusee desu.

3 たけし ： そうですか。せんこうは なんですか。
　Takeshi　　　　Soo desu ka.　　Senkoo wa　　nan desu ka.

4 メアリー ： にほんごです。いま にねんせいです。
　Mearii　　　　Nihongo desu.　　Ima　ninensee desu.

Ⅰ

Mary: Excuse me. What time is it now?

Takeshi: It's half past twelve.

Mary: Thank you.

Takeshi: You're welcome.

Ⅱ

Takeshi: Um . . . are you an international student?

Mary: Yes, I am a student at the University of Arizona.

Takeshi: I see. What is your major?

Mary: Japanese. I am a sophomore now.

たんご
Vocabulary

 K01-05

* あの	ano	um . . .
* いま	ima	now
えいご	eego	English (language)
* ええ	ee	yes
* がくせい	gakusee	student
* 〜ご	. . . go	. . . language ex. にほんご (nihongo) Japanese language
こうこう	kookoo	high school
ごご	gogo	P.M.
ごぜん	gozen	A.M.
〜さい	. . . sai	. . . years old
〜さん	. . . san	Mr./Ms. . . .
* 〜じ	. . . ji	o'clock ex. いちじ (ichiji) one o'clock
〜じん	. . . jin	. . . people ex. にほんじん (nihonjin) Japanese people
* せんこう	senkoo	major
せんせい	sensee	teacher; Professor . . .
そうです	soo desu	That's right.
* そうですか	soo desu ka	I see.; Is that so?
* だいがく	daigaku	college; university
でんわ	denwa	telephone
ともだち	tomodachi	friend
なまえ	namae	name
* なん／なに	nan/nani	what
* にほん	Nihon	Japan
* 〜ねんせい	. . . nensee	. . . year student ex. いちねんせい (ichinensee) first-year student
はい	hai	yes
* はん	han	half ex. にじはん (niji han) half past two
ばんごう	bangoo	number
* りゅうがくせい	ryuugakusee	international student
わたし	watashi	I

* Words that appear in the dialogue

ADDITIONAL VOCABULARY

 K01-06

Countries

アメリカ	Amerika	U.S.A.
イギリス	Igirisu	Britain
オーストラリア	Oosutoraria	Australia
かんこく	Kankoku	Korea
スウェーデン	Suweeden	Sweden
ちゅうごく	Chuugoku	China

Majors

かがく	kagaku	science
アジアけんきゅう	ajia kenkyuu	Asian studies
けいざい	keezai	economics
こくさいかんけい	kokusaikankee	international relations
コンピューター	konpyuutaa	computer
じんるいがく	jinruigaku	anthropology
せいじ	seeji	politics
ビジネス	bijinesu	business
ぶんがく	bungaku	literature
れきし	rekishi	history

Occupations

しごと	shigoto	job; work; occupation
いしゃ	isha	doctor
かいしゃいん	kaishain	office worker
こうこうせい	kookoosee	high school student
しゅふ	shufu	housewife
だいがくいんせい	daigakuinsee	graduate student
だいがくせい	daigakusee	college student
べんごし	bengoshi	lawyer

Family

おかあさん	okaasan	mother
おとうさん	otoosan	father
おねえさん	oneesan	older sister
おにいさん	oniisan	older brother
いもうと	imooto	younger sister
おとうと	otooto	younger brother

ぶんぽう Ｇｒａｍｍａｒ

1 ＸはＹです

"It is 12:30." "I am a student." "My major is the Japanese language." These sentences will all be translated into Japanese using an appropriate noun and the word *desu*.

> ～です。　　　　*It is . . .*

じゅうにじはんです。　　　　*(It) is half past twelve.*
Juuniji han desu.

がくせいです。　　　　*(I) am a student.*
Gakusee desu.

にほんごです。　　　　*(My major) is the Japanese language.*
Nihongo desu.

Note that none of these sentences has a "subject," like the "it," "I," and "my major," found in their English counterparts. Sentences without subjects are very common in Japanese; Japanese speakers actually tend to omit subjects whenever they think it is clear to the listener what or who they are referring to.

What are we to do, then, when it is not clear what is being talked about? To make explicit what we are talking about, we can say:

_____ は にほんごです。　　　　_____ *is the Japanese language.*
　　　　　　wa　nihongo desu.

Where _____ stands for the thing that is talked about, or the "topic," which is later in the sentence identified as *nihongo*. For example,

せんこうは にほんごです。　　　　*(My) major is the Japanese language.*
Senkoo wa　　nihongo desu.

Similarly, one can use the pattern *X wa Y desu* to identify a person or a thing X as item Y.

> ＸはＹです。　　　　*X is Y. As for X, it is Y.*

わたしは スー・キムです。　　　　*I am Sue Kim.*
Watashi wa　Suu Kimu desu.

やましたさんは　せんせいです。
Yamashita san wa　　sensee desu.

Mr. Yamashita is a teacher.

メアリーさんは　アメリカじんです。
Mearii san wa　　　amerikajin desu.

Mary is an American.

Wa is a member of the class of words called "particles." So is the word *no*, which we will turn to later in this lesson. Particles attach themselves to phrases and indicate how the phrases relate to the rest of the sentence.

Note also that nouns like *gakusee* and *sensee* in the above examples stand alone, unlike their English translations "student" and "teacher," which are preceded by "a." In Japanese, there is no item that corresponds to "a," nor is there any item that corresponds to the plural "-s" at the end of a noun. Without background situations, a sentence like *gakusee desu* is therefore ambiguous between the singular and the plural interpretations; it may mean "We are/you are/they are students," as well as "I am/you are/she is a student."

2　Question Sentences

It is very easy to form questions in Japanese. Basically, all you need to do is add *ka* at the end of a statement.

りゅうがくせいです。
Ryuugakusee desu.
(I am) an international student.

りゅうがくせいですか。[1]
Ryuugakusee desu ka.
(Are you) an international student?

The above sentence, *Ryuugakusee desu ka*, is a "yes/no" question. Question sentences may also contain a "question word" like *nan*[2] (what). In this lesson, we learn how to ask, and answer, questions using the following question words: *nanji* (what time), *nansai* (how old), *nannensee* (what year in school).

せんこうは　なんですか。
Senkoo wa　　nan desu ka.
What is your major?

（せんこうは）　えいごです。
(Senkoo wa)　　eego desu.
(My major) is English.

---

[1] It is not customary to write a question mark at the end of a question sentence in Japanese.

[2] The Japanese question word for "what" has two pronunciations: *nan* and *nani*. *Nan* is used immediately before *desu* or before a "counter" like *ji* (o'clock). The other form, *nani*, is used before a particle. *Nani* is also used in the combination *nanijin* (person of what nationality).

いま なんじですか。
Ima　 nanji desu ka.
What time is it now?

（いま）　くじです。
(Ima)　 kuji desu.
It is nine o'clock.

メアリーさんは なんさいですか。
Mearii san wa　　　 nansai desu ka.
How old are you, Mary?

じゅうきゅうさいです。
Juukyuusai desu.
I'm nineteen years old.

なんねんせいですか。
Nannensee desu ka.
What year are you in college?

にねんせいです。
Ninensee desu.
I'm a sophomore.

でんわばんごうは なんですか。
Denwa bangoo wa　　 nan desu ka.
What is your telephone number?

186 の 7343 です。
Ichi hachi roku no nana san yon san desu.
It is 186-7343.

3　noun₁ の noun₂

No is a particle that connects two nouns. The phrase *Sakura daigaku no gakusee* means "a student at Sakura University." The second noun *gakusee* provides the main idea[3] (being a student) and the first one *Sakura daigaku* makes it more specific (not a high school, but a college student). *No* is very versatile. In the first example below, it acts like the possessive ("x's") in English, but that is not the only role *no* can play. See how it connects two nouns in the following examples.

たけし さんの　でんわばんごう		*Takeshi's phone number*
Takeshi san no　 denwa bangoo		
だいがくの　せんせい		*a college professor*
daigaku no　 sensee		
にほんごの　がくせい		*a student of the Japanese language*
nihongo no　 gakusee		
にほんの　だいがく		*a college in Japan*
Nihon no　 daigaku		

Observe that in the first two examples, the English and Japanese words are arranged in the same order, while in the last two, they are in the opposite order. Japanese seems to be more consistent in arranging ideas here; the main idea always comes at the end, with any further description placed before it.

---

[3] Here is what we mean by the "main idea." In the phrase *Takeshi san no denwa bangoo* (Takeshi's phone number), the noun *denwa bangoo* (phone number) is the main idea, in the sense that if something is Takeshi's phone number, it is a phone number. The other noun *Takeshi san* is not the main idea, because Takeshi's phone number is not Takeshi.

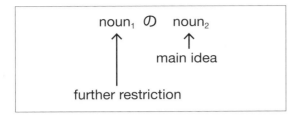

A phrase of the form "noun₁ *no* noun₂" acts more or less like one big noun. You can put it wherever you can put a noun, as in the following example:

| たけしさんの おかあさん | は | こうこうの せんせい | です。 |

Takeshi san no   okaasan wa   kookoo no   sensee desu.

| *Takeshi's mother* | *is* | *a high school teacher* | . |

Culture Note

にほんじんの なまえ Japanese Names
Nihonjin no namae

When Japanese give their name, they say their family name first and given name last (middle names do not exist). When introducing themselves, they often say only their family name. Here are some typical Japanese names.

Family name		Given name			
		Men		Women	
さとう	Satoo	たくや	Takuya	えりか	Erika
すずき	Suzuki	しょうた	Shoota	あい	Ai
たかはし	Takahashi	いちろう	Ichiroo	なおみ	Naomi
たなか	Tanaka	ひろし	Hiroshi	ゆうこ	Yuuko
いとう	Itoo	まさひろ	Masahiro	みさき	Misaki

Most Japanese names are written in kanji. For example, Tanaka is usually written as 田中, which means "middle of the rice field." Family names are often related to nature or geographical features. Because many kanji share the same reading, names with the same pronunciation may be written with different kanji, such as 裕子 and 優子 for the feminine name *Yuuko*.

表現ノート………2
ひょう　げん

あの ▸ *Ano* indicates that you have some reservations about saying what you are going to say next. You may be worried about interrupting something someone is currently doing, or sounding rude and impolite for asking personal questions, for example.

はい/ええ ▸ Both *hai* and *ee* means "yes" in response to yes-no questions. Compared to *hai*, *ee* is more conversational and relaxed. In more informal situations, *un* is used.

　Hai is also used to respond to a knock at the door or to the calling of one's name, meaning "Here," as follows. (*Ee* cannot be replaced in this case.)

Teacher:	スミスさん？ すみす Sumisu san?	*Mr. Smith?*
Student:	はい。 Hai.	*Here.*

そうですか ▸ *Soo desu ka* acknowledges that you have understood what was just said. "Is that so?" or "I see."

Pronunciation of は ▸ The particle は is pronounced "*wa*," not "*ha*." It should be written with は. All other instances "*wa*" are written with わ.

わたしの　でんわばんごうは 37- 8667です。
Watashi no　denwa bangoo wa　　　san nana no hachi roku roku nana desu.
My telephone number is 37-8667.

There are few exceptions, such as *konnichiwa* (good afternoon) and *konbanwa* (good evening). They are usually written with こんにちは and こんばんは.

Numbers ▸ Many number words have more than one pronunciation. Refer to the table at the end of this book for a general picture.

0　ゼロ and れい are both commonly used.
ぜ ろ
1　いち, but pronounced as いっ in いっぷん (one minute) and いっさい (one year old).
2　に all the time. When you are reading out each digit separately, as when you give your phone number, it may be pronounced with a long vowel, as にい.
3　さん all the time. The part that follows it may change shape, as in さん ぷん, instead of さんふん.

4 よん is the most basic, but fourth-year student is よねんせい and four o'clock is よじ. In some combinations that we will later learn, it is read as し (as in しがつ, April). The part that follows this number may change shape too, as in よんぷん.

5 ご all the time. When read out separately, it may be pronounced with a long vowel, as ごう.

6 ろく, but pronounced as ろっ in ろっぷん.

7 なな is the most basic, but seven o'clock is しちじ.

8 はち, but usually pronounced as はっ in はっぷん and はっさい.

9 きゅう is the most basic, but nine o'clock is くじ.

10 じゅう, but pronounced as じゅっ or じっ in じゅっぷん/じっぷん and じゅっさい/じっさい.

Giving one's telephone number ▶ The particle *no* is usually placed in between the local exchange code and the last four digits. Therefore, the number 012-345-6789 is *zero ichi ni, san yon go no, roku nana hachi kyuu*.

せんせい ▶ The word *sensee* is usually reserved for describing somebody else's occupation. *Watashi wa sensee desu* makes sense, but may sound slightly arrogant, because the word *sensee* actually means an "honorable master." If you (or a member of your family) are a teacher, and if you want to be really modest, you can use the word *kyooshi* instead.

さん ▶ *San* is placed after a name as a generic title. It goes both with a given name and a family name. Children are referred to as *chan* (and boys in particular as *kun*), rather than *san*. Professors and doctors are usually referred to with the title *sensee*. *San* and other title words are never used in reference to oneself.

Referring to the person you are talking to ▶ The word for "you," *anata*, is not very commonly used in Japanese. Instead, we use the name and a title like *san* and *sensee* to refer to the person you are talking to. Therefore, a sentence like "Ms. Hart, are you Swedish?" should be:

ハートさんは スウェーデンじんですか。
Haato san wa　　　suweedenjin desu ka.

instead of ハートさん、あなたは スウェーデンじんですか。
　　　　　　Haato san,　　　anata wa　　　suweedenjin desu ka.

れんしゅう Ｐｒａｃｔｉｃｅ

Ⅰ すうじ (Numbers)

🔊 K01-07

0	ゼロ／れい zero　ree				
1	いち ichi	11	じゅういち juuichi	30	さんじゅう sanjuu
2	に ni	12	じゅうに juuni	40	よんじゅう yonjuu
3	さん san	13	じゅうさん juusan	50	ごじゅう gojuu
4	よん／し／（よ） yon　shi　(yo)	14	じゅうよん／じゅうし juuyon　juushi	60	ろくじゅう rokujuu
5	ご go	15	じゅうご juugo	70	ななじゅう nanajuu
6	ろく roku	16	じゅうろく juuroku	80	はちじゅう hachijuu
7	なな／しち nana　shichi	17	じゅうなな／じゅうしち juunana　juushichi	90	きゅうじゅう kyuujuu
8	はち hachi	18	じゅうはち juuhachi	100	ひゃく hyaku
9	きゅう／く kyuu　ku	19	じゅうきゅう／じゅうく juukyuu　juuku		
10	じゅう juu	20	にじゅう nijuu		

A. Read the following numbers. 🔊 K01-08

(a) 5　　　　(b) 9　　　　(c) 7　　　　(d) 1　　　　(e) 10

(f) 8　　　　(g) 2　　　　(h) 6　　　　(i) 4　　　　(j) 3

B. Read the following numbers. 🔊 K01-09

(a) 45　　　(b) 83　　　(c) 19　　　(d) 76　　　(e) 52

(f) 100　　(g) 38　　　(h) 61　　　(i) 24　　　(j) 97

C. What are the answers? 🔊 K01-10

(a) $5+3$　(b) $9+1$　(c) $3+4$　(d) $6-6$　(e) $10+9$　(f) $8-7$　(g) $40-25$

Ⅱ じかん (Time)

K01-11

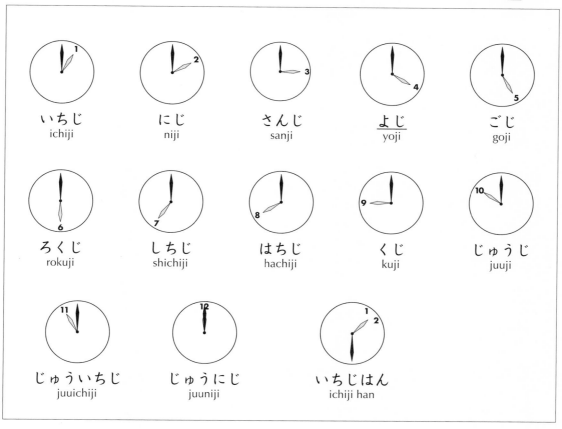

いちじ ichiji	にじ niji	さんじ sanji	<u>よじ</u> yoji	ごじ goji
ろくじ rokuji	しちじ shichiji	はちじ hachiji	くじ kuji	じゅうじ juuji
じゅういちじ juuichiji	じゅうにじ juuniji	いちじはん ichiji han		

A. Look at the following pictures and answer the questions. K01-12

Example:　Q：いま　なんじですか。
　　　　　　　　Ima　　nanji desu ka.

　　　　　　Ａ：いちじはんです。
　　　　　　　　Ichiji han desu.

Ex.

(1) (2) (3) (4)

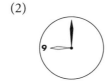 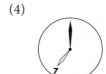

(5) (6) (7) (8)

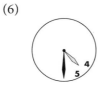  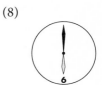

B. Answer the questions. 🔊 K01-13

Example: Q：とうきょうは いま なんじですか。
Tookyoo wa　　　ima　　nanji desu ka.

A：ごぜん さんじです。
Gozen　　sanji desu.

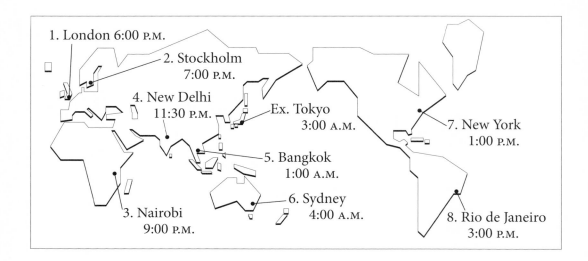

1. London 6:00 P.M.
2. Stockholm 7:00 P.M.
4. New Delhi 11:30 P.M.
Ex. Tokyo 3:00 A.M.
7. New York 1:00 P.M.
5. Bangkok 1:00 A.M.
6. Sydney 4:00 A.M.
3. Nairobi 9:00 P.M.
8. Rio de Janeiro 3:00 P.M.

Ⅲ でんわばんごう (Telephone Numbers)

A. Read the following people's telephone numbers. 🔊 K01-14

Example: やました　283-9547　→　にはちさんの　きゅうごよんなな
Yamashita　　　　　　　　　　　　ni hachi san no　　kyuu go yon nana

1. だいがく　　951-0326
daigaku

2. せんせい　　362-4519
sensee

3. メアリー　　020-6921-4236
め あ り い
Mearii

4. たけし　　　030-8522-1032
Takeshi

B. Pair Work—Read the dialogue below with your partner. 🔊 K01-15

A：でんわばんごうは なんですか。
Denwa bangoo wa　　　nan desu ka.

B：283-9547 です。
Ni hachi san no kyuu go yon nana desu.

A：283-9547 ですね。*　　（＊ね＝ right?)
Ni hachi san no kyuu go yon nana desu ne.

B：はい、そうです。
Hai,　　soo desu.

C. Group Work—Use the dialogue above and ask three classssmates their telephone numbers.

| name | telephone number |

    (　　　　　　)　(　　　　　　　　　　　　)

    (　　　　　　)　(　　　　　　　　　　　　)

    (　　　　　　)　(　　　　　　　　　　　　)

Ⅳ にほんごの がくせい

Translate the following phrases into Japanese using の (no). 🔊 K01-16

Example:　student of Japanese language　→　にほんごの がくせい
nihongo no　gakusee

1. my teacher
2. my telephone number
3. my name
4. Takashi's major
5. Mary's friend
6. student of the University of London
7. teacher of the Japanese language
8. high school teacher

Ⅴ メアリーさんは アメリカじんです

A. Look at the chart on the next page and describe each person using the cues in (a) through (e).

1. たけしさん　2. スーさん　3. ロバートさん　4. やましたせんせい
Takeshi san　　Suu san　　　Robaato san　　　Yamashita sensee

(a) Nationality 🔊 K01-17
Example:　メアリーさん　→　メアリーさんは アメリカじんです。
Mearii san　　　　　　Mearii san wa　amerikajin desu.

(b) Year in school 🔊 K01-18
Example:　メアリーさん　→　メアリーさんは にねんせいです。
Mearii san　　　　　　Mearii san wa　ninensee desu.

(c) Age 🔊 K01-19
Example:　メアリーさん　→　メアリーさんは じゅうきゅうさいです。
Mearii san　　　　　　Mearii san wa　juukyuu sai desu.

(d) School 🔊 K01-20

Example:　メアリーさん　→　メアリーさんは　アリゾナだいがくの
　　　　　　　Mearii san　　　　　　 Mearii san wa　　　　Arizona daigaku no

　　　　　　　がくせいです。
　　　　　　　gakusee desu.

(e) Major 🔊 K01-21

Example:　メアリーさん　→　メアリーさんの　せんこうは　にほんごです。
　　　　　　　Mearii san　　　　　　 Mearii san no　　senkoo wa　　nihongo desu.

	Hart, Mary	きむら たけし Kimura Takeshi	Kim, Sue	Smith, Robert	やましたせんせい Yamashita sensee
Nationality	American	Japanese	Korean (かんこくじん) kankokujin	British (イギリスじん) igirisujin	Japanese
Year	2nd year	4th year	3rd year	4th year	
Age	19	22	20	22	47
School	U. of Arizona	Sakura Univ.	Seoul Univ.	U. of London	Sakura Univ.
Major	Japanese	history (れきし) rekishi	computer (コンピューター) konpyuutaa	business (ビジネス) bijinesu	(Japanese teacher)

B.　Ask and answer questions using the given cues. 🔊 K01-22

Example 1:　メアリーさん／アメリカじん
　　　　　　 Mearii san　　　amerikajin

　　　→　Q：メアリーさんは　アメリカじんですか。
　　　　　　　　 Mearii san wa　　amerikajin desu ka.

　　　　　A：ええ、そうです。
　　　　　　　 Ee,　　soo desu.

Example 2: メアリーさん／さんねんせい
めありい　　　　　　　sannensee
Mearii san

→ Q：メアリーさんは　さんねんせいですか。
　　　　めありい
　　　　Mearii san wa　　　　sannensee desu ka.

A：いいえ、にねんせいです。
　　　Iie,　　　ninensee desu.

1. メアリーさん／アリゾナだいがくの　がくせい
　めありい　　　　ありぞな
　Mearii san　　　Arizona daigaku no　　　gakusee

2. メアリーさん／いちねんせい
　めありい
　Mearii san　　　ichinensee

3. たけしさん／にほんじん
　Takeshi san　　nihonjin

4. たけしさん／にほんだいがくの　がくせい
　Takeshi san　　Nihon daigaku no　　gakusee

5. たけしさん／じゅうきゅうさい
　Takeshi san　　juukyuusai

6. スーさん／スウェーデンじん
　すう　　　　　すうぇえでん
　Suu san　　　suweedenjin

7. スーさんの　せんこう／けいざい (economics)
　すう
　Suu san no　　senkoo　　keezai

8. ロバートさんの　せんこう／ビジネス
　ろばあと　　　　　　　　　びじねす
　Robaato san no　　senkoo　　bijinesu

9. ロバートさん／よねんせい
　ろばあと
　Robaato san　　yonensee

10. ロバートさん／にじゅういっさい
　ろばあと
　Robaato san　　nijuuissai

11. やましたせんせい／にほんじん
　Yamashita sensee　　nihonjin

12. やましたせんせい／ハワイだいがくの　せんせい
　　　　　　　　　　　　はわい
　Yamashita sensee　　Hawai daigaku no　　sensee

Ⅵ おとうさんは　かいしゃいんです

A. Look at the chart about Mary's host family and describe each person with regard to (a) and (b).

1. おかあさん　　2. おにいさん　　3. いもうと
　okaasan　　　　oniisan　　　　imooto

(a) Occupation/School 🔊 K01-23

Example：おとうさん　→　おとうさんは　かいしゃいんです。
　　　　　otoosan　　　　　Otoosan wa　　　kaishain desu.

(b) Age 🔊 K01-24

Example:　おとうさん　→　おとうさんは　よんじゅうはっさいです。
　　　　　　 otoosan　　　　　Otoosan wa　　　yonjuuhassai desu.

Mary's host family

	おとうさん otoosan (father)	おかあさん okaasan (mother)	おにいさん oniisan (elder brother)	いもうと imooto (younger sister)
Occupation/ School	かいしゃいん kaishain (works for a company)	しゅふ shufu (housewife)	だいがくいんせい daigakuinsee (graduate student)	こうこうせい kookoosee (high school student)
Age	48	45	23	16

B. **Answer the questions using the chart above.** 🔊 K01-25

1. おとうさんは　かいしゃいんですか。
   Otoosan wa　　kaishain desu ka.

2. おとうさんは　なんさいですか。
   Otoosan wa　　nansai desu ka.

3. おかあさんは　せんせいですか。
   Okaasan wa　　sensee desu ka.

4. おかあさんは　なんさいですか。
   Okaasan wa　　nansai desu ka.

5. おにいさんは　かいしゃいんですか。
   Oniisan wa　　kaishain desu ka.

6. おにいさんは　なんさいですか。
   Oniisan wa　　nansai desu ka.

7. いもうとは　だいがくせいですか。
   Imooto wa　　daigakusee desu ka.

8. いもうとは　なんさいですか。
   Imooto wa　　nansai desu ka.

Ⅶ まとめの れんしゅう (Review Exercises)

A. Class Activity—Ask five classmates questions and find in the chart below.

Q : おなまえは？ (What is your name?)
Onamae wa?

A : メアリー・ハートです。
Mearii Haato desu.

Q : ごしゅっしんは？ (Where do you come from?)
Goshusshin wa?

A : アリゾナです。
Arizona desu.

Q : おしごとは？ (What is your occupation?)
Oshigoto wa?

A : がくせいです。
Gakusee desu.

Q : なんねんせいですか。
Nannensee desu ka.

A : にねんせいです。
Ninensee desu.

Q : なんさいですか。
Nansai desu ka.

A : じゅうきゅうさいです。
Juukyuusai desu.

Q : せんこうは なんですか。
Senkoo wa   nan desu ka.

A : にほんごです。
Nihongo desu.

Name	Nationality/ Hometown	Occupation/ School	Age	Major, etc.

B. Self-introduction—Introduce yourself to the class.

Example:

はじめまして。 メアリー・ハートです。
Hajimemashite.   Mearii Haato desu.

アリゾナだいがくの がくせいです。
Arizona daigaku no   gakusee desu.

いま にねんせいです。 せんこうは にほんごです。
Ima   ninensee desu.   Senkoo wa   nihongo desu.

じゅうきゅうさいです。 よろしく おねがいします。
Juukyuusai desu.   Yoroshiku   onegaishimasu.

C. Class Activity—Ask your classmates what their majors are, and find someone who has the following major.

Example:　Q：せんこうは　なんですか。
　　　　　　　Senkoo wa　　　nan desu ka.

　　　　　　A：にほんごです。
　　　　　　　Nihongo desu.

　　　　　　　　　　　　　　　　　name

1. Japanese　　　_____

2. economics　　_____

3. English　　　 _____

4. history　　　 _____

5. business　　　_____

D. Role Play—Using Dialogue as a model, make skits in the following situations.

1. You don't have a watch with you, but you need to know what time it is.

2. You've just met a Japanese person and want to get to know the person.

Useful Expressions
じかん・とし
T i m e / A g e

Time

Hours			
1	いちじ ichiji		
2	にじ niji		
3	さんじ sanji		
4	よじ yoji		
5	ごじ goji		
6	ろくじ rokuji		
7	しちじ shichiji		
8	はちじ hachiji		
9	くじ kuji		
10	じゅうじ juuji		
11	じゅういちじ juuichiji		
12	じゅうにじ juuniji		

Minutes			
1	いっぷん ippun	11	じゅういっぷん juuippun
2	にふん nifun	12	じゅうにふん juunifun
3	さんぷん sanpun	13	じゅうさんぷん juusanpun
4	よんぷん yonpun	14	じゅうよんぷん juuyonpun
5	ごふん gofun	15	じゅうごふん juugofun
6	ろっぷん roppun	16	じゅうろっぷん juuroppun
7	ななふん nanafun	17	じゅうななふん juunanafun
8	はっぷん happun / はちふん hachifun	18	じゅうはっぷん juuhappun / じゅうはちふん juuhachifun
9	きゅうふん kyuufun	19	じゅうきゅうふん juukyuufun
10	じゅっぷん juppun / じっぷん jippun	20	にじゅっぷん nijuppun / にじっぷん nijippun
		30	さんじゅっぷん sanjuppun / さんじっぷん sanjippun

Age

なんさいですか。／おいくつですか。　(How old are you?)
Nansai desu ka.　　Oikutsu desu ka.

The counter suffix ～さい (. . . *sai*) is used to indicate " . . . years old."

1	いっさい issai	5	ごさい gosai	9	きゅうさい kyuusai
2	にさい nisai	6	ろくさい rokusai	10	じゅっさい jussai ／じっさい jissai
3	さんさい sansai	7	ななさい nanasai	11	じゅういっさい juuissai
4	よんさい yonsai	8	はっさい hassai	20	はたち* hatachi

*For 20 years old, はたち(*hatachi*) is usually used, although にじゅっさい／にじっさい (*nijussai/nijissai*) can be used.

第2課 L E S S O N ·········2
だい に か
かいもの Shopping

かいわ D i a l o g u e

Ⅰ Mary goes to a flea market. 🔊 K02-01/02

1 メアリー： すみません。これは いくらですか。
　め あ り い
　Mearii　　　　 Sumimasen.　　 Kore wa　ikura desu ka.

2 みせのひと： それは さんぜんえんです。
　Mise no hito　　 Sore wa　 sanzen en desu.

3 メアリー： たかいですね。じゃあ、あのとけいは いくらですか。
　め あ り い
　Mearii　　　　 Takai desu ne.　　 Jaa,　　 ano tokee wa　　 ikura desu ka.

4 みせのひと： あれは さんぜんごひゃくえんです。
　Mise no hito　　 Are wa　 sanzengohyaku en desu.

5 メアリー： そうですか。あれも たかいですね。
　め あ り い
　Mearii　　　　 Soo desu ka.　　 Are mo　 takai desu ne.

6 みせのひと： これは せんはっぴゃくえんですよ。
　Mise no hito　　 Kore wa　 senhappyaku en desu yo.

7 メアリー： じゃあ、そのとけいを ください。
　め あ り い
　Mearii　　　　 Jaa,　　　 sono tokee o　　 kudasai.

＊　　　＊　　　＊

A man finds a wallet on the ground.

8 しらないひと：これは だれの さいふですか。
　Shiranai hito　　 Kore wa　 dare no　 saifu desu ka.

9 メアリー： わたしの さいふです。
　め あ り い
　Mearii　　　　 Watashi no　 saifu desu.

　　　　　　 ありがとう ございます。
　　　　　　 Arigatoo　　　 gozaimasu.

Ⅱ After shopping, Mary goes to a restaurant. 🔊 K02-03/04

1 ウエートレス：いらっしゃいませ。メニューを どうぞ。
　う え え と れ す　　　　　　　　 め に ゅ う
　Ueetoresu　　　 Irasshaimase.　　 Menyuu o　 doozo.

2 メアリー： どうも。これは なんですか。
　め あ り い
　Mearii　　　　 Doomo.　 Kore wa　 nan desu ka.

3 ウエートレス： どれですか。 ああ、 とんかつです。
　Ueetoresu　　　Dore desu ka.　　Aa,　　tonkatsu desu.

4 メアリー： とんかつ？ さかなですか。
　Mearii　　　Tonkatsu?　Sakana desu ka.

5 ウエートレス： いいえ、 さかなじゃないです。 にくです。 おいしいですよ。
　Ueetoresu　　　Iie,　　sakana ja nai desu.　　Niku desu.　　Oishii desu yo.

6 メアリー： じゃあ、 これを おねがいします。
　Mearii　　　Jaa,　　kore o　onegaishimasu.

　　　　　　　　　＊　　　　　＊　　　　　＊

7 メアリー： すみません。 トイレは どこですか。
　Mearii　　　Sumimasen.　Toire wa　doko desu ka.

8 ウエートレス： あそこです。
　Ueetoresu　　　Asoko desu.

9 メアリー： ありがとう ございます。
　Mearii　　　Arigatoo　gozaimasu.

Ⅰ

Mary: Excuse me. How much is this?

Vendor: It is 3,000 yen.

Mary: It's expensive. Well then, how much is that watch?

Vendor: That is 3,500 yen.

Mary: I see. That is expensive, too.

Vendor: This is 1,800 yen.

Mary: Then, I'll take that watch.
　　　＊　　　＊　　　＊
Stranger: Whose wallet is this?

Mary: It's my wallet. Thank you very much.

Ⅱ

Waitress: Welcome. Here's the menu.

Mary: Thank you. What is this?

Waitress: Which one? Oh, it is *tonkatsu* (pork cutlet).

Mary: *Tonkatsu*? Is it fish?

Waitress: No, it is not fish. It is meat. It is delicious.

Mary: Then, I'll have this.
　　　＊　　　＊　　　＊
Mary: Excuse me. Where is the restroom?

Waitress: It is over there.

Mary: Thank you very much.

たんご

 K02-05

Vocabulary

Words That Point

* これ	kore	this one
* それ	sore	that one
* あれ	are	that one (over there)
* どれ	dore	which one
この	kono	this . . .
* その	sono	that . . .
* あの	ano	that . . . (over there)
どの	dono	which . . .
ここ	koko	here
そこ	soko	there
* あそこ	asoko	over there
* どこ	doko	where
* だれ	dare	who

Food

* おいしい	oishii	delicious
* さかな	sakana	fish
* とんかつ	tonkatsu	pork cutlet
* にく	niku	meat
* メニュー	menyuu	menu
やさい	yasai	vegetable

Things

えんぴつ	enpitsu	pencil
かさ	kasa	umbrella
かばん	kaban	bag
くつ	kutsu	shoes
* さいふ	saifu	wallet
ジーンズ	jiinzu	jeans
じしょ	jisho	dictionary
じてんしゃ	jitensha	bicycle
しんぶん	shinbun	newspaper
Tシャツ	tiishatsu	T-shirt
* とけい	tokee	watch; clock

* Words that appear in the dialogue

ノート	nooto	notebook
ペン	pen	pen
ぼうし	booshi	hat; cap
ほん	hon	book

Places

きっさてん	kissaten	cafe
ぎんこう	ginkoo	bank
*トイレ	toire	toilet; restroom
としょかん	toshokan	library
ゆうびんきょく	yuubinkyoku	post office

Countries

アメリカ	Amerika	U.S.A.
イギリス	Igirisu	Britain
かんこく	Kankoku	Korea
ちゅうごく	Chuugoku	China

Majors

けいざい	keezai	economics
コンピューター	konpyuutaa	computer
ビジネス	bijinesu	business
れきし	rekishi	history

Family

| おかあさん | okaasan | mother |
| おとうさん | otoosan | father |

Money Matters

*いくら	ikura	how much
*〜えん	. . . en	. . . yen
*たかい	takai	expensive; high

Expressions

*いらっしゃいませ	irasshaimase	Welcome (to our store).
*(〜を)おねがいします	(. . . o) onegaishimasu	. . . , please.
*(〜を)ください	(. . . o) kudasai	Please give me . . .
*じゃあ	jaa	then . . . ; if that is the case, . . .
*どうぞ	doozo	Please.; Here it is.
*どうも	doomo	Thank you.

ぶんぽう Grammar

1 これ それ あれ どれ

What do we do when we want to talk about things that we do not know the names of? We say "this thing," "that one," and so forth. In Japanese, we use *kore*, *sore*, and *are*.

これは いくらですか。 *How much is this?*
Kore wa ikura desu ka.

それは さんぜんえんです。 *That is 3,000 yen.*
Sore wa sanzen en desu.

Kore refers to a thing that is close to you, the speaker ("this thing here"). *Sore* is something that is close to the person you are talking to ("that thing in front of you"), and *are* refers to a thing that is neither close to the speaker nor the listener ("that one over there").

あれは わたしの ペンです。
Are wa watashi no pen desu.

これは わたしの ペンです。   それは わたしの ペンです。
Kore wa watashi no pen desu.   Sore wa watashi no pen desu.

There is also an expression *dore* for "which." Here we will learn to use *dore* in sentences like:

どれですか。 *Which one is it (that you are talking about)?*
Dore desu ka.

In this lesson, we will not explore the full extent to which the word *dore* can be put to use, because there is a slight complication with question words like *dore*. Question words like *dore* and *nani* cannot be followed by the particle *wa*. Instead, you must use the particle *ga* and say:

どれが あなたの ペンですか。 *Which one is your pen?*
Dore ga   anata no   pen desu ka.

2　この/その/あの/どの ＋ noun

If you want to be slightly more specific than *kore*, *sore*, and *are*, you can use *kono*, *sono*, and *ano* together with a noun. (Note here that the *re* series must always stand alone, while the *no* series must always be followed by a noun.) Thus, if you know that the item in your hand is a watch (*tokee*), instead of:

これは いくらですか。 *How much is this?*
Kore wa   ikura desu ka.

you can say:

このとけいは いくらですか。 *How much is this watch?*
Kono tokee wa   ikura desu ka.

Similarly, if you are talking about a watch that is held by the person you are talking to, you can say:

そのとけいは さんぜんえんです。 *That watch is 3,000 yen.*
Sono tokee wa   sanzen en desu.

And if the watch is far from both the speaker and the listener, you can say:

あのとけいは さんぜんごひゃくえんです。 *That watch over there is 3,500 yen.*
Ano tokee wa   sanzengohyaku en desu.

If you already know that one of several watches is 3,500 yen but do not know which, you can say:

どのとけいが さんぜんごひゃくえんですか。 *Which watch is 3,500 yen?*
Dono tokee ga   sanzengohyaku en desu ka.

Since *dono* is a question word, just like *dore* discussed above, we cannot use the particle *wa* with it; we must use *ga*.

To summarize:

これ（は〜）	この noun（は〜）	close to the person speaking
それ（は〜）	その noun（は〜）	close to the person listening
あれ（は〜）	あの noun（は〜）	far from both people
どれ（が〜）	どの noun（が〜）	unknown

3　ここ そこ あそこ どこ

We will learn just one more *ko-so-a-do* set in this lesson: *koko, soko, asoko,* and *doko* are words for places.

ここ	*here, near me*
そこ	*there, near you*
あそこ	*over there*
どこ	*where*

You can ask for directions by saying:

すみません。ゆうびんきょくは どこですか。　　*Excuse me. Where is the post office?*
Sumimasen.　　Yuubinkyoku wa　　doko desu ka.

If you are close by, you can point toward the post office and say:

（ゆうびんきょくは）あそこです。　　*(The post office is) right over there.*
(Yuubinkyoku wa)　　asoko desu.

We will learn how to give more specific directions in Lesson 4.

4　だれの noun

In Lesson 1, we learned how to say things like *Mearii san no denwa bangoo* (Mary's phone number) and *Takeshi san no okaasan* (Takeshi's mother). We now learn how to ask who something belongs to. The question word for "who" is *dare*, and for "whose," we simply add the particle *no*.

これは だれの かばんですか。　　　　それは スーさんの かばんです。
Kore wa　dare no　kaban desu ka.　　Sore wa　Suu san no　kaban desu.
Whose bag is this?　　　　　　　　　*That is Sue's bag.*

5   noun も

In Lesson 1, we learned how to say "Item A is this, item B is that." We now learn how to say "Item A is this, and item B is this, too."

たけしさんは　にほんじんです。
Takeshi san wa　　nihonjin desu.

Takeshi is a Japanese person.

みちこさんも　にほんじんです。
Michiko san mo　　nihonjin desu.

Michiko is Japanese, <u>too</u>.

Note that these two sentences are almost identical in shape. This is natural, as they both claim that a certain person is Japanese. The second sentence, however, is different from the first in that we do not find the particle *wa* in it. We have *mo* instead. *Mo* is a particle that indicates that that item, *too*, has the given property. One thing that you should watch out for is exactly where the particle is placed. In English, the word "too" can be placed after the sentence as a whole, as in the example above. Not so in Japanese. In the above example, *mo* must directly follow *Michiko san*.

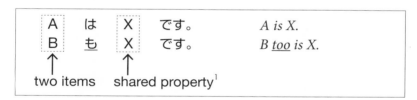

6   noun じゃないです

To negate a statement of the form *X wa Y desu*, where Y is a noun, you replace *desu* with *ja nai desu*.[2]

やまださんは　がくせいじゃないです。
Yamada san wa　　gakusee ja nai desu.

Mr. Yamada is not a student.

---

[1] We cannot use *mo* to describe a situation like the following: Our friend, Pat, has dual citizenship; Pat is a Japanese, but at the same time, she is an American. To describe the second half of this situation, we cannot say, *Patto mo amerikajin desu*, because the sentence would mean that Pat, in addition to somebody that has been mentioned, is an American. Neither can we say, *Patto wa amerikajin mo desu*. (Japanese speakers would say, *Patto wa amerikajin demo arimasu*.)

[2] In the dialogues, there are two sentences that end with *desu*, which call for special attention: *Are mo takai desu ne* (That one too is expensive), and *Oishii desu yo* (It is delicious). These sentences cannot be negated by replacing *desu* with *ja nai desu*, because *takai* and *oishii* are not nouns. *Are mo takai ja nai desu* and *oishii ja nai desu* are therefore not grammatical. Instead, one would have to say *takaku nai desu* and *oishiku nai desu*. We will learn about the conjugation pattern of adjectives in Lesson 5.

You find several stylistic variants in negative sentences. *Ja nai desu* is very colloquial. The more formal replacement for *nai desu* is *arimasen*. *Ja* is a contraction of *de wa*, which is more formal and more appropriate in the written language. Thus in addition to the above sentence, you also find:

やまださんは　がくせいじゃありません。　　(more conservative speech style)
Yamada san wa　　gakusee ja arimasen.

やまださんは　がくせいではありません。　　(formal, appropriate for writing)
Yamada san wa　　gakusee de wa arimasen.

affirmative:	(X は) Y です。		X is Y.
negative:	(X は) Y	じゃないです。 じゃありません。 ではありません。	X is not Y.

7　～ね/～よ

Statements often end with the tags *ne* or *yo*, depending on the way the speaker views the interaction with the listener. If the speaker is seeking the listener's confirmation or agreement to what has been said, then *ne* ("right?") could be added.

リーさんの　せんこうは　ぶんがくですね。　　*Ms. Lee, your major is literature, right?*
Rii san no　　senkoo wa　　bungaku desu ne.

これは　にくじゃないですね。　　*This is not meat, is it?*
Kore wa　niku ja nai desu ne.

Another particle, *yo* ("I tell you"), is added to a statement if the speaker wants to assure the listener of what has been said. With *yo* added, a statement becomes an authoritative decree.

とんかつは　さかなじゃないですよ。
Tonkatsu wa　　sakana ja nai desu yo.
Let me assure you. "Tonkatsu" is not fish.

スミスさんは　イギリスじんですよ。
Sumisu san wa　　igirisujin desu yo.
(In case you're wondering,) Mr. Smith is British.

表現ノート……3
<ruby>表<rt>ひょう</rt></ruby><ruby>現<rt>げん</rt></ruby>

（〜を）ください▶ *(. . . o) kudasai* is "Please give me X." You can use it to request (concrete) items in general.

（〜を）おねがいします▶ *(. . . o) onegaishimasu* too is a request for item X. When used to ask for a concrete object, *(. . . o) onegaishimasu* sounds slightly more upscale than *(. . . o) kudasai.* It is heard often when ordering food at a restaurant ("I will have . . ."). *(. . . o) onegaishimasu* can also be used to ask for "abstract objects," such as repairs, explanations, and understanding.

（〜を）どうぞ▶ *(. . . o) doozo* is used when an offer is made with respect to item X. In the dialogue, the restaurant attendant uses it when she is about to hand the menu to the customer. It may also be used when a person is waiting for you to come forth with item X; a telephone operator, asking for your name, would probably say *Onamae o doozo.* (*O* is a politeness marker. Therefore *onamae* is "your honorable name.")

On the pronunciation of number words ▶ Note that the words for 300, 600, 800, 3,000, and 8,000 involve sound changes. "Counters" whose first sound is *h*, like *hyaku* (hundred), generally change shape after 3, 6, and 8. Some counters that begin with *s*, like *sen* (thousand), change shape after 3 and 8. Refer to the table at the end of the volume.

Big numbers ▶ In addition to the digit markers for tens (*juu*), hundreds (*hyaku*), and thousands (*sen*), which are found in Western languages as well, Japanese uses the marker for tens of thousands (*man*). Thus 20,000, for example, is *niman* ($= 2 \times 10,000$), rather than *nijuusen* ($= 20 \times 1,000$). While the next unit marker in Western languages is one million, Japanese describes that number as $100 \times 10,000$, that is, *hyakuman*.

More complicated numbers can be considered the sums of smaller numbers, as in the following examples.

234,567	=	$23 \times 10,000$	にじゅうさんまん	(*nijuusanman*)
		$4 \times 1,000$	よんせん	(*yonsen*)
		5×100	ごひゃく	(*gohyaku*)
		6×10	ろくじゅう	(*rokujuu*)
		7	なな	(*nana*)

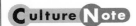

にほんの おかね Japanese Currency
Nihon no okane

Japan's official currency is the yen, which is pronounced *en* in Japanese. The bills and coins currently in circulation are the following:

10,000-yen bill	5,000-yen bill	2,000-yen bill

A portrait of Yukichi Fukuzawa (1835-1901), a philosopher and the founder of Keio University.

A portrait of Ichiyoo Higuchi (1872-1896), a writer and poet.

Shurei Gate, the second gate of Shuri Castle in Okinawa.

1,000-yen bill	500-yen coin	100-yen coin

A portrait of Hideyo Noguchi (1876-1928), a bacteriologist who devoted himself to yellow fever research.

50-yen coin	10-yen coin	5-yen coin	1-yen coin

All bills and coins are different sizes. For example, the bills slightly descend in length from 10,000 yen to 1,000 yen. Although credit cards are now widespread in Japan, some small shops and restaurants do not accept them, even in major cities. Consequently, most people usually carry a certain amount of cash with them, and ATMs can be found almost everywhere.

Pre-paid cards are available for use for public transportation and shopping. Personal checks are not used in Japan.

れんしゅう P r a c t i c e

① すうじ (Numbers)

K02-06

100	ひゃく hyaku	1,000	せん sen	10,000	いちまん ichiman
200	にひゃく nihyaku	2,000	にせん nisen	20,000	にまん niman
300	さんびゃく sanbyaku	3,000	さんぜん sanzen	30,000	さんまん sanman
400	よんひゃく yonhyaku	4,000	よんせん yonsen	40,000	よんまん yonman
500	ごひゃく gohyaku	5,000	ごせん gosen	50,000	ごまん goman
600	ろっぴゃく roppyaku	6,000	ろくせん rokusen	60,000	ろくまん rokuman
700	ななひゃく nanahyaku	7,000	ななせん nanasen	70,000	ななまん nanaman
800	はっぴゃく happyaku	8,000	はっせん hassen	80,000	はちまん hachiman
900	きゅうひゃく kyuuhyaku	9,000	きゅうせん kyuusen	90,000	きゅうまん kyuuman

A. Read the following numbers. K02-07

(a) 34   (b) 67   (c) 83   (d) 99   (e) 125

(f) 515   (g) 603   (h) 850   (i) 1,300   (j) 3,400

(k) 8,900   (l) 35,000   (m) 64,500   (n) 92,340

B. Look at the pictures and answer how much the things are. K02-08

Example:　Q：ペンは いくらですか。
　　　　　　　Pen wa　　ikura desu ka.

　　　　　　A：はちじゅうえんです。
　　　　　　　Hachijuu en desu.

Ex. ペン

¥80

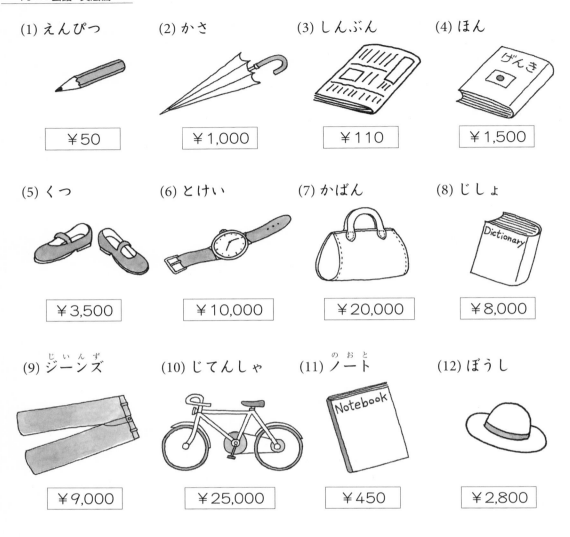

(1) えんぴつ ¥50

(2) かさ ¥1,000

(3) しんぶん ¥110

(4) ほん ¥1,500

(5) くつ ¥3,500

(6) とけい ¥10,000

(7) かばん ¥20,000

(8) じしょ ¥8,000

(9) ジーンズ ¥9,000

(10) じてんしゃ ¥25,000

(11) ノート ¥450

(12) ぼうし ¥2,800

C. Pair Work—One of you looks at picture A and the other looks at picture B (p. 80). (Don't look at the other picture.) Find out the price of all items.

Example:　A：えんぴつは　いくらですか。
　　　　　　　Enpitsu wa　　　ikura desu ka.

　　　　　　B：ひゃくえんです。
　　　　　　　Hyaku en desu.

¥

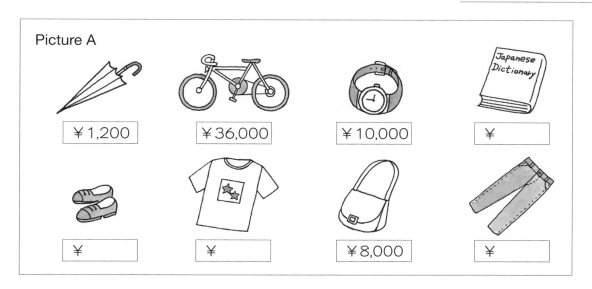

Picture A

Ⅱ これは なんですか

A. Items (1) through (6) are near you, and items (7) through (12) are near your friend. Your friend asks what these things are called in Japanese. Pay attention to これ (*kore*) and それ (*sore*). 🔊 K02-09

Example 1:
Friend：それは なんですか。
　　　　Sore wa　nan desu ka.
　You：これは ペンです。
　　　　Kore wa　pen desu.

Example 2:
Friend：これは なんですか。
　　　　Kore wa　nan desu ka.
　You：それは Tシャツです。
　　　　Sore wa　tiishatsu desu.

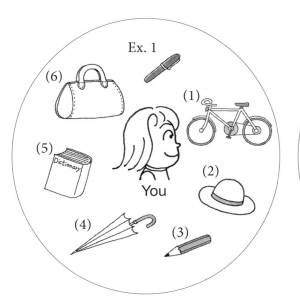

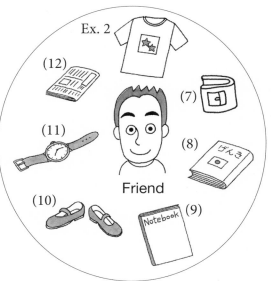

B. Look at the picture and tell what each building is. 🔊 K02-10

Example:　Q：あれは　なんですか。
　　　　　　　　Are wa　　nan desu ka.

　　　　　　A：あれは　としょかんです。
　　　　　　　　Are wa　　toshokan desu.

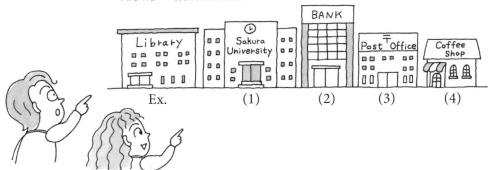

　　　　　　　　　　Ex.　　　　（1）　　　（2）　　　（3）　　　（4）

C. Pair Work—Point out five things in the classroom and ask your partner what they are using これ (kore), それ (sore), or あれ (are). Refer the picture on p. 83 for the vocabulary.

Example 1:
A：あれは　なんですか。
　　Are wa　　nan desu ka.

B：あれは　とけいです。
　　Are wa　　tokee desu.

Example 2:
A：それは　なんですか。
　　Sore wa　　nan desu ka.

B：これは　ペンです。
　　　　　べん
　　Kore wa　　pen desu.

Ⅲ このほんは　いくらですか

A. Look at the pictures and make sentences using この (kono), その (sono), or あの (ano). 🔊 K02-11

Example:　このえんぴつは　ろくじゅうえんです。
　　　　　　　Kono enpitsu wa　　rokujuu en desu.

Ex.　　　　　　　　　（1）　　　　　　　　　　（2）

　　¥60　　　　　　　　　¥290　　　　　　　　　　　　　　　　¥68,000

(3)　　　　　　　(4)　　　　　　　(5)

¥4,300　　　　　¥3,500　　　　　¥17,000

B.　Pair Work—One of you looks at card A and the other looks at card B (p. 81). Ask and answer questions to find out the price of each item. Use この (kono), その (sono), or あの (ano) appropriately. After finding out the price of all items, decide on one item you want to buy.

Example:　Customer :　このほんは いくらですか。
　　　　　　　　　　　　Kono hon wa　　ikura desu ka.

　　　　　Store attendant :　にせんひゃくえんです。
　　　　　　　　　　　　　　　Nisen hyaku en desu.

　　　　　　　　　　*　　　　*　　　　*

　　　　　Customer :　じゃあ、そのかさを ください。
　　　　　　　　　　　　Jaa,　　sono kasa o　　kudasai.

Card A

¥12,600

¥4,200

Wallet

¥315

Book

Ex.　¥2,100

(1) ¥

(2) ¥

(3) ¥

¥1,800

ABC

(4) ¥

¥7,350

(5) ¥

Part I.　You are a store attendant. Tell the customer how much each item is.

Part II.　You are a customer. Ask for the prices of items (1)-(5).

Ⅳ ぎんこうは あそこです

Look at the pictures and answer where the following are. 🔊 K02-12

Ex.

Example:
A：すみません。ぎんこうは どこですか。
　　Sumimasen.　　Ginkoo wa　　doko desu ka.
B：あそこです。
　　Asoko desu.
A：ありがとう ございます。
　　Arigatoo　　gozaimasu.

(1) トイレ
　　toire

(2) としょかん
　　toshokan

(3) くつ
　　kutsu

(4) やましたせんせい
　　Yamashita sensee

(5) メニュー
　　menyuu

(6) じしょ
　　jisho

Ⅴ これは だれの かさですか

Pair Work—Point at each item below (picture A) and ask whose it is. Your partner will refer to the picture B (p. 82) and tell you who it belongs to.

Example:　　A：これは だれの かさですか。
　　　　　　　　Kore wa　dare no　　kasa desu ka.
　　　　　　　B：メアリーさんの かさです。
　　　　　　　　Mearii san no　　　　kasa desu.

Picture A

(1)   (2)   (3)   (4)   (5)

Switch roles with your partner.

(6)   (7)   (8)   (9)  (10)

Ⅵ おかあさんも にほんじんです

Look at the pictures below and describe each picture. 🔊 K02-13

Example:

おとうさんは　にほんじんです。
Otoosan wa　　　nihonjin desu.

おかあさんも　にほんじんです。
Okaasan mo　　　nihonjin desu.

Ex. Japanese

Father　　　　　　Mother

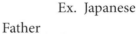

(1) second year

Mary　　　　Carlos

(2) ¥5,800

(3) 22-years old

Takeshi　　　Robert

(4) 7:00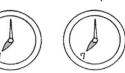

Seoul　　Tokyo

(5) vegetable

(6) U. of London students

Robert　　Nancy

Ⅶ メアリーさんは にほんじんじゃないです

めありい

A. Look at the chart on the next page and answer the questions. 🔊 K02-14

Example: Q：メアリーさんは にほんじんですか。
　　　　　　　めありい　　　　　　Mearii san wa　　　　　nihonjin desu ka.

　　　　　A：いいえ、にほんじんじゃないです。アメリカじんです。
　　　　　　　Iie,　　　nihonjin ja nai desu.　　あめりか　Amerikajin desu.

1. たけしさんは ちゅうごくじんですか。
　Takeshi san wa　　chuugokujin desu ka.

2. ロバートさんは アメリカじんですか。
　ろばあと　　　　　あめりか
　Robaato san wa　　amerikajin desu ka.

3. やましたせんせいは かんこくじんですか。
　Yamashita sensee wa　　kankokujin desu ka.

4. ロバートさんの せんこうは にほんごですか。
　ろばあと
　Robaato san no　　senkoo wa　　nihongo desu ka.

5. スーさんの せんこうは けいざいですか。
　すう
　Suu san no　　senkoo wa　　keezai desu ka.

6. たけしさんは さくらだいがくの がくせいですか。
　Takeshi san wa　　Sakura daigaku no　　gakusee desu ka.

7. メアリーさんは ロンドンだいがくの がくせいですか。
　めありい　　　　　ろんどん
　Mearii san wa　　Rondon daigaku no　　gakusee desu ka.

8. たけしさんは にねんせいですか。
　Takeshi san wa　　ninensee desu ka.

9. スーさんは いちねんせいですか。
　すう
　Suu san wa　　ichinensee desu ka.

10. ロバートさんは よねんせいですか。
　ろばあと
　Robaato san wa　　yonensee desu ka.

	Hart, Mary	きむら たけし Kimura　Takeshi	Kim, Sue	Smith, Robert	やましたせんせい Yamashita sensee
Nationality	American	Japanese	Korean	British	Japanese
School	U. of Arizona	Sakura Univ.	Seoul Univ.	U. of London	Sakura Univ.
Major	Japanese	history	computer	business	(Japanese teacher)
Year	2nd year	4th year	3rd year	4th year	

B. Pair Work—Ask your partner whose belongings items (1) through (7) (picture A) are. Your partner will refer to the picture B (p. 78) and answer the questions.

Example:　A：これは メアリーさんの さいふですか。
　　　　　　　Kore wa　Mearii san no　　　　saifu desu ka.

　　　　　　B：いいえ、 メアリーさんの さいふじゃないです。
　　　　　　　Iie,　　　Mearii san no　　　　saifu ja nai desu.

　　　　　　A：リーさんの さいふですか。
　　　　　　　Rii san no　　　saifu desu ka.

　　　　　　B：ええ、 リーさんの さいふです。
　　　　　　　Ee,　　Rii san no　　　saifu desu.

Ex.

Picture A

(1) 　　(2) 　　(3) 　　(4)

(5) 　　(6) 　　(7)

Picture B

めありい
メアリー
Mearii

りい
リー
Rii

ようこ
Yooko

Ⅷ まとめの れんしゅう (Review Exercises)

A.　Role Play—One student is a store attendant. The other is a customer.
　　Use Dialogue Ⅰ as a model.

B. Role Play—One student is a waiter/waitress. The other student goes to a restaurant. Look at the menu below and order some food or drink, using Dialogue II as a model. (See Culture Note in Lesson 8 [p. 207] for more information on Japanese food.)

C. Look at the picture and ask who each person is. Then, add more questions about their nationality, occupation, etc., as in the example.

Example:　A：これは　だれですか。
Kore wa　dare desu ka.

　　　　　　B：メアリーさんです。
Mearii san desu.

　　　　　　A：イギリスじんですか。
Igirisujin desu ka.

　　　　　　B：いいえ、イギリスじんじゃないです。
Iie,　　　igirisujin ja nai desu.
アメリカじんです。
Amerikajin desu.
アリゾナだいがくの　がくせいです。
Arizona daigaku no　　　gakusee desu.

　　　　　　A：そうですか。
Soo desu ka.

(1)　(2)　(3)　(4)　Ex.

Pair Work (I) C.

(→ p. 70)

Example:　A：えんぴつは　いくらですか。
Enpitsu wa　　　ikura desu ka.

　　　　　　B：ひゃくえんです。
Hyaku en desu.

￥100

Picture B

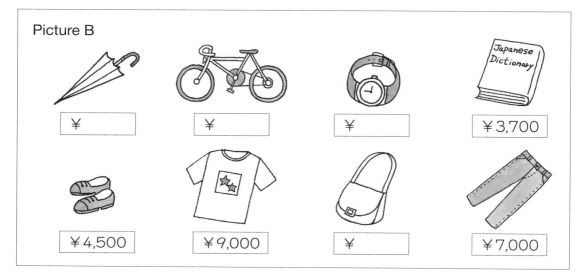

￥　　　￥　　　￥　　　￥3,700

￥4,500　￥9,000　￥　　　￥7,000

Pair Work (Ⅲ) B.

(→ p. 73)

Example: Customer :   このほんは　いくらですか。
Kono hon wa　　ikura desu ka.

Store attendant : にせんひゃくえんです。
Nisen hyaku en desu.

*　　　　*　　　　*

Customer :   じゃあ、そのかさを　ください。
Jaa,　　　sono kasa o　　kudasai.

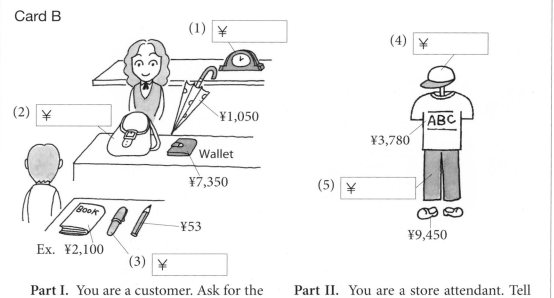

Card B

(1) ¥

(2) ¥

¥1,050

Wallet

¥7,350

BOOK

¥53

Ex.　¥2,100

(3) ¥

(4) ¥

¥3,780

(5) ¥

¥9,450

Part I. You are a customer. Ask for the prices of items (1)-(5).

Part II. You are a store attendant. Tell the customer how much each item is.

Pair Work Ⅴ

(→ p. 74)

Example: A : これは だれの かさですか。
Kore wa   dare no   kasa desu ka.

B : メアリーさんの かさです。
Mearii san no   kasa desu.

Picture B

スー
Suu

たけし
Takeshi

メアリー
Mearii

ロバート
Robaato

やましたせんせい
Yamashita sensee

Useful Expressions

きょうしつ

In the Classroom

こくばん
kokuban

でんき
denki

カーテン
kaaten

ドア
doa

まど
mado

ほん
hon

じしょ
jisho

えんぴつ
enpitsu

ペン
pen

いす
isu

けしゴム
keshigomu

つくえ
tsukue

かばん
kaban

わかりましたか。 Wakarimashita ka.	Do you understand?
わかりました。 Wakarimashita.	I understand./I understood.
わかりません。 Wakarimasen.	I don't understand./I don't know.
ゆっくり いってください。 Yukkuri　itte kudasai.	Please say it slowly.
もういちど いってください。 Moo ichido　itte kudasai.	Please say it again.
ちょっと まってください。 Chotto　matte kudasai.	Please wait.
きいてください。 Kiite kudasai.	Please listen./Please ask.
10ページを みてください。 Juppeeji o　mite kudasai.	Please look at page 10.

第3課 | L E S S O N ·············3

デートの約束 Making a Date
やく そく

会 話 Dialogue
かい わ

Ⅰ Mary and Takeshi are talking. 🔊 K03-01/02

1 たけし : メアリーさん、週末はたいてい何をしますか。
しゅうまつ　　　　なに

2 メアリー : そうですね。たいていうちで勉強します。でも、ときどき映画を見
べんきょう　　　　　　　　　　　　　　えいが　み

3 ます。

4 たけし : そうですか……。じゃあ、土曜日に映画を見ませんか。
どようび　えいが　み

5 メアリー : 土曜日はちょっと……。
どようび

6 たけし : じゃあ、日曜日はどうですか。
にちようび

7 メアリー : いいですね。

Ⅱ On Sunday morning, at Mary's host family's. 🔊 K03-03/04

1 メアリー : おはようございます。

2 お母さん : おはよう。早いですね。
かあ　　　　　　　　はや

3 メアリー : ええ、今日は京都に行きます。京都で映画を見ます。
きょう　きょうと　い　　　きょうと　えいが　み

4 お母さん : いいですね。何時ごろ帰りますか。
かあ　　　　　　　　なんじ　　　かえ

5 メアリー : 九時ごろです。
くじ

6 お母さん : 晩ご飯は？
かあ　　　　ばん　はん

7 メアリー : 食べません。
た

8 お母さん : そうですか。じゃあ、いってらっしゃい。
かあ

9 メアリー : いってきます。

（I）

Takeshi: Mary, what do you usually do on the weekend?

Mary: Let's see. I usually study at home. But I sometimes see movies.

Takeshi: I see. . . . Then, would you like to see a movie on Saturday?

Mary: Saturday is not a good day. (lit., Saturday is a little bit [inconvenient] . . .)

Takeshi: Then, how about Sunday?

Mary: That's fine.

（II）

Mary: Good morning.

Host mother: Good morning. You are early, aren't you?

Mary: Yes, I'm going to Kyoto today. I will see a movie in Kyoto.

Host mother: Good. Around what time will you come back?

Mary: Around nine.

Host mother: How about dinner?

Mary: I will not eat.

Host mother: I see. Well, have a nice day.

Mary: Good-bye.

単語
たん　ご

V o c a b u l a r y

 K03-05

Nouns

Entertainment and Sports

* えいが	映画	movie
おんがく	音楽	music
ざっし	雑誌	magazine
スポーツ		sports
デート		date (romantic, not calendar)
テニス		tennis
テレビ		TV

Foods and Drinks

アイスクリーム		ice cream
あさごはん	朝ご飯	breakfast
おさけ	お酒	sake; alcohol
おちゃ	お茶	green tea
コーヒー		coffee
* ばんごはん	晩ご飯	dinner
ハンバーガー		hamburger
ひるごはん	昼ご飯	lunch
みず	水	water

Places

いえ	家	home; house
* うち		home; house; my place
がっこう	学校	school

Time

あさ	朝	morning
あした	明日	tomorrow
いつ		when
* きょう	今日	today
* ～ごろ		at about . . .
こんばん	今晩	tonight
* しゅうまつ	週末	weekend
* どようび	土曜日	Saturday

* Words that appear in the dialogue

* にちようび	日曜日	Sunday
まいにち	毎日	every day
まいばん	毎晩	every night

U-verbs

* いく	行く	to go （destination に/へ）
* かえる	帰る	to go back; to return （destination に/へ）
きく	聞く	to listen; to hear （〜を）
のむ	飲む	to drink （〜を）
はなす	話す	to speak; to talk （language を/で）
よむ	読む	to read （〜を）

Ru-verbs

おきる	起きる	to get up
* たべる	食べる	to eat （〜を）
ねる	寝る	to sleep; to go to sleep
* みる	見る	to see; to look at; to watch （〜を）

Irregular Verbs

くる	来る	to come （destination に/へ）
* する		to do （〜を）
* べんきょうする	勉強する	to study （〜を）

Adjectives

| * いい | | good |
| * はやい | 早い | early |

Adverbs

あまり + negative		not much
ぜんぜん + negative	全然	not at all
* たいてい		usually
* ちょっと		a little
* ときどき	時々	sometimes
よく		often; much

Expressions

* そうですね		That's right.; Let me see.
* でも		but
* どうですか		How about . . . ?; How is . . . ?

文法 Grammar
ぶん ぽう

1 Verb Conjugation

Verbs in Japanese conjugate, or take various shapes. In this lesson, we learn three forms: (1) the "dictionary forms," (2) the present tense affirmative forms, and (3) the present tense negative forms.[1] There are two kinds of verbs that follow regular conjugation patterns, and an example of each is below.

	ru-verb	u-verb
verb bases	tabe	ik
dictionary forms	食べる (to eat)	行く (to go)
present, affirmative	食べます	行きます
present, negative	食べません	行きません[2]
stems	食べ	行き

食べる belongs to the group of verbs called the "ru-verbs." Ru-verbs are so called, because you add the suffix ru to the verb base (tabe, in the above example) to form the dictionary form. For the two long forms we learn in this lesson, you simply add the suffixes masu and masen, instead of ru, to the bases. We learn four ru-verbs in this lesson:

食べる	寝る	起きる	見る
た	ね	お	み
食べます	寝ます	起きます	見ます
た	ね	お	み

Another major group of verbs is called the "u-verbs." The dictionary form of an u-verb like 行く can be broken down into the base (ik in the above example) and the suffix u. The long forms like 行きます and 行きません, then, are formed with the base plus suffixes imasu and imasen. In u-verb conjugations you find letters shifting in the same row of the hiragana chart (see inside front cover). In 行く, for example, you see く and き, both in the か row of the hiragana chart, 飲む has む and み, both in the ま row, and so forth. We learn six u-verbs in this lesson:

---

[1] The use of the term "dictionary form" is by no means restricted to listings in a dictionary. They also appear in various constructions in actual sentences. We will learn their uses in later chapters. Don't be misled by the names given to the long forms too; the "present tense" in Japanese can indicate both the "present" and the "future." We will return to this issue in Section 2 below. For the moment, we will concentrate on the forms, not the meaning of these verbs.

[2] In addition to the standard negative forms like 食べません and 行きません, you may also hear the much more colloquial sub-standard negative forms like 食べないです and 行かないです used by Japanese speakers. We will briefly come back to these increasingly popular new negative forms in Lesson 8.

飲む	読む	話す	聞く	行く	帰る
の	よ	はな	き	い	かえ
飲みます	読みます	話します	聞きます	行きます	帰ります
の	よ	はな	き	い	かえ

In later lessons, we will have many opportunities to refer to the parts like 食べ and 行き, which come before ます and ません in the long forms. For the sake of ease of reference, we will call these parts (same as bases with *ru*-verbs, and bases plus *i* with *u*-verbs) "stems."

In addition to *ru*-verbs and *u*-verbs, there are two "irregular verbs." Note that the vowels in their bases are different in the short (dictionary) forms and the long forms.

	irregular verbs	
dictionary forms	する (to do)	くる (to come)
present, affirmative	します	きます
present, negative	しません	きません
stems	し	き

These two verbs are also used to form compound verbs. In this lesson, we learn the verb 勉強する, which conjugates just like verb する.

It is important to remember which verb belongs to which conjugation class. It is a good idea, therefore, to memorize each verb as a set: instead of memorizing just the dictionary form, try to memorize the dictionary form *and* the present tense affirmative, like 行く—行きます. This is especially important with verbs that end with the *hiragana* る, because they may be irregular verbs like する and くる, or *ru*-verbs, or *u*-verbs whose bases just happen to end with the consonant *r*. If you know the verb classes and the rules that apply to them, you know why it is wrong to say ×見ります and ×帰ます.

	見る (= a *ru*-verb)	帰る (= an *u*-verb that ends with る)
verb bases	*mi*	*kaer*
long forms	見ます／見ません	帰ります／帰りません
stems	見	帰り

Look at the second from the last syllable in the dictionary form; み and え in 見る and 帰る, for example. The irregular verbs set aside, if you see the vowels *a*, *u*, or *o* right before the final る, you can be absolutely sure that they are *u*-verbs. (We have not learned any such verbs yet.) If you see the vowels *i* and *e* before the final る, in most cases, the verbs are *ru*-verbs. 寝る is such a *ru*-verb. There are exceptions, however; there are also *u*-verbs that have the vowels *i* and *e* before the final る. 帰る is such an exceptional *u*-verb.

2　Verb Types and the "Present Tense"

In this lesson we learn about a dozen verbs that describe basic human actions. These are often called "action verbs," and the "present tense" of these verbs either means (1) that a person habitually or regularly engages in these activities, or (2) that a person will, or is planning to, perform these activities in the future.

Habitual actions:

私はよくテレビを見ます。 　　　　　　　　　*I often watch TV.*

メアリーさんはときどき朝ご飯を食べません。 *Mary sometimes doesn't eat breakfast.*

Future actions:

私はあした京都に行きます。 　　　　　　　　*I will go to Kyoto tomorrow.*

スーさんは今日うちに帰りません。 　　　　　*Sue will not return home today.*

3　Particles

Nouns used in sentences generally must be followed by particles, which indicate the relations that the nouns bear to the verbs.[3] In this lesson, we learn four particles: を, で, に, and へ.

を　The particle を indicates "direct objects," the kind of things that are directly involved in, or affected by, the event. Note that this particle is pronounced "*o*."

コーヒーを飲みます。 　　　　　　　*I drink coffee.*

音楽を聞きます。 　　　　　　　　　*I listen to music.*

テレビを見ます。 　　　　　　　　　*I watch TV.*

で　The particle で indicates where the event described by the verb takes place.[4]

図書館で本を読みます。 　　　　　　*I will read books in the library.*

うちでテレビを見ます。 　　　　　　*I will watch TV at home.*

---

[3] In spoken language, particles are often "dropped." We will learn more about such cases in Lesson 15.

[4] In later lessons, we will be introduced to verbs that require particles other than で to express location.

に   The particle に has many meanings, but here we will learn two: (1) the goal toward which things move, and (2) the time at which an event takes place.

(1) goal of movement

私は今日学校に行きません。
わたし　きょう　がっこう　い

I will not go to school today.

私はうちに帰ります。
わたし　　　　かえ

I will return home.

(2) time

日曜日に京都に行きます。
にちよう び　　きょうと　い

I will go to Kyoto on Sunday.

十一時に寝ます。
じゅういち じ　ね

I will go to bed at eleven.

(Some time words stand alone, without the particle に tagging along, which will be discussed in Section 4 below.)

Approximate time references can be made by substituting ごろ or ごろに for に. Thus,

十一時ごろ(に)寝ます。
じゅういち じ　　　　　ね

I will go to bed at about eleven.

へ   The particle へ, too, indicates the goal of movement. The sentences in (1) above therefore can be rewritten using へ instead of に. Note that this particle is pronounced "*e.*"

私は今日学校へ行きません。
わたし　きょう　がっこう　い

I will not go to school today.

私はうちへ帰ります。
わたし　　　　かえ

I will return home.

Note that へ may replace the particle に only in the goal-of-movement sense. The particle に for time references and other uses, which we will learn about in later lessons, cannot be so replaced.

4   Time Reference

You need the particle に with (1) the days of the week like "on Sunday," and (2) numerical time expressions, like "at 10:45," and "in September."

日曜日に行きます。
にちよう び　い

I will go on Sunday.

十時四十五分に起きます。
じゅう じ　よんじゅう ご ふん　お

I get up at 10:45.

九月に帰ります。
く がつ　かえ

I will go back in September.

You do not use the particle に with (1) time expressions defined relative to the present moment, such as "today," and "tomorrow," (2) expressions describing regular intervals, such as "every day," and (3) the word for "when."

あした来ます。	*I will come tomorrow.*
毎晩テレビを見ます。	*I watch TV every evening.*
いつ行きますか。	*When will you go?*

You normally do not use に with (1) the parts of a day, like "in the morning" and "at night," and (2) the word for "weekend." Unlike words like あした and 毎晩 above, however, these words can be followed by に, depending on styles, emphases, and personal preferences.

朝(に)新聞を読みます。	*I read the newspaper in the morning.*
週末(に)何をしますか。	*What will you do on weekends?*

5　〜ませんか

You can use ませんか (= the present tense negative verb, plus the question particle) to extend an invitation. It should be noted that its affirmative counterpart, ますか, *cannot* be so used. Thus a sentence like 昼ご飯を食べますか can only be construed as a question, not as an invitation.

昼ご飯を食べませんか。	*What do you say to having lunch with me?*
いいですね。	*Sounds great.*
テニスをしませんか。	*Will you play tennis with me?*
うーん、ちょっと。	*Um, it's slightly (inconvenient for me at this moment).*

6　Word Order

Japanese sentences are fairly flexible in the arrangement of elements that appear in them. Generally, sentences are made up of several noun-particle sequences followed by a verb or an adjective, which in turn is often followed by a sentence-final particle such as か, ね, or よ. Among the noun-particle sequences, their relative orders are to a large extent free. A typical sentence, therefore, looks like the following, but several other arrangements of noun-particle sequences are also possible.

私は 今日 図書館で 日本語を 勉強します。
topic **time** **place** **object** **verb**

I will study Japanese in the library today.

私は よく 七時ごろ うちへ 帰ります。
topic **frequency** **time** **goal** **verb**

I often go back home at around seven.

---

7 Frequency Adverbs

You can add a frequency adverb such as 毎日 (everyday), よく (often), and ときどき (sometimes) to a sentence to describe how often you do something.

私はときどき喫茶店に行きます。   *I sometimes go to a coffee shop.*

In this lesson, we also learn two adverbs which describe how *infrequent* an activity or an event is; ぜんぜん (never; not at all) and あまり (not often; not very much). These adverbs anticipate the negative at the end of the sentence. If you use ぜんぜん or あまり, in other words, you need to conclude the sentence with ません.

私はぜんぜんテレビを見ません。   *I do not watch TV at all.*

たけしさんはあまり勉強しません。   *Takeshi does not study much.*

---

8 The Topic Particle は

As we saw in Lesson 1, the particle は presents the topic of one's utterance ("As for item X, it is such that . . ."). It puts forward the item that you want to talk about and comment on. You may have noted that the topic phrases in sentences such as メアリーさんは二年生です (Mary is a sophomore), and 私の専攻は日本語です (My major is the Japanese language), are the subjects of those sentences. A topic phrase, however, need not be the subject of a sentence. We see three sentences in the dialogue of this lesson where nonsubject phrases are made topics with the help of the particle は.

メアリーさん、週末はたいてい何をしますか。
Mary, what do you usually do on the weekend?

今日は京都に行きます。
I'm going to Kyoto today.

In the above two examples, は promotes time expressions as the topic of each sentence. Its effects can be paraphrased like these: "Let's talk about weekends; what do you do on weekends?" "Let me say what I will do today; I will go to Kyoto."

晩ご飯は？
ばん　はん
How about dinner?

—————

食べません。
た
I will not eat.

In this example, は is used in directing the listener's attention and thereby inviting a comment or completion of a sentence. You may also note that the broached topic, 晩ご飯, does not stand in subject relation to the verb, but is rather its direct object.
ばん　はん

表現ノート………4
ひょう　げん

Expression Notes 4

行く/来る▶When you move to a place where the hearer is, you say "I'm com-
い　　く
ing." in English. However in the same situation, 私は行きます is used in Japa-
わたし　い
nese. 来る is a movement toward the place where the speaker is, while 行く is a
く　　　　　　　　　　　　　　　　　　　　　　　　　　　い
movement in a direction away from the speaker.

speaker's viewpoint

I'm coming.

私は
わたし
行きます。
い

speaker's viewpoint

ちょっと▶ちょっと literally means "a little," "a bit," "a small amount," as in ちょっ
とください (Please give me a little) and ちょっと待ってください (Please wait
ま
for a moment). It is commonly used for a polite refusal. In this case, it means "inconvenient," "impossible," and so on. Japanese people don't normally reject requests, suggestions, or invitations with いいえ (No), because it sounds too direct.

A：土曜日に映画を見ませんか。　*Will you see a movie on Saturday?*
　　どようび　えいが　み
B：土曜日は、ちょっと。　　　　　*Saturday is not convenient.*
　　どようび
　　　　　　　　　　　　　　　　　(lit., Saturday is a little bit.)

練習 P r a c t i c e
れん しゅう

Ⅰ 図書館で雑誌を読みます
と しょ かん ざっ し よ

A. Change the following verbs into 〜ます and 〜ません. 🔊 K03-06/07

Example:　たべる　→　たべます

　　　　　　たべる　→　たべません

1. のむ
2. きく
3. みる
4. する
5. はなす
6. いく
7. くる
8. かえる
9. ねる
10. よむ
11. おきる
12. べんきょうする

B. Look at the pictures below and make sentences using the cues.

(a) Add the appropriate verbs to the following direct objects. 🔊 K03-08

Example:　雑誌　→　雑誌を読みます。
　　　　　ざっ し　　　ざっ し　よ

Ex. 雑誌
ざっ し

library/2:00

(1) 音楽
おんがく

home/4:30

(2) テニス

school/Saturday

(3) ハンバーガー

McDonald's/5:00

(4) コーヒー

coffee shop/3:00

(5) テレビ

home/tonight

(6) 日本語
に ほん ご

college/every day

(b) Add the place to the above sentences. 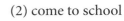 K03-09

Example:　library　→　図書館で雑誌を読みます。
　　　　　　　　　　　　としょかん　ざっし　　　よ

C.　Look at the pictures below and make sentences using the cues. 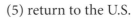 K03-10

Example:　go to the post office　→　郵便局に行きます。
　　　　　　　　　　　　　　　　　ゆうびんきょく　　い

Ex. go to the post office　　　(1) go to the library　　　(2) come to school

　　　　1:00　　　　　　　　　　　3:00　　　　　　　　　　8:30

(3) come to the coffee shop　　(4) return home　　　(5) return to the U.S.

　　　Sunday　　　　　　　　　　5:30　　　　　　　　　tomorrow

D.　Pair Work—Make questions, using verbs we have learned in this lesson.

Example:　Ａ：図書館で雑誌を読みますか。
　　　　　　　　としょかん　ざっし　　　よ
　　　　　　　Ｂ：ええ、読みます。／いいえ、読みません。
　　　　　　　　　　　　よ　　　　　　　　　　　　よ

E. Pair Work—Guessing game
Ask questions and find out the items your partner has chosen.

> 1. Before you start, both of you will choose one item in each row of the table and mark it.
> 2. In each row, using the verb and one of the four items, make a yes-or-no-question sentence and find out which item your partner has chosen.
> 3. You can ask at most two questions with one verb. If you have guessed correctly the item your partner has chosen, you score a point. Your partner will not give away the right answer when you ask a wrong question.
> 4. When you have asked questions about all the verbs in the table, switch roles with your partner and answer their questions.
> 5. Tabulate the score. You win the game if you have scored higher than your partner.

Example:　A：学校に行きますか。
　　　　　B：いいえ、行きません。
　　　　　A：喫茶店に行きますか。
　　　　　B：はい、行きます。(A guessed what B marked, therefore A won.)

～に行きます	post office	school	coffee shop	library
～を見ます	sports	movie	news（ニュース）	cartoon（まんが）
～を飲みます	sake	green tea	water	coffee
～を読みます	book	newspaper	magazine	Japanese book
～をします	date	study	telephone	tennis

(II) 何時に起きますか

A. Look at Mary's schedule and answer the following questions. 🔊 K03-11

7:30 A.M.	get up
8:00	eat breakfast
8:30	go to school
12:00	eat lunch
3:00 P.M.	drink coffee
4:00	play tennis
5:00	go home
6:30	eat dinner
7:00	watch TV
8:00	study
11:30	go to bed

1. メアリーさんは何時に起きますか。
2. メアリーさんは何時に学校に行きますか。
3. メアリーさんは何時に昼ご飯を食べますか。
4. メアリーさんは何時にコーヒーを飲みますか。
5. メアリーさんは何時にうちに帰りますか。
6. メアリーさんは何時に勉強しますか。
7. メアリーさんは何時に寝ますか。

B. Pair Work—Ask your partner what time they do the following things.

Example:　A：何時に起きますか。／何時ごろ起きますか。
　　　　　　B：八時に起きます。／八時ごろ起きます。

Your partner's schedule

time	
(　　　　　)	get up
(　　　　　)	eat breakfast
(　　　　　)	go to school
(　　　　　)	eat lunch
(　　　　　)	go home
(　　　　　)	go to bed

C. Look at the pictures in I-B (p. 95) and I-C (p. 96), and add the time expressions to the sentences. 🔊 K03-12/13

Example:　(I-B) 2:00　→　二時に図書館で雑誌を読みます。
　　　　　　(I-C) 1:00　→　一時に郵便局に行きます。

Ⅲ コーヒーを飲みませんか

A. Make suggestions using the cues below. 🔊 K03-14

Example: drink coffee → コーヒーを飲みませんか。

1. see a movie
2. come to my house
3. play tennis
4. eat dinner
5. study in the library
6. talk at a coffee shop
7. drink tea at home
8. listen to the music

B. Pair Work—Ask your friend out for the activities in the pictures.

Example: A：日曜日に図書館で勉強しませんか。
B：いいですね。／すみませんが、ちょっと……。

Ex.　　　　(1)　　　　(2)　　　　(3)

(4)　　　　(5)　　　　(6)

Ⅳ 毎日本を読みます

How often do you do the following activities? Answer the questions using the expressions below.

Example: Q：本を読みますか。
A：ええ、よく読みます。／いいえ、あまり読みません。

1. スポーツをしますか。
2. 雑誌を読みますか。
3. 図書館に行きますか。
4. 映画を見ますか。
5. コーヒーを飲みますか。
6. 日本の音楽を聞きますか。
7. 朝ご飯を食べますか。

毎日	
よく	〜ます
ときどき	
あまり	
ぜんぜん	〜ません

Ⓥ まとめの練習 (Review Exercises)

A. Answer the following questions.

1. 何時に起きますか。
2. どこで勉強しますか。
3. いつテレビを見ますか。
4. スポーツをしますか。

5. 週末はどこに行きますか。
6. 朝、何を食べますか。
7. 今晩、何をしますか。
8. 毎晩、何時ごろ寝ますか。

B. Tell your classmates what your plans are today/tomorrow/on the weekend.

Example: 今日は一時ごろ昼ご飯を食べます。三時に図書館で日本語を勉強します。六時ごろ家に帰ります。

C. Class Activity—Find someone who . . .

name

1. gets up at 7 o'clock. _____

2. eats breakfast every day. _____

3. speaks French. _____

4. watches TV at home. _____

5. listens to Japanese music. _____

6. plays tennis. _____

D. Suggest to a classmate that you do something together over the weekend. Use Dialogue I as a model.

Example:　A：Ｂさんはテニスをしますか。

　　　　　B：はい。

　　　　　A：じゃあ、日曜日<small>にちようび</small>にテニスをしませんか。

　　　　　B：日曜日<small>にちようび</small>はちょっと……。

　　　　　A：そうですか。じゃあ、土曜日<small>どようび</small>はどうですか。

　　　　　B：ええ、いいですね。

Culture Note

日本の家<small>にほんいえ</small> Japanese Houses

Traditionally, Japanese buildings were made of wood. Rooms were floored with *tatami* (rice-straw mats) and divided by *fusuma* or *shooji* (two types of sliding doors).

Fusuma　　Tatami　　　Shooji

Modern Japanese houses have mainly Western-style rooms, and are equipped with Western-style toilets. However, most bathrooms retain traditional characteristics—they are separated from toilets and sinks, and have some space for washing one's body outside the bathtub. Usually, all family members share the same bathtub water, so it is necessary to clean one's body before getting into the bathtub.

Another traditional feature of Japanese homes is the *genkan*, a space inside the entrance where people remove their shoes.

Japanese-style toilet

Bathroom

Genkan

第4課 | L E S S O N ·················4

初めてのデート The First Date
はじ

会話 D i a l o g u e
かい わ

(I) Mary goes downtown. 🔊 K04-01/02

1 メアリー： すみません。マクドナルドはどこですか。

2 知らない人： あそこにデパートがありますね。
　し　　ひと

3 　　　　　　マクドナルドはあのデパートの前ですよ。
　　　　　　　　　　　　　　　　　　　　　まえ

4 メアリー： ありがとうございます。

(II) In the evening, at Mary's host family's house. 🔊 K04-03/04

1 メアリー： ただいま。

2 お父さん： おかえりなさい。映画はどうでしたか。
　とう　　　　　　　　　　　えい が

3 メアリー： 見ませんでした。たけしさんは来ませんでした。
　　　　　み　　　　　　　　　　　　　　　　き

4 お父さん： えっ、どうしてですか。
　とう

5 メアリー： わかりません。だから、一人で本屋とお寺に行きました。
　　　　　　　　　　　　　　　ひとり　ほん や　　てら　い

6 お父さん： 人がたくさんいましたか。
　とう　　　ひと

7 メアリー： はい。お寺で写真をたくさん撮りました。
　　　　　　　　　てら　しゃしん　　　　　と

8 　　　　　デパートにも行きました。
　　　　　　　　　　　　い

9 　　　　　はい、おみやげです。

10 お父さん： ありがとう。
　　とう

Ⅲ Next day at school. 🔊 K04-05/06

1 メアリー： 　あっ、たけしさん。きのう来ませんでしたね。

2 たけし： 　行きましたよ。モスバーガーの前で一時間待ちました。

3 メアリー： 　モスバーガーじゃないですよ。マクドナルドですよ。

4 たけし： 　マクドナルド……ごめんなさい！

Ⓘ

Mary: Excuse me. Where is McDonald's?

Stranger: There is a department store over there. McDonald's is in front of the department store.

Mary: Thank you.

Ⅱ

Mary: I'm home.

Host father: Welcome home. How was the movie?

Mary: I didn't see it. Takeshi didn't come.

Father: Oh, why?

Mary: I don't know. So, I went to a bookstore and a temple alone.

Host father: Were there a lot of people?

Mary: Yes. I took many pictures at the temple. I also went to a department store.
　　　Here's a souvenir for you.

Host father: Thank you.

Ⅲ

Mary: Oh, Takeshi. You didn't come yesterday, did you?

Takeshi: I went there. I waited for one hour in front of the Mos Burger place.

Mary: Not Mos Burger. McDonald's!

Takeshi: McDonald's . . . I'm sorry!

単語
たん ご

 K04-07

V o c a b u l a r y

Nouns

Activities

アルバイト		part-time job
かいもの	買い物	shopping
クラス		class

People and Things

あなた		you
いす		chair
いぬ	犬	dog
*おみやげ	お土産	souvenir
こども	子供	child
ごはん	ご飯	rice; meal
*しゃしん	写真	picture; photograph
つくえ	机	desk
てがみ	手紙	letter
ねこ	猫	cat
パン		bread
*ひと	人	person
メール		e-mail

Places

*おてら	お寺	temple
こうえん	公園	park
スーパー		supermarket
*デパート		department store
バスてい	バス停	bus stop
びょういん	病院	hospital
ホテル		hotel
*ほんや	本屋	bookstore
まち	町	town; city
レストラン		restaurant

* Words that appear in the dialogue

Time

* きのう	昨日	yesterday
* 〜じかん	〜時間	. . . hours
cf. いちじかん	一時間	one hour
せんしゅう	先週	last week
とき	時	when . . . ; at the time of . . . （〜の）
げつようび	月曜日	Monday
かようび	火曜日	Tuesday
すいようび	水曜日	Wednesday
もくようび	木曜日	Thursday
きんようび	金曜日	Friday

U - v e r b s

あう	会う	to meet; to see (a person) （*person* に）
* ある		there is . . . （*place* に *thing* が）
かう	買う	to buy （〜を）
かく	書く	to write （*person* に *thing* を）
* とる	撮る	to take (a picture) （〜を）
* まつ	待つ	to wait （〜を）
* わかる		to understand （〜が）

R u - v e r b

* いる		(a person) is in . . . ; stays at . . . （*place* に *person* が）

A d v e r b s   a n d   O t h e r   E x p r e s s i o n s

〜ぐらい		about (approximate measurement)
* ごめんなさい		I'm sorry.
* だから		so; therefore
* たくさん		many; a lot
〜と		together with (a person)
* どうして		why
* ひとりで	一人で	alone

Location Words

みぎ	右	right （〜の）
ひだり	左	left （〜の）
*まえ	前	front （〜の）
うしろ	後ろ	back （〜の）
なか	中	inside （〜の）
うえ	上	on （〜の）
した	下	under （〜の）
ちかく	近く	near; nearby （〜の）
となり	隣	next （〜の）
あいだ	間	between （A と B の）

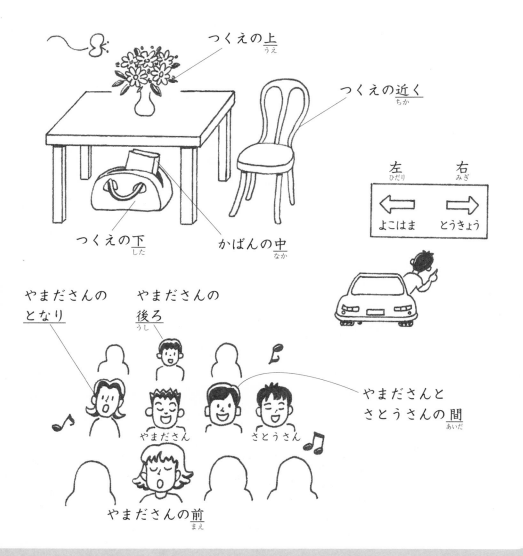

つくえの上
つくえの近く
つくえの下
かばんの中

左　右
よこはま　とうきょう

やまださんの　となり
やまださんの　後ろ
やまださんと　さとうさんの　間
やまださん
さとうさん
やまださんの　前

文法 Grammar

1　Xがあります/います

Xがあります means "there is/are X (nonliving thing)." The particle が introduces, or presents, the item X. You can use あります when you want to say that there is something at a certain location.

あそこにマクドナルドがあります。 　　　*There's a McDonald's over there.*

Note that あります is different from other verbs we have seen so far on the following three counts. One, it calls for the particle に, rather than で, for the place description. Two, the place description usually comes at the beginning of the sentence. Three, the thing description is usually followed by the particle が, rather than は.[1]

You can also use あります to say that you *have* or *own* something.[2]

テレビがありません。 　　　*I don't have a TV.*

時間がありますか。 　　　*Do you have time?*

We also use あります when we want to say that *an event will take place*.[3]

火曜日にテストがあります。 　　　*There will be an exam on Tuesday.*

あしたは日本語のクラスがありません。 　　　*There will be no Japanese class tomorrow.*

---

[1] Another count on which ある differs from other verbs is its colloquial substandard negative form. We have ないです, instead of the expected regular formation あらないです, which is ungrammatical.

[2] Note the difference between:
　　テレビがありません (I don't have a TV), the negative version of テレビがあります, and
　　テレビじゃありません (It isn't a TV), the more conservative negative version of テレビです.

[3] When あります is used in the sense of an event taking place, the place description is followed by the particle で, like normal verbs and unlike the other uses of あります.
　　あした京都でお祭りがあります。　　*There will be a festival in Kyoto tomorrow.*
Note also that some time expressions (such as 日曜日に) come with the particle に, and some others (such as あした) do not (see Lesson 3). The rule applies to the あります sentences as well.

When you want to present a *person* or some other sentient being, rather than a thing, you need to use the verb います.[4] Thus,

あそこに留学生がいます。　　　　*There's an international student over there.*
りゅうがくせい

You can also use います to say that you *have* friends, siblings, and so forth.

日本人の友だちがいます。　　　　*I have a Japanese friend.*
にほんじん　とも

(place に)	thing が	あります	*There is/are . . .*
	person が	います	

2　Describing Where Things Are

We learned in Lesson 2 that to ask for the location of item X, you can use the word どこ (where) and say X はどこですか.

マクドナルドはどこですか。　　　　*Where's McDonald's?*

In response, one can, of course, point and say:

マクドナルドは	あそこ	です。	*McDonald's is*	over there.	
	そこ			right there near you.	
	ここ			right here.	

In this lesson, we will learn to describe locations in more detail. More specifically, we learn to describe the location of an item relative to another item, as in "X is in front of Y." The Japanese version looks like X は Y の前です.
まえ

（マクドナルドは）あのデパートの前です。
まえ

It's in front of that department store.

---

[4] Note that the same verb "is" in English comes out differently in Japanese:

あそこに留学生がいます。　　*There is an international student over there.*
りゅうがくせい

メアリーさんは留学生です。　　*Mary is an international student.*
りゅうがくせい

います and あります are strictly for descriptions of existence and location, while です is for description of an attribute of a person or a thing.

Other useful words describing locations are as follows:

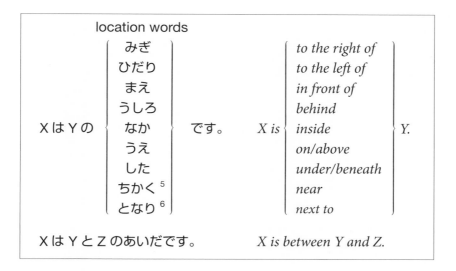

銀行は図書館の<u>となり</u>です。
ぎんこう　としょかん
The bank is next to the library.

かさはテーブルの<u>下</u>です。
した
The umbrella is under the table.

レストランはデパートと病院の<u>間</u>です。
びょういん　　　あいだ
The restaurant is between the department store and the hospital.

One can use any of the above location words together with a verb to describe an event that occur in the place. To use these phrases with verbs such as 食べる and 待つ, one will need
た　　　　　　　ま
the particle で.

私はモスバーガーの<u>前</u>でメアリーさんを待ちました。
わたし　　　　　　　　まえ　　　　　　　　　ま
I waited for Mary in front of the Mos Burger place.

---

[5] Another word for "near" that is also commonly used is そば.

[6] Both X は Y のとなりです and X は Y のよこです describe situations where two items (X and Y) are found side by side. For a となり sentence to be considered appropriate, items X and Y need to belong to the same category; two people, two buildings, and so forth. In contrast, an item can be よこ in relation to another item even if they are quite distinct.

　　　○ かばんはつくえの<u>よこ</u>です。　　　　*The bag is by the desk.*
　　　× かばんはつくえの<u>となり</u>です。　　　(odd)

3 Past Tense of です

The past tense versions of "X は Y です" sentences look like the following.

	affirmative	negative
present tense	～です	～じゃないです
past tense	～でした	～じゃなかったです[7]

山下先生はさくら大学の学生でした。
Mr. Yamashita was a student at Sakura University.

あれは日本の映画じゃなかったです。
That was not a Japanese movie.

4 Past Tense of Verbs

The past tense forms of verbs look like the following, where ～ stands for the stem of a verb.

	affirmative	negative
present tense	～ます	～ません
past tense	～ました	～ませんでした[8]

メアリーさんは九時ごろうちに帰りました。　*Mary returned home at about nine.*

私はきのう日本語を勉強しませんでした。　*I did not study Japanese yesterday.*

The various details of formation of the long forms that we learned in Lesson 3, like the *ru*-verb/*u*-verb/irregular verb distinctions, all apply to the past tense forms as well.

---

[7] As was the case with the present tense じゃないです, you also find a more conservative variant じゃありませんでした along with じゃなかったです. Written language would more likely have ではありませんでした, with the uncontracted form では.

[8] The colloquial substandard form of the past tense negative verbs are なかったです, as in 帰らなかったです. We will learn how to change verbs into these forms in Lesson 8.

5 も

We learned in Lesson 2 that we use the particle も in reference to the second item which shares a common attribute with the first. You can also use も when two or more people perform the same activity.

私はきのう京都に行きました。   *I went to Kyoto yesterday.*

山下先生もきのう京都に行きました。 *Professor Yamashita went to Kyoto*
                yesterday, too.

Or when someone buys, sees, or eats two or more things.

メアリーさんはくつを買いました。 *Mary bought shoes.*

メアリーさんはかばんも買いました。 *Mary bought a bag, too.*

In both cases, も directly marks an item on the list of things or people that have something in common. Observe that も *replaces* the particles は, が, or を in these sentences.

You can also use も when you go to two places, do something on two different occasions, and so forth.

私は先週京都に行きました。   *I went to Kyoto last week.*

大阪にも行きました。   *I went to Osaka, too.*

ロバートさんは土曜日にパーティーに行きました。
           Robert went to a party on Saturday.

日曜日にもパーティーに行きました。
           He went to a party on Sunday, too.

We put も *after* the particle に in these sentences. More generally, particles other than は, が, and を are used together with も, rather than being replaced by it.

6 一時間
いち じ かん

The duration of an activity is expressed with a bare noun, like 一時間. Such a noun stands
いち じ かん
alone (that is, not followed by any particle).

メアリーさんはそこでたけしさんを一時間待ちました。
いち じ かん ま

Mary waited for Takeshi there for an hour.

For an approximate measurement, you can add ぐらい[9] after 〜時間.
じ かん

私はきのう日本語を三時間ぐらい勉強しました。
わたし   に ほん ご さん じ かん   べんきょう

I studied Japanese for about three hours yesterday.

To say one hour and a half, you can add 半 immediately after 〜時間.
はん   じ かん

きのう七時間半寝ました。
しち じ かんはん ね

(I) slept for seven and a half hours last night.

7 たくさん

Expressions of quantity in Japanese are rather different from those in English. In Japanese,
if you want to add a quantity word like たくさん to the direct object of a sentence, you can
either place it before the noun, or after the particle を.

私は京都で⎰ 写真をたくさん ⎱撮りました。   *I took many pictures in Kyoto.*
わたし きょうと しゃしん   と
      ⎱ たくさん写真を ⎰
              しゃしん

⎰ 野菜をたくさん ⎱食べました。   *I ate a lot of vegetables.*
  やさい   た
⎱ たくさん野菜を ⎰
       やさい

---

[9] As we learned in Lesson 3, for "at about a certain time" we have another word ごろ.

[10] You can use と to connect nouns only. We will learn about connecting verbs and sentences in Lesson 6.

[11] "With" as in "with chopsticks" requires another particle. See Lesson 10.

8　と

The particle と has two functions. One is to connect two nouns A and B.[10]

日本語と英語を話します。　　　　　　*I speak Japanese <u>and</u> English.*

京都と大阪に行きました。　　　　　　*I went to Kyoto <u>and</u> Osaka.*

The other meaning of と is "together with"; it describes *with whom* you do something.[11]

メアリーさんはスーさんと韓国に行きます。

Mary will go to Korea <u>with</u> Sue.

表現ノート……5

Expression Notes 5

X の前▶X の前 is often used in the sense of "across (the street) from X" or "opposite X." You may also hear another word that is used in the sense of across, namely, X のむかい.

If something is behind X, or farther away from a street and cannot be directly seen because of the intervening X, in addition to calling it X の後ろ, you can also describe it as being X のうら.

えっ/あっ▶In the dialogues, we observe Mary's host father saying えっ, and Mary saying あっ. えっ is like the incredulous "what?" that you use when you have heard something that is hard to believe. あっ is used when you have suddenly noticed or remembered something. The small っ at the end of these little words indicates that these words, when pronounced, are very short.

日本の祝日 Japanese National Holidays
にほん　　しゅくじつ

1月1日 がつついたち	元日 がんじつ	New Year's Day
1月第2月曜日[1] がつだい　げつよう び	成人の日 せいじん　ひ	Coming-of-Age Day (Celebrates people who turn 20 years old in that year)
2月11日 がつ　にち	建国記念の日 けんこく き ねん　ひ	National Foundation Day
3月20日ごろ[2] がつ はつか	春分の日 しゅんぶん　ひ	Vernal Equinox Day
4月29日 がつ　にち	昭和の日 しょう わ　ひ	Showa Day (Birthday of Emperor Showa [1901-1989])
5月3日 がつみっか	憲法記念日 けんぽう き ねん び	Constitution Day
5月4日 がつよっか	みどりの日 ひ	Greenery Day
5月5日 がついつか	こどもの日 ひ	Children's Day
7月第3月曜日[3] がつだい　げつようび	海の日 うみ　ひ	Marine Day
9月第3月曜日[3] がつだい　げつようび	敬老の日 けいろう　ひ	Respect-for-the-Aged Day
9月23日ごろ[2] がつ　にち	秋分の日 しゅうぶん　ひ	Autumnal Equinox Day
10月第2月曜日[1] がつだい　げつようび	体育の日 たいいく　ひ	Health and Sports Day
11月3日 がつみっか	文化の日 ぶん か　ひ	Culture Day
11月23日 がつ　にち	勤労感謝の日 きんろうかんしゃ　ひ	Labor Thanksgiving Day
12月23日 がつ　にち	天皇誕生日 てんのうたんじょう び	Emperor's Birthday

1: The second Monday　　2: The day varies year to year　　3: The third Monday

The period around April 29 to May 5 encompasses several holidays and is called ゴールデンウィーク (Golden Week). Some businesses close for a whole week or more during that period. (For the names of months and days, see p. 127.)

練習 Practice
れん しゅう

① 病院があります
びょういん

A. Look at the picture and tell what you see, using あります or います.

B. Answer the following questions.

1. あなたの町に日本のレストランがありますか。
   まち　にほん
2. あなたの家に猫がいますか。
   いえ　ねこ
3. あなたの学校に何がありますか。
   がっこう　なに
4. あなたの学校に日本人の学生がいますか。
   がっこう　にほんじん　がくせい
5. デパートに何がありますか。
   なに
6. この教室 (classroom) にだれがいますか。
   きょうしつ
7. 動物園 (zoo) に何がいますか。
   どうぶつえん　　　なに
8. あなたの国 (country) に何がありますか。
   くに　　　　　　　なに
9. あなたの家に何がありますか。
   いえ　なに

C. Look at Takeshi's schedule for the week and answer the following questions.

K04-08

	School	After School
Monday	French English Computer	
Tuesday	History	Club activity
Wednesday	French English Computer	
Thursday	History	Club activity
Friday	English (TEST)	Party
Saturday	NO SCHOOL	Date
Sunday	NO SCHOOL	Part-time job

club activity	サークル
party	パーティー
test	テスト

Example:　Q：月曜日にフランス語のクラスがありますか。
　　　　　　A：はい、あります。

1. 月曜日に英語のクラスがありますか。
2. 火曜日にコンピューターのクラスがありますか。
3. 木曜日にフランス語のクラスがありますか。
4. 土曜日にクラスがありますか。
5. 水曜日に何がありますか。
6. 金曜日に何がありますか。
7. 日曜日に何がありますか。

D. Pair Work—Write down your next week's schedule and ask each other what plans you have on each day of the week.

Example:　A：月曜日に何がありますか。
　　　　　　B：日本語のクラスがあります。

	Your Schedule	Your Partner's Schedule
月曜日 げつようび		
火曜日 かようび		
水曜日 すいようび		
木曜日 もくようび		
金曜日 きんようび		
土曜日 どようび		
日曜日 にちようび		

Ⅱ 図書館はどこですか
としょかん

A. Look at the picture and tell where the following things are. 🔊 K04-09

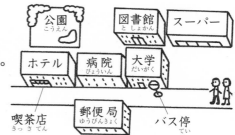

Example: 図書館
としょかん
→ 図書館は大学の後ろです。
としょかん だいがく うし
図書館はスーパーのとなりです。
としょかん

1. 郵便局   3. バス停   5. スーパー
ゆうびんきょく   てい
2. 喫茶店   4. 公園   6. 病院
きっさてん   こうえん   びょういん

B. Look at the picture and tell where the following things are. 🔊 K04-10

Example: 本 → 本はつくえの上です。
ほん   ほん   うえ

1. えんぴつ
2. ラケット
3. 時計
とけい
4. 電話
でんわ
5. かばん
6. ぼうし

ドア (door)

ラケット
(racket)

C. Pair Work—Ask and answer questions to find where the buildings are.
One student looks at map A. The other student looks at map B (p. 126). Don't
look at the other's map.

Example:　A：公園はどこですか。
　　　　　　　　こうえん
　　　　　　B：公園はホテルのとなりです。
　　　　　　　　こうえん

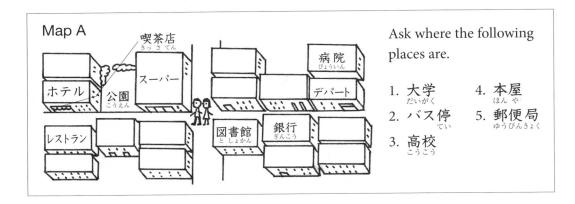

Map A

喫茶店
きっ さ てん
スーパー
ホテル　公園
　　　こうえん
レストラン

病院
びょういん
デパート
図書館　銀行
と しょかん　ぎんこう

Ask where the following places are.

1. 大学　　　4. 本屋
　 だいがく　　　 ほん や
2. バス停　　5. 郵便局
　 　　 てい　　　 ゆうびんきょく
3. 高校
　 こうこう

Ⅲ 先生は大学生でした
　 せん せい　　 だい がく せい

A. Look at the information about Professor Yamashita 25 years ago and answer
the questions. 🔊 K04-11

Twenty-five years ago, Prof. Yamashita was
　・twenty-two years old
　・senior at a college
　・good student
　・his major—Japanese history

Example:

Q：山下先生は大学生 (college student) でしたか。
　 やましたせんせい　　 だいがくせい
A：はい、山下先生は大学生でした。
　　　　　 やましたせんせい　　 だいがくせい

Q：山下先生は十九歳でしたか。
　 やましたせんせい　　 じゅうきゅうさい
A：いいえ、山下先生は十九歳じゃなかったです。
　　　　　　 やましたせんせい　　 じゅうきゅうさい

1. 山下先生は子供でしたか。
　 やましたせんせい　 こ ども
2. 山下先生は一年生でしたか。
　 やましたせんせい　 いちねんせい
3. 山下先生はいい学生でしたか。
　 やましたせんせい　　　 がくせい

4. 山下先生の専攻は英語でしたか。
　 やましたせんせい　 せんこう　 えい ご
5. 山下先生の専攻は歴史でしたか。
　 やましたせんせい　 せんこう　 れき し

B. Pair Work—Guessing game
Ask questions and find out the prices your partner has chosen.

1. Before you start, both of you will choose one price in each row of the table and mark it.
2. In each row, use the item and one of the four prices, make a yes-or-no-question sentence and find out which price your partner has chosen.
3. You can ask at most two questions with one item. If you have guessed correctly the price your partner has chosen, you score a point. Your partner will not give away the right answer when you ask a wrong question.
4. When you have asked questions about all the items in the table, switch the roles with your partner and answer their questions.
5. Tabulate the score. You win the game if you have scored higher than your partner.

Example:　A：そのかばんは二万円でしたか。
　　　　　B：いいえ、二万円じゃなかったです。
　　　　　A：一万五千円でしたか。
　　　　　B：はい、そうです。

かばん	¥5,000	¥10,000	¥15,000	¥20,000
かさ	¥600	¥1,000	¥1,300	¥2,000
ぼうし	¥1,600	¥2,000	¥2,400	¥3,000
Tシャツ	¥3,500	¥4,000	¥6,500	¥8,000
時計	¥3,000	¥10,000	¥17,000	¥25,000

C. Pair Work—Suppose you got one thing as a birthday present (プレゼント) and choose it from the items on the next page. Your partner guesses what you got. Answer your partner's questions.

Example:　A：プレゼントはかばんでしたか。
　　　　　B：ええ、かばんでした。／いいえ、かばんじゃなかったです。

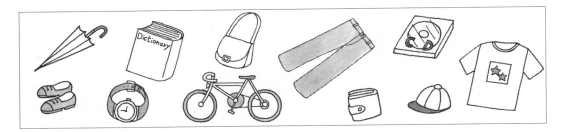

Ⅳ 月曜日に何をしましたか
げつ よう び なに

A. Change the following verbs into 〜ました and 〜ませんでした. 🔊 K04-12/13

Example: たべる　→　たべました

たべる　→　たべませんでした

1. はなす	4. かく	7. おきる	10. とる	13. きく
2. かう	5. くる	8. わかる	11. ある	14. かえる
3. よむ	6. まつ	9. する	12. ねる	15. のむ

B. The pictures below show what Mary did last week. Tell what she did. 🔊 K04-14

Example:　メアリーさんは月曜日に図書館で勉強しました。
げつようび　としょかん　べんきょう

Ex. Monday　　　(1) Tuesday　　　(2) Wednesday　　　(3) Thursday

in the library　　　at home　　　at school　　　at a coffee shop

(4) Friday　　　(5) Saturday　　　(6) Sunday

at her friend's house　　　in Kyoto　　　at a department store

C. Look at the pictures in B and answer the questions. 🔊 K04-15

Example:　Q：メアリーさんは月曜日に図書館で勉強しましたか。
　　　　　A：はい、勉強しました。
　　　　　Q：メアリーさんは月曜日に映画を見ましたか。
　　　　　A：いいえ、見ませんでした。

1. メアリーさんは火曜日に音楽を聞きましたか。
2. メアリーさんは水曜日に手紙を書きましたか。
3. メアリーさんは木曜日に日本人の友だちに会いましたか。
4. メアリーさんは金曜日にお寺に行きましたか。
5. メアリーさんは土曜日にテニスをしましたか。
6. メアリーさんは日曜日に買い物をしましたか。

D. Look at the pictures in B and answer the questions. 🔊 K04-16

Example:　Q：メアリーさんは月曜日に何をしましたか。
　　　　　A：図書館で勉強しました。

1. メアリーさんは水曜日に何をしましたか。
2. メアリーさんは火曜日に何をしましたか。
3. メアリーさんはいつ映画を見ましたか。
4. メアリーさんはいつ買い物をしましたか。
5. メアリーさんは金曜日にどこで晩ご飯を食べましたか。
6. メアリーさんは木曜日にどこで友だちに会いましたか。

E. Pair Work—Ask what your partner did on Monday, Tuesday, etc.

Example:　A：月曜日に何をしましたか。
　　　　　B：テニスをしました。

Ⓥ コーヒーも飲みます

A. Compare sentences (a) and (b), and change the sentence (b) using も.  K04-17

Example:　(a) ハンバーガーは二百円です。
　　　　　(b) コーヒーは二百円です。　→　コーヒーも二百円です。

1. (a) たけしさんは時計を買いました。
   (b) たけしさんはかばんを買いました。

2. (a) ロバートさんは日本語を勉強します。
   (b) メアリーさんは日本語を勉強します。

3. (a) たけしさんは土曜日にアルバイトをします。
   (b) たけしさんは日曜日にアルバイトをします。

4. (a) メアリーさんはうちで日本語を話します。
   (b) メアリーさんは学校で日本語を話します。

5. (a) あした、メアリーさんはたけしさんに会います。
   (b) あした、メアリーさんはスーさんに会います。

6. (a) 先週、デパートに行きました。
   (b) きのう、デパートに行きました。

B. Describe the pictures using も. K04-18

Example:　山本さんは学生です。
　　　　　田中さんも学生です。

Ex. やまもと　たなか

student

(1) きむら　やまぐち

go to a party

(2)

ごはん　パン

(3)

コーヒー　おちゃ

(4)

I speak English　Hablo español

スペイン語

(5)

(6)

(7)

(8)

(9)

Ⅵ 一時間待ちました
いち じ かん ま

A. Mary did a lot yesterday. Describe how many hours Mary did each activity.

K04-19

Example: メアリーさんは八時間寝ました。
はち じ かん ね

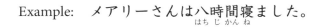

B. Pair Work—Ask your partner the following questions.

Example: A：きのう、何時間テレビを見ましたか。
B：一時間ぐらい見ました。

1. きのう、何時間勉強しましたか。
2. きのう、何時間寝ましたか。
3. ゲーム (game) をしますか。たいてい何時間ぐらいゲームをしますか。
4. インターネット (Internet) をしますか。たいてい何時間ぐらいしますか。

Ⅶ まとめの練習 (Review Exercises)

A. Pair Work—Using the expressions below, ask your partners how often they did the following activities when they were a child or in high school.

Example: A：子供の時／高校の時 よく本を読みましたか。
B：はい、よく読みました。／
いいえ、あまり読みませんでした。

1. 勉強する
2. スポーツをする
3. 映画を見る
4. 公園に行く
5. 手紙を書く
6. デートをする

毎日	
よく	
ときどき	～ました
あまり	
ぜんぜん	～ませんでした

B. Answer the following questions.

1. 毎日、何時に起きますか。
2. たいてい何時間ぐらい寝ますか。
3. 毎日、何時間勉強しますか。
4. よくだれと昼ご飯を食べますか。
5. よく友だちにメールをしますか。
6. 先週、スポーツをしましたか。

7. きのう、どこで晩ご飯を食べましたか。
   ばん はん た
8. 先週、写真をたくさん撮りましたか。
   せんしゅう しゃしん と
9. きのうは何曜日でしたか。
   なんよう び

C. Pair Work—A and B want to play badminton together. The following is A's schedule for this week. (B's schedule is on p. 126.) Play the roles of A and B with your partner. Ask each other what the other is doing and decide on what day you will play badminton.

Example:

A：バドミントン (badminton) を
   しませんか。

B：いいですね。

A：月曜日はどうですか。
   げつよう び

B：月曜日は図書館で勉強します。
   げつよう び と しょかん べんきょう
   火曜日は？
   か よう び

A's Schedule

SUN	
MON	
TUE	Go to bank at 3 o'clock
WED	
THU	Part-time job
FRI	Date
SAT	Part-time job (12-5 p.m.)

Pair Work Ⅱ C.

(→ p. 118)

Example:　A：公園はどこですか。
　　　　　　　　こうえん

　　　　　　B：公園はホテルのとなりです。
　　　　　　　　こうえん

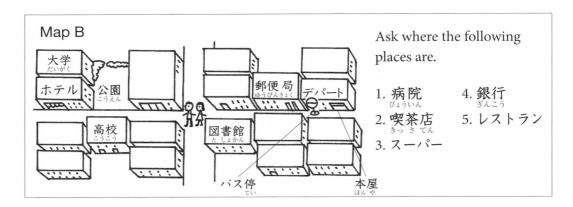

Map B

Ask where the following places are.

1. 病院　　　　4. 銀行
　びょういん　　　ぎんこう

2. 喫茶店　　　5. レストラン
　きっさてん

3. スーパー

Pair Work Ⅶ C.

(→ p. 125)

Example:

A：バドミントン (badminton) を
　しませんか。

B：いいですね。

A：月曜日はどうですか。
　げつようび

B：月曜日は図書館で勉強します。
　げつようび　としょかん　べんきょう
　火曜日は？
　かようび

B's Schedule

SUN	6 p.m. Jogging
MON	Study in the library
TUE	
WED	Shopping in town
THU	Dinner at friend's house
FRI	
SAT	

Useful Expressions

日・週・月・年
ひ・しゅう・つき・とし

Days / Weeks / Months / Years

Days

日曜日 にちようび	月曜日 げつようび	火曜日 かようび	水曜日 すいようび	木曜日 もくようび	金曜日 きんようび	土曜日 どようび
	1 ついたち	**2** ふつか	**3** みっか	**4** よっか	**5** いつか	**6** むいか
7 なのか	**8** ようか	**9** ここのか	**10** とおか	**11** じゅういちにち	**12** じゅうににち	**13** じゅうさんにち
14 じゅうよっか	**15** じゅうごにち	**16** じゅうろくにち	**17** じゅうしちにち	**18** じゅうはちにち	**19** じゅうくにち	**20** はつか
21 にじゅういちにち	**22** にじゅうににち	**23** にじゅうさんにち	**24** にじゅうよっか	**25** にじゅうごにち	**26** にじゅうろくにち	**27** にじゅうしちにち
28 にじゅうはちにち	**29** にじゅうくにち	**30** さんじゅうにち	**31** さんじゅういちにち			

Months

いちがつ（一月）——January　　しちがつ（七月）——July
にがつ（二月）——February　　はちがつ（八月）——August
さんがつ（三月）——March　　くがつ（九月）——September
しがつ（四月）——April　　じゅうがつ（十月）——October
ごがつ（五月）——May　　じゅういちがつ（十一月）——November
ろくがつ（六月）——June　　じゅうにがつ（十二月）——December

Time Words

Day	Week	Month	Year
おととい the day before yesterday	にしゅうかんまえ （二週間前） two weeks ago	にかげつまえ （二か月前） two months ago	おととし the year before last
きのう(昨日) yesterday	せんしゅう(先週) last week	せんげつ(先月) last month	きょねん(去年) last year
きょう(今日) today	こんしゅう(今週) this week	こんげつ(今月) this month	ことし(今年) this year
あした(明日) tomorrow	らいしゅう(来週) next week	らいげつ(来月) next month	らいねん(来年) next year
あさって the day after tomorrow	さらいしゅう （再来週） the week after next	さらいげつ （再来月） the month after next	さらいねん （再来年） the year after next

第5課 | L E S S O N ⋯⋯⋯⋯⋯⋯5

沖縄旅行 A Trip to Okinawa
おき なわ りょ こう

会 話 D i a l o g u e
かい わ

Ⅰ Robert and Ken are vacationing in Okinawa. 🔊 K05-01/02

1 ロバート： いい天気ですね。
てんき

2 け　ん： そうですね。でも、ちょっと暑いですね。
あつ

3 ロバート： ええ。わあ、きれいな海！
うみ

4 け　ん： 泳ぎましょう。
およ

＊　　　　＊　　　　＊

5 け　ん： ロバートさんはどんなスポーツが好きですか。
す

6 ロバート： サーフィンが好きです。
す

7 　　　　　 あした一緒にやりましょうか。
いっしょ

8 け　ん： でも、難しくないですか。
むずか

9 ロバート： 大丈夫ですよ。
だいじょうぶ

Ⅱ At the post office. 🔊 K05-03/04

1 ロバート： すみません。はがきは、イギリスまでいくらですか。

2 郵便局員： 七十円です。
ゆうびんきょくいん　ななじゅうえん

3 ロバート： じゃあ、七十円切手を二枚お願いします。それから、五十円切手を
ななじゅうえんきって　にまい　ねが　　　　　　　　　　ごじゅうえんきって

4 　　　　　 一枚ください。
いちまい

On Monday at school. (◖))) K05-05/06

1 たけし： 　ロバートさん、はがき、ありがとう。旅行は楽しかったですか。

2 ロバート： 　ええ。沖縄の海はすごくきれいでしたよ。

3 たけし： 　よかったですね。ぼくも海が大好きです。

4 　飛行機の切符は高かったですか。

5 ロバート： 　いいえ、あまり高くなかったです。たけしさんのデートはどうでし

6 　たか。

7 たけし： 　……

Ⅰ

Robert: Nice weather.

Ken: Yes. But it is a little hot.

Robert: Yes. Wow, beautiful sea!

Ken: Let's swim.

　　　　*　　　*　　　*

Ken: What kind of sports do you like, Robert?

Robert: I like surfing. Shall we do it together tomorrow?

Ken: But isn't it difficult?

Robert: No.

Ⅱ

Robert: Excuse me. How much is a postcard to Britain?

Person at the post office: 70 yen.

Robert: Then, two 70-yen stamps, please. And one 50-yen stamp, please.

Ⅲ

Takeshi: Robert, thank you for the postcard. Did you enjoy the trip?

Robert: Yes. The sea was very beautiful in Okinawa.

Takeshi: Good. I like the sea very much, too. Was the airline ticket expensive?

Robert: No, it wasn't so expensive. How was your date, Takeshi?

Takeshi: . . .

単語
たん ご

 K05-07

Ｖｏｃａｂｕｌａｒｙ

Ｎｏｕｎｓ

* うみ	海	sea
* きって	切手	postal stamps
* きっぷ	切符	ticket
* サーフィン		surfing
しゅくだい	宿題	homework
たべもの	食べ物	food
たんじょうび	誕生日	birthday
テスト		test
* てんき	天気	weather
のみもの	飲み物	drink
* はがき	葉書	postcard
バス		bus
* ひこうき	飛行機	airplane
へや	部屋	room
* ぼく	僕	I (used by men)
やすみ	休み	holiday; day off; absence
* りょこう	旅行	travel

い-ａｄｊｅｃｔｉｖｅｓ

あたらしい	新しい	new
* あつい	暑い	hot (weather)
あつい	熱い	hot (thing)
いそがしい	忙しい	busy (people/days)
おおきい	大きい	large
おもしろい	面白い	interesting; funny
かっこいい		good-looking (conjugates like いい)
こわい	怖い	frightening
さむい	寒い	cold (weather—not used for things)
* たのしい	楽しい	fun
ちいさい	小さい	small
つまらない		boring
ふるい	古い	old (thing—not used for people)
* むずかしい	難しい	difficult

* Words that appear in the dialogue

| やさしい | | easy (problem); kind (person) |
| やすい | 安い | inexpensive; cheap (thing) |

な-adjectives

きらい（な）	嫌い	disgusted with; to dislike （〜が）
*きれい（な）		beautiful; clean
げんき（な）	元気	healthy; energetic
しずか（な）	静か	quiet
*すき（な）	好き	fond of; to like （〜が）
だいきらい（な）	大嫌い	to hate （〜が）
*だいすき（な）	大好き	very fond of; to love （〜が）
にぎやか（な）		lively
ひま（な）	暇	not busy; to have a lot of free time

U-verbs

*およぐ	泳ぐ	to swim
きく	聞く	to ask （*person* に）
のる	乗る	to ride; to board （〜に）
*やる		to do; to perform （〜を）

Ru-verb

| でかける | 出かける | to go out |

Adverbs and Other Expressions

*いっしょに	一緒に	together
*すごく		extremely
*それから		and then
*だいじょうぶ	大丈夫	It's okay.; Not to worry.; Everything is under control.
とても		very
*どんな		what kind of . . .
*〜まい	〜枚	[counter for flat objects]
*〜まで		to (a place); as far as (a place); till (a time)

文法 G r a m m a r
ぶん ぽう

1 Adjectives

There are two types of adjectives in Japanese. One type is called "い-adjectives," and the other type "な-adjectives." い and な are their last syllables when they modify nouns.

い-adjectives:

おもしろい映画　*an interesting movie*
えいが

きのう、おもしろい映画を見ました。　*I saw an interesting movie yesterday.*
えいが　み

こわい先生　*a scary teacher*
せんせい

山下先生はこわい先生です。　*Professor Yamashita is a scary teacher.*
やましたせんせい　せんせい

な-adjectives:

きれいな写真　*a beautiful picture*
しゃしん

京都できれいな写真を撮りました。　*I took a beautiful picture in Kyoto.*
きょうと　しゃしん　と

元気な先生　*an energetic teacher*
げんき　せんせい

山下先生は元気な先生です。　*Professor Yamashita is an energetic teacher.*
やましたせんせい　げんき　せんせい

Japanese adjectives conjugate for tense (present and past), polarity (affirmative and negative), and so forth, just as verbs do. The two types of adjectives follow different conjugation patterns.

い-adjectives 　い-adjectives change shape as follows.

さむい		
	affirmative	negative
present	さむい<u>です</u>	さむ<u>くない</u>です (or さむ<u>くありません</u>)
	It is cold.	*It is not cold.*
past	さむ<u>かったです</u>	さむ<u>くなかった</u>です (or さむ<u>くありませんでした</u>)
	It was cold.	*It was not cold.*

In the negative, you can use the more colloquial variant ないです, or the more conservative variant ありません. Both these forms involve the change of the last い syllable into く.

Unlike verbs, adjectives conjugate fairly uniformly. The only irregularity worth noticing at this stage is the behavior of the adjective いい (good). The first syllable of いい is changed to よ in all forms except the dictionary form and the long present tense affirmative form.[1]

いい (irregular)		
	affirmative	negative
present	いいです	<u>よ</u>くないです (or <u>よ</u>くありません)
past	<u>よ</u>かったです	<u>よ</u>くなかったです (or <u>よ</u>くありませんでした)

Compound adjectives like かっこいい that are built with いい follow this syllable change.

な-adjectives　The conjugation pattern of な-adjectives is exactly the same as the conjugation table of です which follows a noun, as discussed in Lesson 4.

元気(な) _{げん き}		
	affirmative	negative
present	元気です _{げん き}	元気じゃないです _{げん き} (or 元気じゃありません) _{げん き}
	She is healthy.	*She is not healthy.*
past	元気でした _{げん き}	元気じゃなかったです _{げん き} (or 元気じゃありませんでした) _{げん き}
	She was healthy.	*She was not healthy.*

The final syllable な is dropped in these long forms of な-adjectives. The two forms shown in the negative column are the colloquial and the conservative variants, respectively. In addition to these two forms in the negative, you can also substitute では for じゃ as in ではありません and ではありませんでした which are more often used in the written language than in the spoken language.

---

[1] There actually are alternate forms, よい and よいです, but they are much less frequently used than いい and いいです in the spoken language.

If you want to say things like "very hot," and "a little hot," you can add "degree adverbs" like すごく (extremely), とても (very) and ちょっと (a little; slightly) before adjectives.

沖縄の海は<u>とても</u>きれいでした。
The sea was very beautiful in Okinawa.

この部屋は<u>ちょっと</u>暑いです。
This room is a little hot.

2 好き(な)/きらい(な)

In this lesson, we learn two な-adjectives that are very important from the grammatical point of view. They are 好き (な) (to be fond of; to like), and きらい（な） (to be disgusted with; to dislike). The meaning of these adjectives is relational, and you need two terms: a person to like or dislike something on the one hand, and a person or a thing on the other hand that is liked or disliked. In sentences, these two terms usually appear with the particles は and が, respectively.[2]

X は Y が	好き / きらい	です。	X	likes / dislikes	Y.

ロバートさんは日本語のクラスが好きです。
Robert likes his Japanese classes.

山下先生は魚がきらいです。
Professor Yamashita dislikes fish.

The item that is liked or disliked can also be a person. You may want to be cautious using these words in reference to your preference for a specific person, however, because 好きです is usually taken to be an admission of one's *romantic* interest.[3]

---

[2] In contexts where you are contrasting two or more items, the particle は is used instead of が. Thus,

私は野菜は好きですが、肉はきらいです。　　I *like* vegetables, *but I don't like* meat.

[3] In the expression of romantic or familial affection, the complex particle のことが can replace が. Thus,

たけしさんはメアリーさん<u>のこと</u>が好きです。　＝メアリーさんが好きです。
Takeshi is in love with Mary.

Let us note three more things about 好き（な） and きらい（な） before we go on. One, if you like or dislike something (or somebody) very much, you can use the intensified forms of 好きです and きらいです, namely, 大好きです (like very much) and 大きらいです (hate), which are more often used than the degree modifier とても in combination with 好きです and きらいです.

たけしさんはコーヒーが大好きです。
Takeshi likes coffee a lot.

キムさんはなっとうが大きらいです。
Ms. Kim hates natto (a Japanese fermented soybean delicacy).

Furthermore, when Japanese people want to say that they neither like nor dislike something, they usually say:

好きでもきらいでもないです。　　　　　*I neither like nor dislike (it).*

Three, you can use 好きな and きらいな as modifiers of nouns. For example, you can say things like:

これは私の好きな本です。　　　　　*This is <u>my favorite book</u>.*

3　〜ましょう/〜ましょうか

Take a long form of a verb and replace the ending with ましょう or ましょうか and you will get the Japanese expression for "let's . . . ," which you can use to suggest a plan of action.

一緒に図書館で勉強しましょう。
Let's study in the library together.

喫茶店でコーヒーを飲みましょうか。
Shall we drink coffee at a coffee shop?

4 Counting

There are two important things you should know about counting items in Japanese. Firstly, we use different number words for different kinds of items; the words used for counting people are different from the words used for counting books, for example. Secondly, number words often come *after*, rather than *before*, the items counted in a sentence.

リーさんは　切手を　三枚　買いました。　　*Lee bought three stamps.*
　　　　　　 きって　 さんまい　か
　　　　　　 item　 **number**

The number word, 三枚, is made up of the numeral 三 and the "counter" 枚. This counter is
　　　　　　　　　 さんまい　　　　　　　　　 さん　　　　　　　　 まい
used for sheets of paper and other flat objects. There will be other counters in later lessons—for people, for books, for sticklike objects, and so forth.

表現ノート……6
ひょう　げん

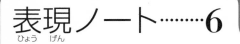忙しい/にぎやか（な）▶忙しい is used when we describe people and is not used
いそが　　　　　　　　　 いそが
for places. When you want to say that Tokyo is busy, you should use にぎやか（な）.

　　たけしさんは忙しいです。　　*Takeshi is busy.*
　　　　　　　　 いそが
　　東京はにぎやかです。　　　 *Tokyo is busy / lively.*
　　とうきょう

Note that the sentence below is also acceptable, since the subject "I" is omitted in the sentence.

　　日曜日は忙しいです。　　＝日曜日は（私は）忙しいです。
　　にちよう び　いそが　　　 にちよう び　わたし　いそが
　　I am busy on Sunday.

練 習 Practice
れん しゅう

①高いです
たか

A. Change the following adjectives into the affirmatives. 🔊 K05-08

Example: たかい   → たかいです
        げんきな → げんきです

1. やすい   4. おもしろい   7. ふるい   10. にぎやかな
2. あつい   5. つまらない   8. いい   11. きれいな
3. さむい   6. いそがしい   9. しずかな   12. ひまな

B. Change the following adjectives into the negatives. 🔊 K05-09

Example: やすい → やすくないです
        ひまな → ひまじゃないです

1. さむい   4. あたらしい   7. ちいさい   10. しずかな
2. ふるい   5. むずかしい   8. いい   11. きれいな
3. こわい   6. かっこいい   9. げんきな   12. にぎやかな

C. Look at the pictures below and make sentences.

Example: この時計は高いです。
        と けい たか
        この時計は安くないです。
        と けい やす

Ex.   (1)   (2)   (3)

¥100,000   ¥480

(4) (5) (6) (7)

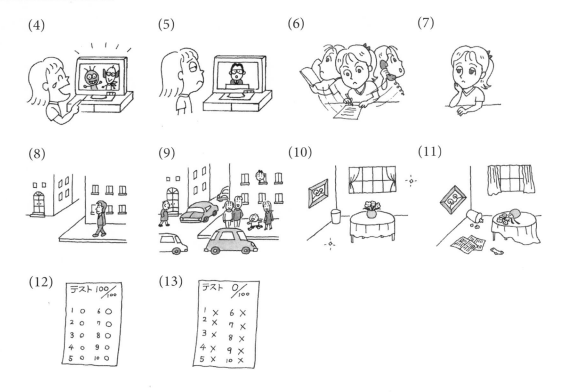

(8) (9) (10) (11)

(12) (13)

D. Answer the following questions.

Example: Q：日本語のクラスは難しいですか。
　　　　　　A：ええ、難しいです。／いいえ、難しくないです。

1. 今日はひまですか。
2. 先生はやさしいですか。
3. 学校は大きいですか。
4. 部屋はきれいですか。

5. 日本の食べ物はおいしいですか。
6. クラスはおもしろいですか。
7. 宿題は難しいですか。
8. あなたの町は静かですか。

E. Pair Work—Make affirmative and negative sentences with your partner.

Example: きれいな

→　友だちの部屋はきれいです。でも、私の部屋はきれいじゃない
　　です。

1. おもしろい　　3. こわい　　5. 高い　　7. 元気な
2. いい　　　　　4. おいしい　6. かっこいい　8. ひまな

F. Pair Work—Make your own sentences on the topics below using adjectives, and tell your partner.

Example: テストは難しくないです。やさしいです。
むずか

1. 私は
わたし
3. 私のとなりの人は
わたし　　　　ひと
5. 東京は
とうきょう
2. 私の町は
わたし　まち
4. 私の部屋は
わたし　へ　や
6. ハワイ (Hawaii) は

Ⅱ 高かったです
たか

A. Change the following adjectives into the past affirmatives. K05-10

Example: たかい　　→　たかかったです
げんきな　→　げんきでした

1. やすい
2. あつい
3. さむい
4. おもしろい
5. つまらない
6. いそがしい
7. たのしい
8. いい
9. しずかな
10. にぎやかな
11. きれいな
12. ひまな

B. Change the following adjectives into the past negatives. K05-11

Example: やすい　→　やすくなかったです
ひまな　→　ひまじゃなかったです

1. たかい
2. たのしい
3. やさしい
4. つまらない
5. おおきい
6. いい
7. いそがしい
8. かっこいい
9. にぎやかな
10. しずかな
11. きれいな
12. げんきな

C. This is what Robert wrote down about the trip to Okinawa. Look at the memo and make sentences. K05-12

Example: 沖縄は暑かったです。
おきなわ　あつ

Ex. Okinawa—hot	4. hotel—new
1. food—not expensive	5. restaurant—not quiet
2. food—delicious	6. sea—beautiful
3. hotel—not big	7. surfing—interesting

D. Pair Work—Practice a dialogue with your partner, substituting the underlined parts. A and B are talking about A's vacation.

Example:

went to Okinawa　—　very hot

→　A：休みに沖縄に行きました。
　　　やす　　おきなわ　い
　　B：そうですか。どうでしたか。
　　A：とても暑かったです。
　　　　　　あつ

1. saw a movie　　　　　　　—　scary

2. stayed home（うちにいる）—　very boring

3. went to a party　　　　　—　not fun

4. went to a restaurant　　　—　not delicious

5. (your own)

(Ⅲ) 高い時計ですね
　　　たか　とけい

A. Look at the pictures and make comments on them. K05-13

Example:　時計　→　高い時計ですね。
　　　　　　とけい　　たか　とけい

Ex.

¥100,000

(1) ホテル

(2) テレビ

(3) 宿題
　　しゅくだい

(4) 人
　　ひと

(5) 人
　　ひと

(6) 町
　　まち

(7) 部屋
　　へや

B. Answer the questions using the given cues. 🕪 K05-14

Example:　Q：メアリーさんはどんな人ですか。
　　　　　　A：メアリーさんはやさしい人です。

Ex. メアリー　　(1) スー　　　(2) ロバート　　(3) たけし

kind　　　　　beautiful　　　interesting　　　energetic

Ⅳ 魚が好きですか

A. Pair Work—Choose the items from the following categories and ask your partners whether they like them.

Example:　A：魚が好きですか。
　　　　　　B：はい、好きです／大好きです。
　　　　　　　　いいえ、きらいです／大きらいです。

1. Foods: meat ／なっとう (fermented beans) ／アイスクリーム (ice cream)

2. Sports: サッカー (soccer) ／スキー (skiing) ／ゴルフ (golf)

3. Music: ロック (rock) ／ジャズ (jazz) ／クラシック (classical music)

4. School work: test ／ Japanese class ／ homework

5. Drinks: sake ／ green tea ／ coffee

＊If you neither like it nor dislike it, you can use 好きでもきらいでもないです.

B. Answer the following questions.

1. どんなスポーツが好きですか。
2. どんな食べ物が好きですか。
3. どんな飲み物が好きですか。
4. どんな映画が好きですか。
5. どんな音楽が好きですか。

Ⓥ 映画を見ましょう
えいが み

A. Change the following into ましょう sentences. 🔊 K05-15

Example:　テニスをする　→　テニスをしましょう。

1. いっしょに帰る
   かえ
2. 先生に聞く
   せんせい き
3. 映画を見る
   えいが み
4. おみやげを買う
   か
5. 出かける
   て

6. 待つ
   ま
7. 泳ぐ
   およ
8. 写真を撮る
   しゃしん と
9. バスに乗る
   の
10. 六時に会う
    ろくじ あ

B. Pair Work—Make follow-up suggestions using ましょうか.

Example:　寒いですね。
さむ
　　　→　　A：寒いですね。お茶を飲みましょうか。
さむ ちゃ の
　　　　　B：そうしましょう。

1. 暑いですね。
   あつ
2. 十二時ですね。
   じゅうに じ
3. この宿題は難しいですね。
   しゅくだい むずか
4. あしたは先生の誕生日ですよ。
   せんせい たんじょうび
5. あのレストランはおいしいですよ。
6. あしたはテストがありますね。

Ⓥ まとめの練習 (Review Exercises)
れんしゅう

A. Pair Work—Ask your partner the following questions.

1. Were you busy last week?

2. Were you fine last week?

3. Was your high school big/old?

4. Was your watch expensive?

5. Is your bag new?

6. Is your room small/clean?

7. Is your teacher kind?

B. Class Activity—Show and tell
Bring pictures you took on a trip. Explain to your class where you went, what you did, how it was, etc. And later, other students will ask in detail about the trip.

Example questions:

どこに行きましたか。

天気はどうでしたか。

だれと行きましたか。

飛行機の切符はいくらでしたか。

C. Role Play—Use Dialogue Ⅱ as a model, buy some stamps and postcards.

日本の祭り Japanese Festivals
にほん まつ

There are many festivals in Japan. Some are famous, while others are known only to the locals. Some are very traditional, while others are rather new. Here are some examples of well-known festivals. Where do you want to visit?

札幌　雪祭り
さっぽろ　ゆきまつり

The Sapporo Snow Festival is held for a week in early February. It features large snow sculptures constructed in a park on the main avenue.

京都　祇園祭
きょうと　ぎおんまつり

The Kyoto Gion Festival is held in July. On the 17th, beautifully decorated floats parade on the main streets in Kyoto.

青森　ねぶた祭り
あおもり　まつ

The Aomori Nebuta Festival is held August 2–7. Huge colorful lanterns are pulled through the streets, accompanied by people dancing and playing flutes and drums.

徳島　阿波踊り
とくしま　あわおど

The Tokushima Awa Dance Festival is held August 12–15. Groups of people form lines and dance around the center of town.

仙台　七夕祭り
せんだい　たなばたまつり

The Sendai Tanabata Festival is held August 6–8, and is famous for its large, elaborate decorations made with colorful Japanese paper.

写真提供：（財）徳島県観光協会

Useful Expressions

郵便局で
ゆうびんきょく

At the Post Office

Expressions

これ、お願いします。──────── Can you take care of this, please?
　　ねが

五十円切手を三枚ください。──── Give me three 50-yen stamps, please.
ご じゅうえんきって　さんまい

（航空便）でお願いします。──── Make this (an airmail), please.
こうくうびん　　ねが

何日ぐらいかかりますか。──── How many days will it take?
なんにち

百五十円になります。──────── It will be 150 yen.
ひゃく ご じゅうえん

Vocabulary

窓口──────── counter
まどぐち

はがき──────── postcard

切手──────── postal stamps
きって

小包──────── parcel
こづみ

航空便──────── airmail
こうくうびん

船便──────── surface mail
ふなびん

速達──────── special delivery
そくたつ

書留──────── registered mail
かきとめ

保険──────── insurance
ほ けん

第6課 ｜ L E S S O N ⋯⋯⋯⋯6

ロバートさんの一日 A Day in Robert's Life
いち にち

会 話 D i a l o g u e
かい わ

Ⅰ In the class. 🔊 K06-01/02

1 山下先生： ロバートさん、次のページを読んでください。
やましたせんせい つぎ よ
2 ロバート： ……
3 山下先生： ロバートさん、起きてください。クラスで寝てはいけませんよ。
やましたせんせい お ね
4 ロバート： 先生、教科書を忘れました。
せんせい きょうかしょ わす
5 山下先生： 教科書を持ってきてくださいね。毎日使いますから。
やましたせんせい きょうかしょ も まいにちつか
6 ロバート： はい、すみません。

Ⅱ After class. 🔊 K06-03/04

1 スー： ロバートさん、今日は大変でしたね。
きょう たいへん
2 ロバート： ええ。後でスーさんのノートを借りてもいいですか。
あと か
3 スー： いいですよ。
4 ロバート： ありがとう。すぐ返します。
かえ
5 スー： ロバートさん、あしたテストがありますよ。
6 ロバート： えっ。本当ですか。
ほんとう
7 スー： ええ。ロバートさん、金曜日に休みましたからね。
きんようび やす
8 ロバート： じゃあ、今日は家に帰って、勉強します。
きょう いえ かえ べんきょう

Ⅲ On the bus. 🔊 K06-05/06

1 おばあさん： あの、すみません。このバスは市民病院へ行きますか。
しみんびょういん い
2 ロバート： ええ、行きますよ。……あの、どうぞ座ってください。
い すわ
3 おばあさん： いいえ、けっこうです。すぐ降りますから。
お

4 ロバート：　　そうですか。じゃあ、荷物を持ちましょうか。

5 おばあさん：　あ、どうもすみません。

Ⅰ

Prof. Yamashita: Robert, please read the next page.

Robert: . . .

Prof. Yamashita: Robert, please wake up. You cannot sleep in the class.

Robert: Mr. Yamashita, I forgot to bring the textbook.

Prof. Yamashita: Please bring your textbook with you. We use it every day.

Robert: I understand. I'm sorry.

Ⅱ

Sue: Robert, you had a hard time today.

Robert: Yes. May I borrow your notebook later, Sue?

Sue: Yes.

Robert: Thank you. I'll return it soon.

Sue: Robert, we will have a test tomorrow.

Robert: Really?

Sue: Yes. You were absent from the class last Friday. (That's why you didn't know about it.)

Robert: Well then, I'll go home and study today.

Ⅲ

Old woman: Excuse me. Does this bus go to the city hospital?

Robert: Yes, it does. Take this seat, please.

Old woman: No, thank you. I'll get off soon.

Robert: Is that so? Then, shall I carry your bag?

Old woman: Thank you.

単語
たん　　ご

🔊 K06-07

V o c a b u l a r y

N o u n s

おかね	お金	money
おふろ	お風呂	bath
かんじ	漢字	kanji; Chinese character
* きょうかしょ	教科書	textbook
こんしゅう	今週	this week
ＣＤ（シーディー）		CD
* しみんびょういん	市民病院	municipal hospital
シャワー		shower
* つぎ	次	next
でんき	電気	electricity
でんしゃ	電車	train
* にもつ	荷物	baggage
パソコン		personal computer
* ページ		page
まど	窓	window
よる	夜	night
らいしゅう	来週	next week
らいねん	来年	next year

な - a d j e c t i v e

* たいへん（な）	大変	tough (situation)

U - v e r b s

あそぶ	遊ぶ	to play; to spend time pleasantly
いそぐ	急ぐ	to hurry
おふろにはいる	お風呂に入る	to take a bath
* かえす	返す	to return (a thing) (*person* に *thing* を)
けす	消す	to turn off; to erase （〜を）
しぬ	死ぬ	to die
* すわる	座る	to sit down （*seat* に）
たつ	立つ	to stand up
たばこをすう	たばこを吸う	to smoke

* Words that appear in the dialogue

* つかう	使う	to use（〜を）
てつだう	手伝う	to help (*person/task* を)
はいる	入る	to enter（〜に）
* もつ	持つ	to carry; to hold（〜を）
* やすむ	休む	(1) to be absent (from . . .)（〜を） (2) to rest

Ru-verbs

あける	開ける	to open (something)（〜を）
おしえる	教える	to teach; to instruct (*person* に *thing* を)
* おりる	降りる	to get off（〜を）
* かりる	借りる	to borrow (*person* に *thing* を)
しめる	閉める	to close (something)（〜を）
シャワーをあびる	シャワーを 浴びる	to take a shower
つける		to turn on（〜を）
でんわをかける	電話をかける	to make a phone call（〜に）
* わすれる	忘れる	to forget; to leave behind（〜を）

Irregular Verbs

つれてくる	連れてくる	to bring (a person)（〜を）
* もってくる	持ってくる	to bring (a thing)（〜を）

Adverbs and Other Expressions

* あとで	後で	later on
おそく	遅く	(do something) late
* 〜から		because . . .
* けっこうです	結構です	That would be fine.; That wouldn't be necessary.
* すぐ		right away
* ほんとうですか	本当ですか	Really?
ゆっくり		slowly; leisurely; unhurriedly

文 法 Grammar
ぶん ぽう

1 Te-form

The main topic of this lesson is a new conjugation of verbs called the "*te*-form." *Te*-forms are a *very* important part of Japanese grammar. In this lesson, we will learn, among their various uses, to use them in:

- making requests (". . . , please.")
- giving and asking for permission ("You may . . . /May I . . . ?")
- stating that something is forbidden ("You must not . . .")
- forming a sentence that describes two events or activities. ("I did this and did that.")

The conjugation paradigm of *te*-forms is complex, as we need to learn separate rules for *ru*-, *u*-, and irregular verbs. Furthermore, the rule for *u*-verbs is divided into five subrules.

First, with *ru*-verbs, the rule is very simple: Take る off and add て.

ru-verbs		
食べる	→	食べて

U-verbs come in several groups, based on the final syllable of their dictionary forms.

u-verbs with final う, つ, and る[1]		
会う	→	会って
待つ	→	待って
とる	→	とって

u-verbs with final む, ぶ, and ぬ		
読む	→	読んで
遊ぶ	→	遊んで
死ぬ	→	死んで

---

[1] As we discussed in Lesson 3 (see page 89), some verbs that end with the *hiragana* る are *ru*-verbs and some others are *u*-verbs. Review the discussion on how the vowel before the final る syllable determines which verb belongs to which class. As far as *te*-forms are concerned, we observe that *u*-verbs that end with る will have a small っ, *ru*-verbs that end with る do not.

u-verbs with final く

書く → 書いて
か   か

There is an important exception in this class:

行く → 行って
い   い

u-verbs with final ぐ

泳ぐ → 泳いで
およ   およ

u-verbs with final す

話す → 話して
はな   はな

The irregular verbs する and くる, and compound verbs built with them, conjugate as follows.

irregular verbs

する → して

くる → きて

Note that *te*-forms and stems (the forms you find before ます) are totally different constructs in the *u*-verb camp. A common mistake is to assume that the simple paradigm provided by the *ru*-verbs (食べて and 食べます) covers the *u*-verbs also, thus coming up with unwarranted forms such as ×会いて (see 会います) and ×読みて (see 読みます). It is probably easier, at this stage of learning, to memorize each verb as a set, as in 書く―書きます―書いて, than to apply the conjugation rules on the spot. Refer to the verb conjugation table at the end of this volume (p. 382).

2 ～てください

Use a verbal *te*-form together with ください to make a polite request to another person "please do . . . for me.[2]"

教科書を読んでください。
きょう か しょ　　よ
Please read the textbook.

すみません。ちょっと教えてください。
おし
Excuse me. Please teach me a little. (= Tell me, I need your advice.)

---

[2] If you are talking to a very close friend or a member of your family, a *te*-form, by itself, can be used as a request.
窓を開けて。　　*Open the window, will you?*
まど　あ

3   〜てもいいです

A verbal *te*-form plus もいいです means "you may do . . . ," which describes an activity that is permitted.[3] To ask for permission, you can turn it into a question sentence, 〜てもいいですか. If somebody asks for permission and if you want to grant it, you can either repeat the whole verb *te*-form plus もいいです construction, or just say いいです. ✕てもいいです and ✕もいいです do not stand alone.

教科書を見てもいいですか。	*May I see the textbook?*
——はい、見てもいいですよ。	*—Yes, you may.*
いいですよ。	*You may.*
どうぞ。	*Please.*

4   〜てはいけません

A verbal *te*-form plus はいけません means "you must not do . . . ," a strong prohibition statement, as in rules and regulations.

ここで写真を撮ってはいけません。	*You must not take pictures here.*

If somebody asks you for permission and if you want to deny it, you can use てはいけません, but the sentence may sound too harsh unless you are in a place of authority. We will learn a softer way to say "please don't" in Lesson 8.

5   Describing Two Activities

You can use a *te*-form if you want to combine two or more verbs, as in describing a sequence of events or actions ("I did this and then I did that"). In other words, the *te*-form does the work of "and" with verbs. (Note that two verbs cannot be joined by と, which only connects nouns.) This *te*-form conjunction can be used for present and future, as in the first and third examples below, and for the past, as in the second example. The tense of the verb at the end of each sentence determines when these events take place.

---

[3] In casual speech, you can drop も and say 食べていいです as well as 食べてもいいです. In contrast, は in the construction てはいけません, which is discussed in the next section, cannot be dropped.

ノートを借りて、コピーします。
I will borrow her notebook and photocopy it.

今日は、六時に起きて、勉強しました。
Today I got up at six and studied.

食堂に行って、昼ご飯を食べましょう。
Let's go to the cafeteria and have lunch.

The *te*-form of a verb can also be used to connect a verb more "loosely" with the rest of a sentence. In the first example below, the verb in the *te*-form describes the manner in which the action described by the second verb is performed. In the second example, the *te*-form describes the situation for which the apology is made.

バスに乗って、会社に行きます。
I go to work by bus. (I take a bus to work.)

教科書を忘れて、すみません。
I am sorry for not bringing in the textbook. (I left the book at home, and I am sorry.)

6　～から

A sentence that ends with から (because) explains the reason or the cause of a situation, a proposal, and so forth.

> (situation)。(explanation) から。[4]

私は今晩勉強します。あしたテストがありますから。
I will study this evening. (Because) we will have an exam tomorrow.

バスに乗りましょう。タクシーは高いですから。
Let's go by bus. (Because) taxis are expensive.

---

[4] The explanation clause may also precede the situation clause. Thus the first example above can also be para-phrased as:

あしたテストがありますから、私は今晩勉強します。

We will discuss this further in Lesson 9.

7　〜ましょうか

In Lesson 5 we learned ましょうか meaning "Let's . . . ." ましょうか is also used in the sense of "let me do . . . ," in offering assistance. If you see somebody having a hard time opening the lid of a bottle, for example, you can offer help by saying:

（私が）やりましょうか。　　　　　　　　*I'll do it.*

Or to a person who is carrying a heavy bag:

荷物を持ちましょうか。　　　　　　　　*Shall I carry your bag?*

Culture Note

日本の教育制度（1）Japan's Educational System (1)

Most children in Japan attend kindergartens or nursery schools before entering elementary school. Compulsory education comprises six years of elementary school and three years of junior high school. Although not compulsory, over 95% of junior high students go on to high school for three years. About half of high school graduates attend a university or junior college. Admission to high schools and universities is usually based on an entrance exam.

The Japanese school year starts in April and ends in March, with a long vacation in summer and two shorter breaks in winter and spring.

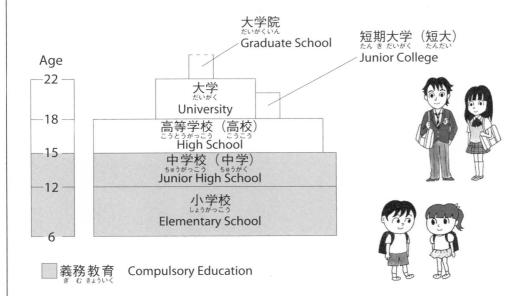

表現ノート……7
ひょう　げん

遅く／遅い▶Although both 遅い and 遅く mean "late," they have different usag-
おそ　おそ　　　　　　　　　　　　　　　おそ　　　　　　　　おそ
es, since 遅い is an adjective and 遅く is an adverb. 遅い modifies nouns or works
　　　　　おそ　　　　　　　　　　　　おそ　　　　　　　　　　　　おそ
as a predicate, and 遅く modifies verbs.
　　　　　　　　　　　おそ

> A：きのう一時に寝ました。　　　*I went to bed at one o'clock yesterday.*
> 　　　　　　いち じ　　ね
> B：遅いですね。　　　　　　　　*It's late.*
> 　　おそ
>
> 週末には、十時ごろ起きて、遅い朝ご飯を食べます。
> しゅうまつ　　　じゅう じ　　　　お　　　　おそ　あさ　はん　た
> 　　　　　　　　　　　　　　　　*On weekends, I get up around 10:00 and*
> 　　　　　　　　　　　　　　　　*eat late breakfast.*
>
> きのう、遅く寝ました。　　　　*I went to bed late yesterday.*
> 　　　　おそ　ね

You can also apply this rule to 早く／早い.
　　　　　　　　　　　　　　　　はや　　はや

どうも▶どうも is normally used with ありがとう, as in どうもありがとう
(Thank you very much), or with すみません, as in どうもすみません (I am very
sorry/Thank you very much). When used alone, it is an abbreviation of どうもあ
りがとう or どうもすみません. Therefore, when you want to show your gratitude or regret, you can just say どうも instead of saying a long sentence. どうも
functions in many ways, depending on the situation. Some people use どうも as
"hello" or "good-bye."

お▶Many words that begin with お can also be used without it. お in such words
simply adds smoothness and nuance of social refinement, without changing the
meaning of the words.

> Example:　お酒　　お金　　お風呂　　お祭り（festival）
> 　　　　　　さけ　　かね　　ふ ろ　　まつ

練習 Practice
れん　しゅう

① 窓を開けてください
　　まど　　あ

A. Change the following verbs into *te*-forms. K06-08

Example:　おきる　→　おきて

1. たべる	4. かく	7. あそぶ	10. いそぐ	13. しぬ
2. かう	5. くる	8. とる	11. いく	14. はなす
3. よむ	6. まつ	9. する	12. ねる	15. かえる

B. Let's sing a *te*-form song! (Battle Hymn of the Republic) K06-09

♪ 1.　　あう　あって　まつ　まって　とる　とって
　　　　よむ　よんで　あそぶ　あそんで　しぬ　しんで
　　　　かく　かいて　けす　けして　いそぐ　いそいで
　　　　みんな　*u*-verb　*te*-form

♪ 2.　　うつる　って　むぶぬ　んで　く　いて　ぐ　いで
　　　　(repeat twice)
　　　　す　して　*u*-verb　*te*-form

C. Make polite requests. K06-10

Example:　日本語を話してください。
　　　　　に ほん ご　　はな

Ex. Please speak Japanese.

1. Please stand up.

2. Please listen.

3. Please read the book.

4. Please look at me.

5. Please bring the textbook.

6. Please teach me kanji.

7. Please return my book.

8. Please speak slowly.

9. Please come with me.

10. Please call me tomorrow.

11. Please bring your friend.

D. What are they saying in the following situations?

Example: 窓を開けてください。
　　　　　まど　あ

Ex.

(1)

(2)

(3)

(4)

(5)

E. Pair Work—Make your own request, such as "Please stand up" and "Please take a picture," and ask your partner to act it out.

Example:　A：コーヒーを飲んでください。　→　B pretends to drink coffee.
　　　　　　　　　　　の

Ⅱ テレビを見てもいいですか

A. You are staying with a host family. Ask your host family for permission to do the following things. 🔊 K06-11

Example: テレビを見る → テレビを見てもいいですか。

1. たばこを吸う
2. 窓を閉める
3. 朝、シャワーを浴びる

4. 遅く帰る
5. 友だちを連れてくる
6. 音楽を聞く

7. 夜、出かける
8. パソコンを使う
9. 自転車を借りる

B. What would you say in the following situations? Make sentences with 〜てもいいですか.

1. You are in class. You realize you need to go to the bathroom as soon as possible.

2. You are in class. You feel sick and want to return home.

3. You have forgotten to do the homework. You are sure you can bring it in tomorrow.

4. You want to ask your teacher something, but you cannot phrase it in Japanese.

5. You have run into a celebrity. Conveniently, you have a camera with you.

6. You and your friend are in a dark room, and you feel somewhat uncomfortable.

C. Pair Work—Ask your partner if it is all right to do the following things.

Example: たばこを吸う

→ A：たばこを吸ってもいいですか。

B：ええ、いいですよ。どうぞ。／すみません。ちょっと……。

1. 夜、電話をかける
2. ペンを借りる
3. 窓を開ける
4. テレビをつける
5. (your partner's name) さんの電話を使う
6. (your partner's name) さんの部屋に行く

Ⅲ テレビを見てはいけません
<small>み</small>

A. You are a strict parent. Tell your child not to do the following things using the cues in Ⅱ-A. 🔊 K06-12

Example: テレビを見る → テレビを見てはいけません。
<small>み</small>　　　　　　　　　<small>み</small>

B. Tell the class what we can and can't do at school and at a place you live.

Example: 学校でたばこを吸ってはいけません。
<small>がっこう</small>　　　　<small>す</small>
ホストファミリーのうちで朝シャワーを浴びてもいいです。
(host family)　　　　　　<small>あさ</small>　　　　　<small>あ</small>

C. Pair Work—Ask your partner if it is all right to do the following things.

Example: 図書館で電話をかける
<small>としょかん　てんわ</small>
→　A：図書館で電話をかけてもいいですか。
<small>としょかん　てんわ</small>
B：はい、電話をかけてもいいです。／
<small>てんわ</small>
いいえ、電話をかけてはいけません。
<small>てんわ</small>

1. 飛行機でたばこを吸う
<small>ひこうき</small>　　　　<small>す</small>
2. クラスで寝る
<small>ね</small>
3. ここでコーヒーを飲む
<small>の</small>
4. 図書館で話す
<small>としょかん　はな</small>

5. 図書館で食べる
<small>としょかん　た</small>
6. 学校へ犬を連れてくる
<small>がっこう　いぬ　つ</small>
7. あなたの国で十八歳の人は
<small>くに　じゅうはっさい　ひと</small>
お酒を飲む
<small>さけ　の</small>

Ⅳ 朝起きて、コーヒーを飲みます
<small>あさ お</small>　　　　　　　<small>の</small>

A. Look at the pictures below and combine the pictures using te-forms. 🔊 K06-13

Example: 朝起きて、コーヒーを飲みます。
<small>あさ お</small>　　　　　　<small>の</small>

Ex.　　　　　　　　　　　　　　　　　(1)

(2)   (3)

(4)   (5)

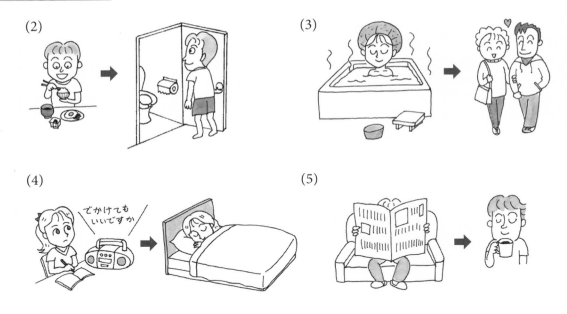

B. Change the following into *te*-forms and make the rest of the sentences.

Example: 朝起きる → 朝起きて、新聞を読みます。
          あさ お   あさ お   しんぶん よ

1. 友だちのうちに行く
   とも   い
2. うちに帰る
     かえ
3. 電車を降りる
   でんしゃ お

4. 友だちに会う
   とも   あ
5. お風呂に入る
    ふ ろ はい
6. 大学に行く
   だいがく い

C. Pair Work—Make questions using the following cues. When you answer, use ～て.

Example: あしたの夜
               よる
          → A：あしたの夜、何をしますか。
                    よる なに
             B：図書館で勉強して、家に帰ります。
               と しょかん べんきょう いえ かえ

1. 今日の夜
   きょう よる
2. あしたの朝
        あさ
3. きのうの朝
        あさ

4. きのうの夜
        よる
5. 今週の週末
   こんしゅう しゅうまつ
6. 先週の週末
   せんしゅう しゅうまつ

Ⅴ 勉強します。あしたテストがありますから。
べんきょう

A. Add reasons to the following sentences.

Example: 勉強します。 → 勉強します。あしたテストがありますから。
べんきょう 　　　　　　　　べんきょう

1. 先週は大変でした。
せんしゅう たいへん

2. あの映画を見ません。
えいが み

3. よくあのレストランに行きます。
い

4. きのうクラスを休みました。
やす

5. (name of a friend) が大好きです。
だいす

6. 友だちに教科書を借りました。
とも きょうかしょ か

B. Pair Work—Ask each other why you think the following.

Example: 昼ご飯を食べません。
ひる はん た

→ Ａ：私は昼ご飯を食べません。
わたし ひる はん た

Ｂ：どうしてですか。

Ａ：あまりお金がありませんから。Ｂさんは？
かね

Ｂ：私も昼ご飯を食べません。クラスがありますから。
わたし ひる はん た

1. 今週は大変です。
こんしゅう たいへん

2. (name of a place) が好きです。
す

3. 週末、(name of a movie) を見ます。
しゅうまつ み

4. (name of a celebrity) がきらいです。

5. お金がぜんぜんありません。
かね

6. 来年は日本語を勉強しません。
らいねん にほんご べんきょう

7. 来週、(name of a place) に行きます。
らいしゅう い

8. 自転車を買います。
じてんしゃ か

Ⅵ テレビを消しましょうか

A. Pair Work—Propose to do the following things, using ましょうか.  K06-14

Example:　A：テレビを消しましょうか。
　　　　　　B：すみません。お願いします。／いいえ、だいじょうぶです。

B. Pair Work—Make a conversation in the following situations.

Example:　You and your partner are in a room. Your partner looks hot.

→　A：窓を開けましょうか。
　　B：ありがとう。お願いします。

1. You and your partner are in a room. Your partner looks cold.
2. Your partner is going to have a party.
3. Your partner has trouble with Japanese homework.
4. You are talking with a Japanese (= your partner) in English, but he doesn't seem to understand English.
5. You come into a room. The room is dark and your partner is studying there.
6. Your partner forgot to bring glasses and cannot read the menu on the wall of a restaurant.

Ⅶ　まとめの練習 (Review Exercises)

A. Role Play—Play the roles of A and B with your partner.

Example:

Example-A	Example-B
You are short of money and want to borrow some money from your friend.	You don't have money to lend to your friend because you went on a trip last week.

　　A：すみませんが、お金を借りてもいいですか。
　　B：お金ですか。どうして。
　　A：あしたは友だちの誕生日ですから。
　　B：でも、私もお金がありません。先週、旅行に行きましたから。

(1)

1-A	1-B
You have a date tomorrow and want to borrow a car（くるま）from your friend.	You just bought a car（くるま）and don't want anyone to use it.

(2)

2-A	2-B
You lost your Japanese textbook, but you need to study for a test tomorrow.	You have a big test in Japanese and need your textbook to prepare for the test.

(3)

3-A	3-B
You are now in your friend's house. You see a cake（ケーキ）that looks very delicious. You love cakes.	You just baked a cake（ケーキ）for your mother's birthday. Your friend is in your house now.

B. Answer the following questions.

1. 今晩、何をしますか。　　　（Answer with "～て、～。"）
2. 図書館で何をしてはいけませんか。
3. 電車の中でたばこを吸ってもいいですか。
4. 大学に何を持ってきますか。
5. よく電車に乗りますか。
6. 先週、宿題を忘れましたか。
7. 子供の時、どこで遊びましたか。
8. 子供の時、よくお母さんを手伝いましたか。
9. 図書館でよく本を借りますか。
10. よくクラスを休みますか。

道を聞く／教える
みち　き　　　　おし

D i r e c t i o n s

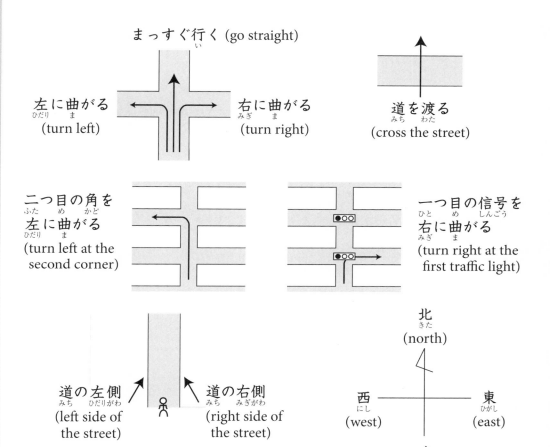

まっすぐ行く (go straight)
い

左に曲がる
ひだり　ま
(turn left)

右に曲がる
みぎ　ま
(turn right)

道を渡る
みち　わた
(cross the street)

二つ目の角を
ふた　め　かど
左に曲がる
ひだり　ま
(turn left at the
second corner)

一つ目の信号を
ひと　め　しんごう
右に曲がる
みぎ　ま
(turn right at the
first traffic light)

道の左側
みち　ひだりがわ
(left side of
the street)

道の右側
みち　みぎがわ
(right side of
the street)

北
きた
(north)

西
にし
(west)

東
ひがし
(east)

南
みなみ
(south)

*　　　　*　　　　*

A：すみません。郵便局はどこですか。
　　　　　　　ゆうびんきょく
Excuse me, where is a post office?

B：まっすぐ行って、三つ目の角を右に曲がって
　　　　　　　みっ　め　かど　みぎ　ま
　　ください。郵便局は右側にありますよ。
　　　　　　　ゆうびんきょく　みぎがわ
Go straight and turn right at the third corner.
The post office is on the right.

A：どうもありがとうございます。
Thank you very much.

第7課 | L E S S O N ⋯⋯⋯⋯⋯⋯ 7

家族の写真 Family Picture
かぞく　しゃしん

会話 D i a l o g u e
かい　わ

(I) Sue is showing a picture of her family to her roommate, Michiko. 🔊 K07-01/02

1 みちこ：　これはスーさんの家族の写真ですか。
　　　　　　　　　　　　かぞく　しゃしん

2 ス　ー：　ええ。

3 みちこ：　スーさんはどれですか。

4 ス　ー：　これです。高校の時はめがねをかけていました。
　　　　　　　　　　こうこう　とき

5 みちこ：　かわいいですね。

6 ス　ー：　これは父です。アメリカの会社に勤めています。
　　　　　　　　　　ちち　　　　　　　かいしゃ　つと

7 みちこ：　背が高くて、かっこいいですね。これはお姉さんですか。
　　　　　　　せ　たか　　　　　　　　　　　　　　　　　　ねえ

8 ス　ー：　ええ。姉は結婚しています。今ソウルに住んでいます。
　　　　　　　　　あね　けっこん　　　　　いま　　　　　す

9 　　　　　　子供が一人います。三歳です。
　　　　　　　こども　ひとり　　　さんさい

10 みちこ：　そうですか。あっ、猫がいますね。
　　　　　　　　　　　　　　　　ねこ

11 　　　　　　でも、ちょっと太っていますね。
　　　　　　　　　　　　　　　ふと

12 ス　ー：　ええ、よく食べますから。
　　　　　　　　　　　　た

Ⅱ Michiko's phone rings. 🔊 K07-03/04

1 ロバート：　もしもし、みちこさん、今何をしていますか。
2 みちこ：　別に何もしていません。今、スーさんの写真を見ています。
3 ロバート：　そうですか。おもしろいＤＶＤを借りましたから、よかったら見に
4 　　　　　　来ませんか。
5 みちこ：　いいですね。スーさんも一緒に行ってもいいですか。
6 ロバート：　もちろん。
7 みちこ：　じゃあ、すぐ行きます。

Ⅰ

Michiko: Is this your family picture, Sue?

Sue: Yes.

Michiko: Which is you?

Sue: This. I was wearing glasses when I was in high school.

Michiko: You are cute.

Sue: This is my father. He works for an American company.

Michiko: He is tall and good-looking. Is this your elder sister?

Sue: Yes. My sister is married. She lives in Seoul now. She has one child. He is three years old.

Michiko: I see. Oh, there is a cat. But he is a little fat.

Sue: Yes, because he eats a lot.

Ⅱ

Robert: Hello, Michiko, what are you doing now?

Michiko: I'm not doing anything especially. I am looking at Sue's pictures.

Robert: I see. I have borrowed a funny DVD, so if you like, won't you come to see it?

Michiko: That sounds good. Is it all right if Sue comes with me?

Robert: Of course.

Michiko: We'll come right now.

単語

Ｖｏｃａｂｕｌａｒｙ

Ｎｏｕｎｓ

* あね	姉	(my) older sister
アパート		apartment
いもうと	妹	younger sister
うた	歌	song
おじいさん		grandfather; old man
おとうと	弟	younger brother
おとこのひと	男の人	man
おにいさん	お兄さん	older brother
* おねえさん	お姉さん	older sister
おばあさん		grandmother; old woman
おんなのひと	女の人	woman
* かいしゃ	会社	company
* かぞく	家族	family
かみ	髪	hair
きょうだい	兄弟	brothers and sisters
くち	口	mouth
くに	国	country; place of origin
くるま	車	car
ゲーム		game
コンビニ		convenience store
サークル		club activity
しょくどう	食堂	cafeteria; dining commons
* ちち	父	(my) father
* ＤＶＤ (ディーブイディー)		DVD
はは	母	(my) mother
め	目	eye
* めがね	眼鏡	glasses

い - ａｄｊｅｃｔｉｖｅｓ

あたまがいい	頭がいい	bright; smart; clever
		(conjugates like いい)
* かわいい		cute
* せがたかい	背が高い	tall (stature)
せがひくい	背が低い	short (stature)
ながい	長い	long

✳ Words that appear in the dialogue

| はやい | 速い | fast |
| みじかい | 短い | short (length) |

な-adjectives

| しんせつ(な) | 親切 | kind |
| べんり(な) | 便利 | convenient |

U-verbs

うたう	歌う	to sing （〜を）
かぶる		to put on (a hat) （〜を）
しる	知る	to get to know （〜を）
しっています	知っています	I know
しりません	知りません	I do not know
*すむ	住む	to live （〜にすんでいます）
はく		to put on (items below your waist) （〜を）
*ふとる	太る	to gain weight
ふとっています	太っています	to be on the heavy side

Ru-verbs

*(めがねを)かける		to put on (glasses)
きる	着る	to put on (clothes above your waist) （〜を）
*つとめる	勤める	to work for （〜につとめています）
やせる		to lose weight
やせています		to be thin

Irregular Verb

| *けっこんする | 結婚する | to get married （〜と） |

Adverbs and Other Expressions

〜が		. . . , but
*なにも + negative	何も	not . . . anything
〜にん	〜人	[counter for people]
*ひとり	一人	one person
ふたり	二人	two people
*べつに + negative	別に	nothing in particular
*もしもし		Hello? (used on the phone)
*もちろん		of course
*よかったら		if you like

文法 Grammar
ぶん ぽう

1 ～ている

A verbal "*te*-form," when followed by the helping verb いる, means either of the following:[1]

   (a) *an action in progress,* or
   (b) *a past event that is connected with the present.*

Which of these two senses a given verb is used in is to a large extent determined by the semantic characteristics of the verb. The verbs we have learned so far can be roughly divided into three groups based on their semantics.

   (1) verbs that describe continuous *states*
   (2) verbs that describe *activities* that last for some time
   (3) verbs that describe *changes* that are more or less instantaneous

We have not seen many Group 1 verbs. So far we only have ある and いる. The *te*-forms of these verbs are never used together with the helping verb いる, so we will have nothing to say about them in this section.

Many verbs belong to Group 2. They include verbs such as 食べる, 読む, and 待つ. When the *te*-form of a verb in this group is followed by the helping verb いる, we have a sentence describing *an action in progress.*

スーさんは今勉強しています。   *Sue is studying right now.*
いまべんきょう

たけしさんは英語の本を読んでいます。   *Takeshi is reading a book in English.*
えい ご　　ほん　　よ

You can also use a ～ています sentence to describe what a person does by occupation or by habit. The first example below therefore has two interpretations: 1. you are teaching English right at this moment; and 2. you are an English-language teacher (but are not necessarily in class right now.) The second example means that Mary is in the habit of studying Japanese (but of course she does not spend 24 hours a day doing so).

私は英語を教えています。
わたし　えい ご　　おし
I teach English. / I am teaching English (right now).

---

[1] The distinction between いる and ある that we learned in Lesson 4 does not apply to this helping verb ～ている: you can use ～ている both for living things and for inanimate objects.

メアリーさんは毎日日本語を勉強しています。
Mary studies Japanese every day.

Verbs in Group 3 describe changes from one state to another. If you get married, or 結婚する, for example, your status changes from being single to being married. With these verbs,[2] ている indicates a past occurrence of a change which has retained its significance until the present moment. In other words, ている describes *the result of a change*.[3]

山下先生は結婚しています。   *Professor Yamashita is married.*[4]

みちこさんは窓の近くに座っています。 *Michiko is seated near the window.*

Here are some more examples of verbs that are commonly used in the 〜ている framework.

持つ	→	持っている (has)	スーさんはお金をたくさん持っています。 *Sue has a lot of money.*
知る	→	知っている[5] (knows)	山下先生は母を知っています。 *Professor Yamashita knows my mother.*
太る	→	太っている (is overweight)	トムさんはちょっと太っています。 *Tom is a little overweight.*
やせる	→	やせている (is thin)	私の弟はとてもやせています。 *My younger brother is very thin.*
着る	→	着ている (wears)	メアリーさんはTシャツを着ています。 *Mary is wearing/wears a T-shirt.*

---

[2] Among the verbs we have learned so far, verbs such as 起きる, 行く, 帰る, 来る, わかる, 出かける, 乗る, 座る, 死ぬ, 消す, 忘れる, 借りる, 降りる, 持ってくる, 連れてくる, 結婚する, 太る, やせる, 着る belong to Group 3. In most cases you can determine whether a verb belongs to Group 2 or 3 by checking if the verb allows for a phrase describing duration, such as 一時間. Compare, for example,

 ○ 私はきのう一時間本を読みました。 *I read a book for an hour yesterday.*
 × 私は一時間死にました。   (Ungrammatical, much as the English translation
            "I died for an hour" which is also odd.)

読む thus belongs to Group 2, and 死ぬ to Group 3.

[3] In Lesson 9, we will observe that this *result of a change* reading is actually not restricted to verbs in Group 3, but can be associated with those in Group 2 in certain contexts.

[4] Note that the sentence does *not* mean Professor Yamashita *is getting married.*

[5] The negation of 知っています is 知りません, without the ている formation.

起きる	→	起きている (is awake)	お父さんは起きています。 *Dad is up and awake.*
住む	→	住んでいる (lives in)	家族は東京に住んでいます。 *My family lives in Tokyo.*
勤める	→	勤めている (works for)	私の姉は日本の会社に勤めています。 *My older sister works for a Japanese company.*

Note that verbs like 行く and 来る belong to this group. Thus 行っている and 来ている indicate the current states that result from prior movements, *not* movements that are currently in progress. You may want to be careful with what the following sentences mean.

中国に行っています。   *Somebody has gone to/is in China.*

Not: *She is going to China.*

うちに来ています。   *Somebody has come over to visit.*

Not: *Somebody is coming over.*

Finally, a note on conjugation. The helping verb いる conjugates as a *ru*-verb. Thus we have long forms as in the following example.

食べ<u>ている</u>

	affirmative	negative
present	食べ<u>ています</u> *He is eating.*	食べ<u>ていません</u> *He is not eating.*
past	食べ<u>ていました</u> *He was eating.*	食べ<u>ていませんでした</u> *He was not eating.*

2 メアリーさんは髪が長いです

To describe somebody who has long hair, one could say:

トムさんの髪は長いです。   *Tom's hair is long.*

But in fact it would be far more natural in Japanese to say:

トムさんは髪が長いです。   *Tom has long hair. (= As for Tom, he has long hair.)*

This applies not only to discussion of the length of one's hair, but to descriptions of a person's physical attributes in general. See the Parts of the Body section at the end of this lesson for the name of body parts.

$$
Aさんは \left\{ \begin{array}{c} 目 \\ 耳 \\ 手 \\ 足 \\ \vdots \end{array} \right\} が \left\{ \begin{array}{c} 大きい \\ 小さい \\ かわいい \\ \vdots \end{array} \right\}
$$

Person A has a body part which is . . .

In idiomatic collocations, we also have:

背が高い
is tall

背が低い
is short

頭がいい
is bright/smart

3　*Te*-forms for Joining Sentences

In the last lesson, we discussed the use of verbal *te*-forms to join sentences. い- and な-adjectives and です after nouns also have *te*-forms, which can be used to combine two elements to form longer sentences.

The *te*-form of an い-adjective is formed by substituting くて for the final い. The *te*-form of a な-adjective and a noun＋です sequence is formed by adding で to the base or the noun.

い-adjectives:	安い	→	安くて
irregular:	いい	→	よくて
な-adjectives:	元気（な）	→	元気で
noun ＋です:	日本人です	→	日本人で

あの店の食べ物は<u>安くて</u>、おいしいです。
The food at that restaurant is <u>inexpensive</u> <u>and</u> delicious.

ホテルは<u>きれいで</u>、よかったです。
The hotel was <u>clean,</u> <u>and</u> we were happy.

山下先生は<u>日本人で</u>、五十歳ぐらいです。
Professor Yamashita is a <u>Japanese</u> <u>and</u> he is about fifty years old.

4 verb stem ＋ に行く

If a person moves to another place in order to do something, we can describe their movement and its purpose this way:

| destination of movement $\left\{\begin{array}{c}に\\へ\end{array}\right\}$ | the purpose of movement | に | $\left\{\begin{array}{c}行く\\来る\\帰る\end{array}\right\}$ |

The purpose of movement is a phrase consisting of a verb, its object, and so forth.[6] Verbs describing the purpose of a movement must be in their stem forms. Stems, as we learned in Lesson 3, are the part you get by removing ます from the verbs' present tense long forms.

| stems: | 食べる → 食べ（ます） | 読む → 読み（ます） etc. |

デパートに かばんを買い に行きました。
I went to a department store to buy a bag.

メアリーさんは日本に 日本語を勉強し に来ました。
Mary has come to Japan to study Japanese.

5 Counting People

The "counter" for people is 人, but "one person" and "two people" are irregular: 一人 and 二人.

ひとり（一人）	one person
ふたり（二人）	two people
さんにん（三人）	three people
よにん（四人）	four people
ごにん（五人）	five people
ろくにん（六人）	six people
しちにん／ななにん（七人）	seven people
はちにん（八人）	eight people
きゅうにん（九人）	nine people
じゅうにん（十人）	ten people

何人いますか。

---

[6] You can also use some nouns like 買い物 (shopping) for the purpose phrase, as in
デパートに買い物に行きました。　*I went to a department store for shopping.*

To count people in a class, for example, you can add ～人 after the noun and the particle が,
and say:

> person が　X人　います

私のクラスに (は) スウェーデン人の学生が一人います。
There is one Swedish student in our class.

The place expressions are often followed by には instead of に in this type of sentence.

表現ノート……8

Expression Notes 8

遊ぶ ▶ 遊ぶ means "to play," "to spend time pleasantly," or "to pay a social call."

子供の時、よく友だちと遊びました。　*When I was a child, I often played with friends.*

先週の週末は東京に遊びに行きました。　*I went to Tokyo to have fun last weekend.*

私のうちに遊びに来てください。　*Please come and see us.*

Note that "to play" as used below requires different words.

Sports:　to play tennis　テニスをする
Games:　to play games　ゲームをする
　　　　to play cards　トランプをする
Music instruments:　to play the guitar　ギターを弾く

知る/わかる ▶ If you don't know the answer to a question but should have thought about it, you should say わかりません instead of 知りません (see Lesson 4 Dialogue 2, for example). 知りません in such a context would sound rude, implying that your ignorance on that matter is none of the inquirer's business.

練習 Practice

Ⅰ 何をしていますか

A. Look at the pictures below and answer the questions. 🔊 K07-06

Example: Q：メアリーさんは何をしていますか。
A：メアリーさんはテレビを見ています。

B. Pair Work—What were you doing at the following times yesterday? Be as specific as possible (where, with whom, and so on).

Example: 2 P.M. → A：午後二時ごろ何をしていましたか。
B：友だちと部屋で勉強していました。

1. 6 A.M.   3. 10 A.M.   5. 6 P.M.   7. 11 P.M.

2. 8 A.M.   4. 12:30 P.M.   6. 8 P.M.

C. Class Activity—Let's play charades. The teacher gives a sentence card to each student. One of the students mimes the sentence. All other students guess what the person is doing and raise their hands when they recognize the action. The person that gets the most points is the winner.

Example:　田中さんは海で泳いでいます。

Ⅱ　お父さんはどこに住んでいますか

A. This is Sue's family. Answer the following questions.

K07-07

Example:　Q：お父さんはどこに住んでいますか。
　　　　　A：お父さんはニューヨークに住んでいます。

1. お姉さんはどこに住んでいますか。
2. 弟さんはアメリカに住んでいますか。
3. お母さんは何をしていますか。
4. お姉さんは何をしていますか。
5. お姉さんは結婚していますか。

6. 弟さんは結婚していますか。
7. お父さんは何歳ですか。
8. 弟さんは何歳ですか。
9. お父さんは日本の会社に勤めていますか。

Father	lives in N.Y.	works for an American company	48 years old
Mother		high school teacher	45 years old
Sister	lives in Seoul	works for a bank; married	27 years old
Brother	lives in London	student; not married	18 years old

B. Pair Work—Ask your partner's family and fill in the blanks below.

	何歳ですか	何をしていますか	どこに住んでいますか	結婚していますか
お父さん				
お母さん				
お兄さん				
お姉さん				
弟さん				
妹さん				

Ⅲ この人は髪が長いです (Describing People)
ひと　かみ　なが

A. Describe the physical characteristics of the following people. 🔊 K07-08

Example:　この人は目が大きいです。
　　　　　ひと　め　おお

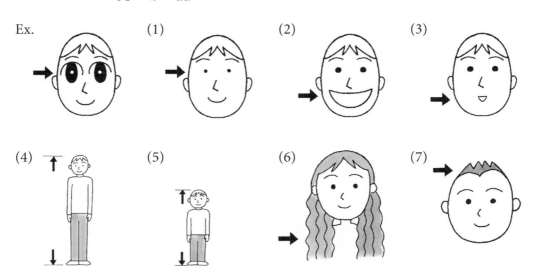

B. Look at the picture below and answer the questions. 🔊 K07-09

Example:　Q：山田さんはやせていますか。
　　　　　　　やまだ
　　　　　　A：はい、山田さんはやせています。
　　　　　　　　　やまだ

1. 山田さんは太っていますか。
   やまだ　　ふと
2. 山田さんはＴシャツを着ていますか。
   やまだ　　ティー　　き
3. 吉川さんは何を着ていますか。
   よしかわ　なに　き
4. 山田さんはジーンズをはいていますか。
   やまだ
5. 吉川さんはめがねをかけていますか。
   よしかわ
6. 吉川さんはかさを持っていますか。
   よしかわ　　　も
7. 山田さんは背が高いですか。
   やまだ　　せ　たか
8. 吉川さんは背が低いですか。
   よしかわ　　せ　ひく
9. 山田さんは髪が長いですか。
   やまだ　　かみ　なが
10. 吉川さんは目が小さいですか。
    よしかわ　　め　ちい

山田　　吉川
やまだ　よしかわ

C. Look at the picture below and describe each person.

Example: 水野さんはぼうしをかぶっています。
みずの

D. Class Activity—One student describes another student without mentioning the name. The rest of the class guesses who the student is.

Example: 髪が短いです。Tシャツを着ています。ジーンズをはいていません。
かみ みじか ティー き

Ⅳ 大学は新しくて、きれいです
だいがく あたら

A. Make sentences using two adjectives. 🔊 K07-10

Example: 大学 — 新しい／きれいな → 大学は新しくて、きれいです。
だいがく あたら だいがく あたら

1. 東京　　　　— 大きい／にぎやかな
とうきょう おお
2. みちこさん — きれいな／やさしい
3. たけしさん — 背が高い／かっこいい
せ たか
4. アパート　　— 静かな／大きい
しず おお
5. 新幹線 (Bullet Train) — 速い／便利な
しんかんせん はや べんり
6. スーさん　　— 頭がいい／親切な
あたま しんせつ
7. 私の国の人 — 元気な／にぎやかな
わたし くに ひと げんき

B. Looking back on your childhood, make sentences using the given cues. 🔊 K07-11

Example:　next-door neighbor — tall & kind

→　となりの人は背が高くて、親切でした。
　　　　　（ひと）（せ）（たか）　　（しんせつ）

1. father　　　— quiet & good-looking
2. teacher　　— big & scary
3. house　　　— old & not clean
4. classes　　— long & not interesting
5. friends　　— kind & interesting
6. school　　— lively & fun
7. homework — difficult & tough
8. myself　　— small & cute

C. Describe the following items using two or more adjectives.

Example:　my mother

→　母はきれいでやさしいです。
　　（はは）
　　母はきれいですが、こわいです。
　　（はは）

1. my hometown
2. my country
3. my Japanese class
4. one of my family members
5. Japanese people
6. people of my country

D. Pair Work—Answer the following questions using two or more adjectives.

Example:　家に犬がいますか。／どんな犬ですか。
　　　　　（いえ）（いぬ）　　　　　　（いぬ）

→　Ａ：家に犬がいますか。
　　　　（いえ）（いぬ）
　　Ｂ：はい。
　　Ａ：どんな犬ですか。
　　　　　　　（いぬ）
　　Ｂ：小さくて、かわいいです。
　　　　（ちい）
　　Ａ：そうですか。

1. どこから来ましたか。／どんな町（国）ですか。
2. パソコンを持っていますか。／どんなパソコンですか。
3. 好きな人がいますか。／どんな人ですか。
4. 週末何をしましたか。／どうでしたか。
5. 休みにどこに旅行しましたか。／どんな町でしたか。

Ⓥ かぶきを見に行きます

A. Sue is going to the following places to do the things below. Make sentences like the example. 🔊 K07-12

Example:　京都 ― かぶき (Kabuki) を見る
　　　　　→　スーさんは京都にかぶきを見に行きます。

1. 図書館　　　　　― 本を借りる
2. 食堂　　　　　　― 昼ご飯を食べる
3. 郵便局　　　　　― 切手を買う
4. 公園　　　　　　― 写真を撮る
5. 友だちのうち　― 勉強する
6. 町　　　　　　　― 遊ぶ
7. デパート　　　　― くつを買う
8. 高校　　　　　　― 英語を教える
9. 喫茶店　　　　　― コーヒーを飲む

B. For what purpose would you go to the following places?

1. コンビニに＿＿＿＿＿＿＿＿＿＿＿＿＿に行きます。

2. 東京に＿＿＿＿＿＿＿＿＿＿＿＿＿＿に行きました。

3. 図書館に＿＿＿＿＿＿＿＿＿＿＿＿に行きます。

4. 家に＿＿＿＿＿＿＿＿＿＿＿＿＿＿＿に帰ります。

5. 大学に＿＿＿＿＿＿＿＿＿＿＿＿＿に来ました。

C. Pair Work—Look at the pictures below and practice the dialogue with your partner.

Example: A：トムさんは友だちのうちに何をしに行きますか。
　　　　　　　　　　とも　　　　　　　なに　　　い

B：遊びに行きます。
　　あそ　　い

Ex. to play (have fun)　　　(1) to borrow　　　(2)

friend's house

Tom

library

Ken

Paul

(3) to buy souvenir　　　(4)　　　(5)

department store

Maria

home

Mary

temple

Yoko

Ⅵ この部屋に女の人が何人いますか
　　　へ　や　　おんな　ひと　　なんにん

Pair Work—Ask your partner the following questions.

Example: A：この部屋に女の人が何人いますか。
　　　　　　　　へ　や　おんな　ひと　なんにん

B：二人います。
　　ふたり

1. この部屋に男の人が何人いますか。
　　へ　や　おとこ　ひと　なんにん

2. この部屋に＿＿＿＿＿＿＿人が何人いますか。
　　へ　や　　　　(nationality)　　じん　なんにん

3. この部屋に髪が長い人が何人いますか。
　　へ　や　かみ　なが　ひと　なんにん

4. この部屋に元気な人が何人いますか。
　　へ　や　げん　き　ひと　なんにん

Ⅶ まとめの練習
れんしゅう

A. Answer the following questions.

1. どこに住んでいますか。
   す

2. 結婚していますか。
   けっこん

3. 自転車／車を持っていますか。
   じてんしゃ　くるま　も

4. 日本の歌を知っていますか。
   にほん　うた　し

5. サークルに入っていますか。
   はい

6. 日本語の先生は今日何を着ていますか／はいていますか。
   にほんご　せんせい　きょうなに　き

7. 兄弟がいますか。何人いますか。
   きょうだい　　　なんにん

8. お父さん／お母さんはどこに勤めていますか。
   とう　　　　かあ　　　　　つと

9. おじいさん／おばあさんはどこに住んでいますか。
   す

10. 子供の時、自転車を持っていましたか。
    こども　とき　じてんしゃ　も

11. 高校の時、日本語を知っていましたか。
    こうこう　とき　にほんご　し

B. Class Activity—Show a picture of your family to the class and describe it.

Ｃulture Ｎote

家族の呼び方 Kinship Terms
かぞく　よ　かた

| | 1. Referring to other families | 2. Referring to yours | | 3. Addressing yours |
		A. formal	B. informal	
Father	お父さん とう	父 ちち	お父さん とう	お父さん／パパ とう
Mother	お母さん かあ	母 はは	お母さん かあ	お母さん／ママ かあ
Older brother	お兄さん にい	兄 あに	お兄さん にい	お兄ちゃん にい
Older sister	お姉さん ねえ	姉 あね	お姉さん ねえ	お姉ちゃん ねえ
Younger brother	弟 さん おとうと	弟 おとうと		——
Younger sister	妹 さん いもうと	妹 いもうと		——
Husband	ご主人 しゅじん	主人／夫 しゅじん　おっと	だんな／うちの人, ひと etc.	お父さん とう
Wife	奥さん おく	家内／妻 かない　つま	奥さん／嫁さん, おく　　よめ etc.	お母さん かあ
Grandfather	おじいさん	祖父 そ　ふ	おじいさん	おじいちゃん
Grandmother	おばあさん	祖母 そ　ぼ	おばあさん	おばあちゃん
Child	お子さん こ	うちの子 こ		——

There are many other kinship terms in addition to those listed in the table above. Equal or younger members of your family can be addressed by their given name instead of the kinship term. As the table indicates, the term used for a particular type of family member varies according to the following situations:

1.　　Speaking about somebody else's family
2-A.　Speaking about your own family in a formal situation, such as a job interview
2-B.　Speaking about your own family in a casual situation
3.　　Speaking to your family

A：田中さんのお父さんは何歳ですか。　　*How old is your father, Mr. Tanaka?*
　　たなか　　　　とう　　　　　なんさい
B：[formal] 父は五十歳です。　　　　　　*My father is 50 years old.*
　　　　　　ちち　ごじゅっさい
　　[informal] お父さんは五十歳です。
　　　　　　　　とう　　　　ごじゅっさい

You can also address members of your family with the terms that the youngest member would use. For example, a wife can call her husband お父さん or パパ, and a mother can call
とう
her oldest son お兄ちゃん.
　　　　　　　にい

Mother: お兄ちゃん、お父さんが待っていますよ。
　　　　　にい　　　　とう　　　　ま
　　　　Son (literally, *older brother*), *your father is waiting.*

体の部分
からだ ぶ ぶん

Parts of the Body

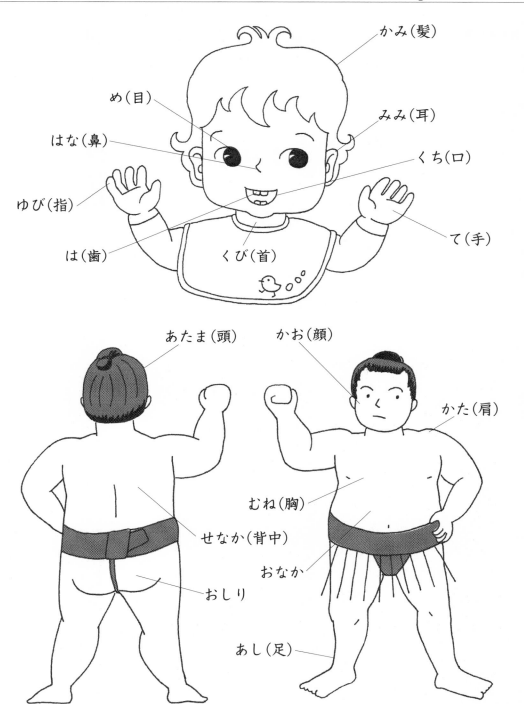

第8課 L E S S O N 8

バーベキュー Barbecue

会 話 Dialogue
かい わ

Ⅰ At school. 🔊 K08-01/02

1 みちこ： たけしさん、あしたみんなでバーベキューをしませんか。

2 たけし： いいですね。だれが来ますか。
き

3 みちこ： スーさんとロバートさんが来ます。メアリーさんも来ると思います。
き く おも

4 たけし： けんさんは？

5 みちこ： けんさんはアルバイトがあると言っていました。
い

6 たけし： 残念ですね。何か持っていきましょうか。
ざんねん なに も

7 みちこ： 何もいらないと思います。
なに おも

Ⅱ Robert is cooking at the barbecue. 🔊 K08-03/04

1 みちこ： 上手ですね。ロバートさんは料理するのが好きですか。
じょう ず りょう り す

2 ロバート： ええ、よく家で作ります。
いえ つく

3 みちこ： 何か手伝いましょうか。
なに てつだ

4 ロバート： じゃあ、トマトを切ってください。
き

　　　　　　　 ＊ 　　　　 ＊ 　　　　 ＊

5 ロバート： 始めましょうか。
はじ

6 みちこ： あっ、まだ飲まないでください。
の

7 　　　　　 メアリーさんも来ると言っていましたから。
く い

8 メアリー： 遅くなってすみません。
おそ

9 みんな： じゃあ、乾杯！
かんぱい

Ⅰ

Michiko: Takeshi, would you like to have a barbecue party tomorrow?

Takeshi: That's nice. Who will come?

Michiko: Sue and Robert will come. I think Mary will come, too.

Takeshi: How about Ken?

Michiko: Ken said he had a part-time job.

Takeshi: Too bad. Shall I bring something?

Michiko: I think nothing is needed.

Ⅱ

Michiko: You are good (at cooking). Do you like cooking, Robert?

Robert: Yes, I often cook at home.

Michiko: Shall I help you with something?

Robert: Well then, cut the tomatoes, please.

        *   *   *

Robert: Shall we start?

Michiko: Don't drink yet. Mary said that she would come.

Mary: I'm sorry for being late.

Everyone: Well then . . . Cheers!

単語
たん ご
V o c a b u l a r y

🔊 K08-05

N o u n s

あさって		the day after tomorrow
あめ	雨	rain
かいしゃいん	会社員	office worker
カメラ		camera
カラオケ		karaoke
くうき	空気	air
けさ	今朝	this morning
こくばん	黒板	blackboard
こんげつ	今月	this month
しごと	仕事	job; work; occupation
だいがくせい	大学生	college student
てんきよほう	天気予報	weather forecast
ところ	所	place
＊トマト		tomato
なつ	夏	summer
＊なにか	何か	something
パーティー		party
＊バーベキュー		barbecue
はし		chopsticks
ふゆ	冬	winter
ホームステイ		homestay; living with a local family
まいしゅう	毎週	every week
らいげつ	来月	next month

な - a d j e c t i v e s

＊じょうず（な）	上手	skillful; good at . . . （～が）
へた（な）	下手	clumsy; poor at . . . （～が）
ゆうめい（な）	有名	famous

U - v e r b s

あめがふる	雨が降る	it rains
あらう	洗う	to wash （～を）
＊いう	言う	to say
＊いる		to need （～が）

＊ Words that appear in the dialogue

* おそくなる	遅くなる	to be late
* おもう	思う	to think
* きる	切る	to cut（〜を）
* つくる	作る	to make（〜を）
* もっていく	持っていく	to take (a thing)（〜を）

Ru-verbs

じろじろみる	じろじろ見る	to stare (at ...)（〜を）
すてる	捨てる	to throw away（〜を）
* はじめる	始める	to begin（〜を）

Irregular Verbs

うんてんする	運転する	to drive（〜を）
せんたくする	洗濯する	to do laundry（〜を）
そうじする	掃除する	to clean（〜を）
でんわする	電話する	to call（〜に）
* りょうりする	料理する	to cook

Adverbs and Other Expressions

いつも		always
ううん		uh-uh; no
うん		uh-huh; yes
* かんぱい	乾杯	Cheers! (a toast)
* ざんねん（ですね）	残念（ですね）	That's too bad.
〜について		about ...; concerning ...
* まだ＋ negative		not ... yet
* みんなで		all (of the people) together

文法 Grammar
ぶん ぼう

1 Short Forms

In this and the next lesson, we will learn a new paradigm of conjugation, which we will call "short forms.[1]" Before we start worrying about their meaning and how they are used, let us first see what they look like. It should be obvious why they are called short forms. We will list the already familiar "long forms" to the right in the table below.

Present tense, affirmative

	short forms	long forms
verbs:	読む[a] よ	読みます よ
い-adjectives:	かわいい[a]	かわいいです
な-adjectives:	静かだ[b] しず	静かです しず
noun＋です：	学生だ[b] がくせい	学生です がくせい

Present tense, negative

	short forms	long forms
verbs:	読まない[c] よ	読みません よ
い-adjectives:	かわいくない[d]	かわいくないです
な-adjectives:	静かじゃない[d] しず	静かじゃないです しず
noun＋です：	学生じゃない[d] がくせい	学生じゃないです がくせい

The following rules summarize how short forms are constructed.

Verbs and い-adjectives in the affirmative (**a** above)
→ same as their dictionary forms

な-adjectives and noun＋です in the affirmative (**b** above)
→ replace です with だ

い- and な-adjectives and noun＋です in the negative (**d** above)
→ drop です after ない

---

[1] Various names have been given to this paradigm. They include "plain forms," "informal forms," and "direct style." Long forms, on the other hand, are often called "polite forms," "formal forms," and "distal style."

As noted in Lesson 5, the adjective いい is irregular. Its negative short form is よくない.

Verbs in the negative need to be analyzed in more detail, because *ru-*, *u-*, and irregular verbs conjugate differently.

Negative short forms of verbs (**c** above)

ru-verbs: Take the final る off and add ない.

食べる → 食べない

u-verbs: Take the final -*u* off and add -*anai*.

書く	→	書かない	作る	→	作らない
話す	→	話さない	泳ぐ	→	泳がない
待つ	→	待たない	呼ぶ	→	呼ばない
死ぬ	→	死なない	買う	→	買わない (1)
読む	→	読まない			

irregular verbs:

する → しない　　　くる → こない (2)

exception:

ある → ない (3)

With verbs in the negative, the following three points are worth noting.

(1) The negative short forms of verbs that end with the *hiragana* う are ～わない instead of ～あない.[2]

(2) The vowel changes with the irregular verbs する and くる.

(3) The verb ある in the negative is ない, as in かさがない (there is no umbrella).

We now turn to discussion of how we utilize short forms. In this lesson, we will learn to use the short forms in the following four contexts:

● In casual conversations, as signs of intimacy (See 2.)
● In represented, or quoted, speech ("I think . . . ," "She said . . . .") (See 3.)
● In making negative requests ("Please don't . . .") (See 4.)
● In expressing ideas like "I like doing . . ." or "I am good at doing . . ." (See 5.)

---

[2] This suggests that the bases of verbs like 買う and 会う actually end with the consonant *w*. This consonant remains dormant when the base is followed by the vowel *i*, thus we have 買います, where *w* is lacking, but it surfaces with the vowel *a* following, 買わない. This mystery consonant also explains why the *te*-form of such a verb has a small つ, just like verbs whose bases obviously end with a consonant, such as とる and 待つ.

2 Informal Speech

Two people who are close friends or family members speak with short forms at the end of sentences, using them as a sign of intimacy. The use of long forms, in contrast, tends to imply the speaker's intention to "keep a proper distance" from the listener. Short forms, then, are like talking on a first name basis, while long forms are like using "Mr." and "Ms."

It may not be easy to decide when it is appropriate to switch to short forms. First of all, Japanese speakers are often very conscious of seniority. A year's difference in age may in many cases totally preclude the possibility of establishing a truly "equal" relationship. Second, license to use short forms is not mutual; senior partners may feel perfectly justified in using short forms while expecting their junior partners to continue addressing them with long forms. Thus if somebody who is older, say, your Japanese language professor, talks to you using short forms, they would be greatly surprised if you should return the favor.

Here are a few observations on the grammar of short forms as they are used in casual conversations.

- In the casual conversational use of short forms, question sentences do not end with the question particle か, but with rising intonation alone.

  どんな音楽を聞く？　（×どんな音楽を聞く<u>か</u>？）
  What kind of music do you listen to?

- The だ ending of な-adjectives and noun ＋ です constructions (**b** in the previous section) is usually dropped at the very end of a sentence, or is followed by sentence-final ね or よ.

  メアリーさんは二年生。 or メアリーさんは二年生だよ。
  　　　　　　　　　　（Rather than: メアリーさんは二年生<u>だ</u>。）
  Mary is a sophomore.

In casual conversations, はい and いいえ are usually replaced by the less formal うん and ううん.

3　～と思います／～と言っていました

To quote a person's utterances or thoughts, you use a clause ending with a predicate in the short form, plus と思います (I think that . . .), と言っていました[3] (They said ". . ."), and so forth. と is a quotation particle, which does the job of both the English word "that" in indirect quotation and of quotation marks (" ") in direct quotation.

あした試験があります。

スーさんは あした試験がある[4] と 言っていました。

スーさんは、あした試験があると言っていました。
Sue said that there would be an exam tomorrow.

（私は）たけしさんはメアリーさんが好きだと思います。[5]
I think Takeshi likes Mary.

---

[3] The action in progress expression in と言っていました indicates that you were there when somebody said that, as in "I heard them saying . . ." If you were not there when the utterance was made, as in "(the long dead) Napoleon said . . . ," と言いました sounds more appropriate.

[4] Note that the present tense in Sue's original utterance is preserved in Mary's report.

[5] To say that you *don't think* something is the case, it is more common in Japanese to say it like ～ないと思います (I *think* that something is *not* the case) than ～と思いません (I *don't think*). Therefore:
　　（私は）メアリーさんはたけしさんが好きじゃないと思います。
　　I don't think Mary likes Takeshi. (= I think Mary doesn't like Takeshi.)

4 〜ないでください

To request that someone refrain from doing something, one can use a negative verbal short form plus でください.

ここで写真を撮らないでください。
しゃしん　と
Please don't take pictures here.

| negative short form ＋ でください | *Please don't . . .* |

5 verb のが好きです
　　　　　　　す

Short forms are used in constructions where verbs and adjectives are to be treated as nouns. Thus 私は〜が好きです／きらいです can, besides describing your preference for items de-
わたし
noted by nouns, such as 猫, also describe your preference for activities, such as swimming,
ねこ
drinking coffee, and studying Japanese. Add の to a verbal short form to express the idea of
"doing x."

（私は）日本語を勉強する のが好きです。
わたし　にほんご　べんきょう　　　　　す
I like studying the Japanese language.

（私は）部屋を掃除する のがきらいです。
わたし　へや　そうじ
I don't like cleaning my room.

"To be good/bad at doing something" is 〜が上手です (is good at . . .) and 〜が下手です (is
じょうず　　　　　　　　　　　　　　　へた
bad at . . .).[6]

ロバートさんは料理を作る のが上手です。
りょうり　つく　　　じょうず
Robert is good at cooking meals.

たけしさんは英語を話す のが下手です。
えいご　はな　　　へた
Takeshi is not a good speaker of English.

---

[6] To describe one's skills or lack thereof, we also often use a different set of expressions, namely, 〜がとくいで
す (is comfortable with . . .) and 〜がにがて です (is uncomfortable with . . .).
　私は日本語を話すのがとくいです。　　*I am good at/comfortable with speaking Japanese.*
わたし　にほんご　はな

$$
\text{person は activity (verb) のが}
\left\{
\begin{array}{l}
好き \\
きらい \\
上手 \\
下手
\end{array}
\right\}
\text{です。}
\qquad
\begin{array}{l}
\textit{likes doing . . .} \\
\textit{doesn't like doing . . .} \\
\textit{is good at doing . . .} \\
\textit{is poor at doing . . .}
\end{array}
$$

It is a common mistake to use the *te*-form of a verb in such contexts, misled by the association between 〜ている and the verb in the *-ing* form in English.

× たけしさんは英語を<u>話して</u>が下手です。

6　が

Consider what ロバートさんは沖縄に行きました means. This sentence of course is about Robert and describes what he did. It is likely to be uttered when the topic of Robert has already been breached. Grammatically speaking, (1) the noun ロバート stands as the subject in relation to the verb 行く (he was the person who performed the going), and (2) the noun is, per the function of the particle は, presented as the topic of the sentence (*as for* Robert, he went to Okinawa).

What if we both know that somebody went to Okinawa recently, and *I* know that it was Robert, but *you* don't. I will say:

ロバートさん<u>が</u>沖縄に行きました。　　　　*ROBERT went to Okinawa.*

This sentence means that *Robert* went to Okinawa, which in English would be uttered with an extra emphasis on the name Robert. His identity is the new piece of information provided by this sentence. It is one of the functions of the particle が to (1) present the subject of a sentence in a way such that (2) the noun will "fill in the blank on the information sheet."

The "blank on the information sheet" is a question word like だれ and 何. The above sentence will fill in the blank left out by:

だれが沖縄に行きましたか。　　　　Compare: × だれ<u>は</u>沖縄に行きましたか。
Who went to Okinawa?

As we learned in Lesson 2, a question word that is the subject of a sentence is never followed by the particle は, but always by the particle が. As we have seen, a noun that will provide the answer to such a question is also followed by the particle が.

どのクラスがおもしろいですか。

Which class is (the most) interesting?

日本語のクラスがおもしろいです。

Japanese class is.

（このクラスで）だれがめがねをかけていますか。

Who wears glasses (in this class)?

山下先生がめがねをかけています。

Professor Yamashita does.

7 何か and 何も

The word for "something" is 何か, and the word for "anything" in negative sentences is 何も.

"Some" and "any" in:		
positive statements	何か	*something*
questions	何か	*anything?*
negative statements	何も + negative	*not . . . anything*

These two words are used in places where the particles は, が, and を are expected. In these contexts, they are used on their own, without the help of particles. We will learn in Lesson 10 what to do in cases where particles other than these are expected.

猫が何か持ってきました。

The cat has brought something.

猫は何か食べましたか。

Did the cat eat anything?

いいえ、猫は何も食べませんでした。

No, the cat did not eat anything.

表現ノート……9
ひょう げん

〜する ▶ Most irregular verbs are compounds of nouns and the verb する. If you have learned an irregular verb, therefore, you have also learned a noun.

verbs	nouns	
勉強する べんきょう *to study*	勉強 べんきょう *study*	ex. 日本語の<u>勉強</u>は楽しいです。 に ほん ご べんきょう たの *Japanese language study is fun.*
料理する りょう り *to cook*	料理 りょう り *cooking*	ex. ロバートさんの<u>料理</u>はおいしいです。 りょう り *Robert's cooking is good.*

Some of these nouns can be used as the "object" of the verb する.

私は日本語の<u>勉強</u><u>を</u>しました。 *I studied Japanese.*
わたし に ほん ご べんきょう
　　Compare: 私は日本語を<u>勉強</u>しました。
　　　　　　 わたし に ほん ご べんきょう

たけしさんは部屋の<u>掃除</u><u>を</u>しました。 *Takeshi cleaned his room.*
へ や そう じ
　　Compare: たけしさんは部屋を<u>掃除</u>しました。
　　　　　　 へ や そう じ

You can use both these nouns and their する verbs in sentences with 好きです
す
and きらいです, for example. You need to add の to the verbs, as we discussed in
Section 5. Pay attention to the particles before these words, too.

日本語<u>の</u>勉強が好きです。／日本語<u>を</u>勉強する<u>の</u>が好きです。
に ほん ご べんきょう す に ほん ご べんきょう す
I like studying Japanese.

練習 P r a c t i c e
れん しゅう

I Short Forms

A. Change the affirmatives into negatives. [🔊] K08-06

Example: かく → かかない

1. みる
2. あける
3. すむ
4. かける
5. はく
6. はじめる
7. つくる
8. せんたくする
9. あらう
10. くる
11. わすれる
12. ある
13. おもう
14. もっていく
15. はいる
16. かえる

B. Change the affirmatives into negatives. [🔊] K08-07

Example: たかい   → たかくない
         げんきだ   → げんきじゃない
         がくせいだ → がくせいじゃない

1. ゆうめいだ
2. あめだ
3. いそがしい
4. かわいい
5. みじかい
6. しんせつだ
7. やすい
8. きれいだ
9. たいへんだ
10. いい
11. かっこいい
12. すきだ

II Informal Speech

A. Answer the following questions in informal speech, first in the affirmative, then in the negative. [🔊] K08-08/09

Example: Q：よく魚を食べる？
         さかな た
         A：うん、食べる。／ううん、食べない。
           た   た

1. 今日、勉強する？
   きょう べんきょう
2. 今日、友だちに会う？
   きょう とも あ
3. よくお茶を飲む？
   ちゃ の
4. よく電車に乗る？
   てんしゃ の
5. 毎日、日本語を話す？
   まいにち にほんご はな
6. 毎日、テレビを見る？
   まいにち み

7. あした、大学に来る？
_{だいがく} _く

8. 今日、宿題がある？
_{きょう} _{しゅくだい}

9. 自転車を持っている？
_{じてんしゃ} _も

10. 来週、カラオケに行く？
_{らいしゅう} _い

11. 毎週、部屋を掃除する？
_{まいしゅう} _へ _や _{そうじ}

12. 毎日、洗濯する？
_{まいにち} _{せんたく}

B. Answer the following questions in informal speech, first in the affirmative, then in the negative. 🔊 K08-10/11

Example:　Q：元気？
_{げんき}
　　　　　　A：うん、元気。／ううん、元気じゃない。
_{げんき} _{げんき}

1. ひま？

2. 忙しい？
_{いそが}

3. この教科書はいい？
_{きょうかしょ}

4. 先生はこわい？
_{せんせい}

5. 料理が上手？
_{りょうり} _{じょうず}

6. お風呂が好き？
_{ふ ろ} _す

7. スポーツがきらい？

8. 今日は月曜日？
_{きょう} _{げつようび}

9. 日本語のクラスはおも
_{にほんご}
しろい？

10. 日本語のクラスは難し
_{にほんご} _{むずか}
い？

（Ⅲ）日本人だと思います
_{にほんじん} _{おも}

A. Make a guess about Mary, using 〜と思います。 🔊 K08-12
_{おも}

Example:　good at Japanese

　　　→　メアリーさんは日本語が上手だと思います。
_{にほんご} _{じょうず} _{おも}

1. often cooks

2. drives a car

3. doesn't smoke

4. speaks Japanese every day

5. doesn't go home late at night

6. doesn't drink coffee much

7. often goes to see movies

8. not married

9. likes Takeshi

10. busy

11. a good student

12. not tall

13. not quiet

14. not a freshman

B. Make a guess about the person or place below and answer the following questions.

Example:　Q：この人は日本人ですか。
_{ひと} _{にほんじん}
　　　　　　A：ええ、日本人だと思います。／
_{にほんじん} _{おも}
　　　　　　　　いいえ、日本人じゃないと思います。
_{にほんじん} _{おも}

Picture A

1. 山下先生はいい先生ですか。
   やましたせんせい　　せんせい
2. 有名ですか。
   ゆうめい
3. ひまですか。
4. 頭がいいですか。
   あたま
5. 背が高いですか。
   せ　たか
6. 忙しいですか。
   いそが
7. 結婚していますか。
   けっこん
8. お金をたくさん持っていますか。
   かね　　　　　　も
9. よく食べますか。
   た
10. よくスポーツをしますか。
11. フランス語を話しますか。
   ご　はな

A

Picture B

1. ここは日本ですか。
   にほん
2. 有名な所ですか。
   ゆうめい　ところ
3. 空気はきれいですか。
   くうき
4. 暑いですか。
   あつ
5. 冬は寒いですか。
   ふゆ　さむ
6. 人がたくさん住んでいますか。
   ひと　　　　　す
7. ここの人は、よく泳ぎますか。
   ひと　　　　　　およ
8. 夏によく雨が降りますか。
   なつ　　　あめ　ふ

B

C. Discuss the following topics in pairs or groups.

Example:　university cafeteria

　→　Ａ：<u>大学の食堂</u>についてどう思いますか。
　　　　　だいがく　しょくどう　　　　　　おも
　　　Ｂ：安くて、おいしいと思います。私はよく食べに行きます。
　　　　　やす　　　　　　おも　　　わたし　　　た　い
　　　　　Ａさんはどう思いますか。
　　　　　　　　　　　おも
　　　Ａ：私は……。
　　　　　わたし

1. this town　　　　　3. Japanese language　　　　5. your own topic

2. this class　　　　　4. Mary and Takeshi

Ⅳ メアリーさんは忙しいと言っていました

A. Report what the following people said, using 〜と言っていました. 📢 K08-13

Example: メアリー／今月は忙しいです。
→ Q：メアリーさんは何と言っていましたか。
A：今月は忙しいと言っていました。

メアリー

Ex. 今月は忙しいです。
1. 来月もひまじゃないです。
2. あしたは買い物をします。
3. 毎日漢字を勉強しています。

ロバート

4. ホームステイをしています。
5. お父さんは親切です。
6. お母さんは料理が上手です。
7. お兄さんは大学生です。
8. 家族は英語を話しません。

天気予報

9. あしたはいい天気です。
10. あしたは寒くないです。
11. あさっては雨が降ります。
12. あさっては寒いです。

B. Pair Work—Ask your partner the following questions. Take notes and report to the class later, using 〜と言っていました.

1. 週末は何をしますか。
2. 日本はどうですか。
3. 日本の友だち／日本の家族はどんな人ですか。
4. どんな人が好きですか。

Ⓥ 見ないでください
ㅤㅤみ

A. What would you say when you want someone . . .  K08-14

ㅤㅤExample:ㅤnot to look at your photoㅤ→ㅤ写真を見ないでください。
ㅤㅤㅤㅤㅤㅤㅤㅤㅤㅤㅤㅤㅤㅤㅤㅤㅤㅤしゃしんㅤㅤみ

1. not to speak English
2. not to call you
3. not to come to your house
4. not to go
5. not to smoke
6. not to sleep in class
7. not to forget
8. not to stare at you
9. not to start the class yet
10. not to be late
11. not to erase the blackboard yet
12. not to throw away the magazine

B. Pair Work—Make a request using the given cues.

ㅤㅤExample:ㅤ窓を開ける
ㅤㅤㅤㅤㅤㅤㅤまどㅤあ
ㅤㅤㅤㅤ→ㅤＡ：窓を開けてもいいですか。
ㅤㅤㅤㅤㅤㅤㅤㅤㅤまどㅤあ
ㅤㅤㅤㅤㅤㅤＢ：すみません。開けないでください。寒いですから。／
ㅤㅤㅤㅤㅤㅤㅤㅤㅤㅤㅤㅤㅤㅤあㅤㅤㅤㅤㅤㅤㅤㅤㅤㅤㅤㅤㅤㅤさむ
ㅤㅤㅤㅤㅤㅤㅤㅤいいですよ。どうぞ。

1. たばこを吸う
ㅤㅤㅤㅤㅤす
2. テレビをつける
3. 写真を撮る
ㅤㅤしゃしんㅤと
4. 電気を消す
ㅤㅤでんきㅤけ
5. パソコンを使う
ㅤㅤㅤㅤㅤㅤつか
6. (your partner's name) に電話する
ㅤㅤㅤㅤㅤㅤㅤㅤㅤㅤㅤㅤㅤㅤㅤㅤㅤでんわ
7. your own request

Ⓥ 勉強するのが好きですか
ㅤㅤべんきょうㅤㅤㅤㅤㅤㅤす

A. Tell what Mary is good/poor at, using 上手です or 下手です.  K08-15
ㅤㅤㅤㅤㅤㅤㅤㅤㅤㅤㅤㅤㅤㅤㅤㅤㅤㅤㅤㅤㅤㅤㅤㅤㅤㅤㅤㅤじょうずㅤㅤㅤㅤㅤㅤㅤへた

ㅤㅤExample:ㅤtennis (good)
ㅤㅤㅤㅤ→ㅤメアリーさんはテニスが上手です。
ㅤㅤㅤㅤㅤㅤㅤㅤㅤㅤㅤㅤㅤㅤㅤㅤㅤㅤじょうず
ㅤㅤㅤㅤswimming (poor)
ㅤㅤㅤㅤ→ㅤメアリーさんは泳ぐのが下手です。
ㅤㅤㅤㅤㅤㅤㅤㅤㅤㅤㅤㅤㅤㅤㅤㅤおよㅤㅤㅤへた

1. French (poor)
2. cooking (good)
3. making sushi (poor)
4. eating <u>with chopsticks</u> (good)
ㅤㅤㅤㅤ（はしで）
5. taking pictures (good)
6. driving a car (good)
7. speaking Japanese (good)
8. writing <u>love letters</u> (good)
ㅤㅤㅤㅤ（ラブレター）

B. Pair Work—Ask if your partner likes to do the following activities.

Example: studying

→ A：勉強するのが好きですか。
 べんきょう　　　　 す

 B：はい、好きです／大好きです。
　　　　 す　　　　　だい す

 いいえ、きらいです／大きらいです。
　　　　　　　　　　　　だい

1. eating
2. sleeping
3. singing
4. doing shopping

5. playing sports
6. studying Japanese
7. doing cleaning
8. doing laundry

9. cooking
10. taking a bath
11. driving a car
12. washing a car

＊If you neither like it nor dislike it, you can use 好きでもきらいでもないです.
　　　　　　　　　　　　　　　　　　　　　　　　す

Ⅶ だれがイギリス人ですか
　　　　　　　　　じん

A. Use the table below and answer the questions. K08-16

Example: Q：だれがイギリス人ですか。
　　　　　　　　　　　じん

 A：ロバートさんがイギリス人です。
　　　　　　　　　　　　　　じん

1. だれが韓国人ですか。
　　　かんこくじん
2. だれが料理をするのが上手ですか。
　　　りょうり　　　　じょうず
3. だれがいつも食堂で食べますか。
　　　　　　しょくどう た
4. だれがデートをしましたか。
5. だれが犬が好きですか。
　　　いぬ す

	Robert	British	is good at cooking	cooks often	went to Okinawa last weekend	doesn't like cats
	Mary	American	is good at skiing	does not cook	had a date last weekend	likes dogs
	Sue	Korean	is good at singing	cooks sometimes	went to Tokyo last weekend	likes cats
	Takeshi	Japanese	is good at swimming	always eats at cafeteria	had a date last weekend	doesn't like cats

B. Pair Work—Use the table above and ask your partner questions with だれが.

Ⅷ 何もしませんでした
なに

A. You went to a party but did nothing there. Make sentences using the cues.

🔊 K08-17

Example:　パーティーに行きましたが、(eat)
い

→　パーティーに行きましたが、何も食べませんでした。
い　　　　　　　　　なに　た

1. パーティーに行きましたが、(drink)
い
2. カラオケがありましたが、(sing)
3. テレビがありましたが、(watch)
4. カメラを持っていましたが、(take)
も
5. ゆみさんに会いましたが、(talk)
あ
6. パーティーに行きましたが、(do)
い

B. Answer the following questions.

Example:　Q：きのうの晩ご飯は何か作りましたか。
ばん　はん　なに　つく
A：はい、スパゲッティ (spaghetti) を作りました。／
つく
いいえ、何も作りませんでした。
なに　つく

1. けさ、何か食べましたか。
なに　た
2. きのう、何か買いましたか。
なに　か
3. きのう、テレビで (on TV) 何か見ましたか。
なに　み
4. 今、何かいりますか。
いま　なに
5. 週末、何かしますか。
しゅうまつ　なに
6. 週末、何か勉強しますか。
しゅうまつ　なに　べんきょう

Ⅸ まとめの練習
れんしゅう

A. Interview one of your classmates about any future plans and report to the class.

Example:　スーさんは来年ソウルへ行くと言っていました。
らいねん　　　　い　い

B. Pair Work/Group Work—You are planning a party. Decide on the following points and fill in the chart.

いつですか	
どこでしますか	
どんなパーティーですか	
何を持っていきますか	
だれが来ますか	

C. Class Activity—Find someone who . . .

1. likes to study Japanese _____

2. hates to do cleaning _____

3. likes to sing _____

4. is poor at driving _____

5. whose mother is good at cooking _____

Then, report to the class:

_____さんは_____と言っていました。

D. Pair Work—A and B are making plans for a one-day trip with two other friends C and D. A knows C's schedule and B knows D's schedule. Play the roles of A and B. Discuss your own and your friend's schedules using 〜と言っていました, and find out which days all four of you are available.

Example:　　A：十六日はひまですか。
　　　　　　B：いいえ、買い物に行きます。十八日は、どうですか。
　　　　　　A：私は、何もしません。でも、Cさんが映画を見に行くと言っていました。
　　　　　　B：そうですか。じゃあ……

Student A

A's schedule

16	17	18	19	20	21	22
				study	quiz	party

23	24	25	26	27	28	29
						part-time job

C told A that he would . . .
   18th: go to see a movie
   24th: meet friends
   26th: go to Osaka to have fun

Pair Work Ⅸ D.

Student B

B's schedule

16	17	18	19	20	21	22
shopping	work					tennis

23	24	25	26	27	28	29
						work

D told B that she would . . .
   19th: do a part-time job
   27th: go to eat Japanese cuisine
   28th: go to Kyoto to see temples

Culture Note

日本の食べ物 Foods in Japan
にほん　た　もの

A traditional Japanese meal consists of a bowl of white rice
(ご飯), a couple of dishes (おかず), and soup (often みそ汁),
はん　　　　　　　　　　　　　　　　　　　　　　　　　しる
and is called 定食 (set menu) in cafeterias. However, many
ていしょく
Japanese don't eat traditional food or rice-based dishes for
every meal. A great variety of food is served in restaurants
and even at home because Japan has adopted and adapted
many foreign dishes over time.

ご飯　おかず　みそ汁
はん　　　　　　しる

Common dishes in Japan

カレーライス　　えびフライ　　　ラーメン　　　　うどん　　　スパゲッティ
Curry with rice　Deep-fried shrimp　Ramen noodles　Udon noodles　Spaghetti

ぎょうざ　　　　牛丼　　　　ハンバーグ　　　さしみ　　　お好み焼き
　　　　　　　ぎゅうどん　　　　　　　　　　　　　　　　　この　や
Dumplings　Beef rice bowl　Hamburger steak　Raw seafood　Savory pancake

What did Michiko and Professor Yamashita eat for breakfast today?

みちこ（20歳）
　　　　はたち

山下先生（47歳）
やましたせんせい　さい

トースト、スープ、ヨーグルト
Toast, soup and yogurt

ご飯、焼き魚、たまご、みそ汁
はん　や　さかな　　　　　しる
Rice, broiled fish, egg and miso soup

第9課 | L E S S O N ·················9
かぶき Kabuki

会話 D i a l o g u e
_{かい わ}

(I) Mary and Takeshi are talking. 📢 K09-01/02

1 たけし： メアリーさんはかぶきが好きですか。

2 メアリー： かぶきですか。あまり知りません。でも、ロバートさんはおもしろ
_す _し

3 　　　　　 かったと言っていました。
_い

4 たけし： かぶきの切符を二枚もらったから、見に行きませんか。
_{きっぷ にまい} _{み い}

5 メアリー： ええ、ぜひ。いつですか。

6 たけし： 木曜日です。十二時から四時までです。
_{もくようび じゅうに じ よじ}

(II) During intermission at a Kabuki theater. 📢 K09-03/04

1 メアリー： きれいでしたね。

2 たけし： 出ている人はみんな男の人ですよ。
_{て ひと おとこ ひと}

3 メアリー： 本当ですか。
_{ほんとう}

4 たけし： ええ。ところで、もう昼ご飯を食べましたか。
_{ひる はん た}

5 メアリー： いいえ、まだ食べていません。
_た

6 たけし： じゃあ、買いに行きましょう。
_{か い}

(III) At a concession stand. 📢 K09-05/06

1 たけし： すみません。お弁当を二つください。
_{べんとう ふた}

2 店の人： はい。
_{みせ ひと}

3 たけし： それから、お茶を一つとコーヒーを一つ。
_{ちゃ ひと ひと}

4 店の人： 二千八百円です。どうもありがとうございました。
_{みせ ひと} _{に せんはっぴゃくえん}

I

Takeshi: Mary, do you like Kabuki?

Mary: Kabuki? I don't know it well. But Robert said it was interesting.

Takeshi: I got two tickets for Kabuki, so would you like to go to see it?

Mary: Sure. When is it?

Takeshi: On Thursday. From twelve noon to four.

II

Mary: It was beautiful.

Takeshi: The people who appear are all men.

Mary: Really?

Takeshi: Yes. By the way, did you already eat lunch?

Mary: No, I haven't eaten it yet.

Takeshi: Then, shall we go to buy it?

III

Takeshi: Excuse me. Two box lunches, please.

Vendor: Here they are.

Takeshi: And then, one tea and one coffee.

Vendor: That is 2,800 yen. Thank you very much.

単 語

たん ご

🔊 K09-07

V o c a b u l a r y

N o u n s

いいこ	いい子	good child
いろ	色	color
* おべんとう	お弁当	boxed lunch
* かぶき	歌舞伎	Kabuki; traditional Japanese theatrical art
ギター		guitar
きょねん	去年	last year
くすり	薬	medicine
くすりをのむ	薬を飲む	to take medicine
コンサート		concert
こんど	今度	near future
さくぶん	作文	essay; composition
しけん	試験	exam
スキー		ski
せんげつ	先月	last month
たんご	単語	word; vocabulary
ピアノ		piano
ピザ		pizza
びょうき	病気	illness; sickness

い - a d j e c t i v e s

あおい	青い	blue
あかい	赤い	red
くろい	黒い	black
さびしい	寂しい	lonely
しろい	白い	white
わかい	若い	young

な - a d j e c t i v e

いじわる(な)	意地悪	mean-spirited

U - v e r b s

おどる	踊る	to dance
おわる	終わる	(something) ends （〜が）

* Words that appear in the dialogue

にんきがある	人気がある	to be popular
はじまる	始まる	(something) begins （〜が）
ひく	弾く	to play (a string instrument or piano) （〜を）
* もらう		to get (from somebody) (*person* に *thing* を)

Ru-verbs

おぼえる	覚える	to memorize （〜を）
* でる	出る	(1) to appear; to attend （〜に）
		(2) to exit （〜を）

Irregular Verbs

うんどうする	運動する	to do physical exercises
さんぽする	散歩する	to take a walk

Adverbs and Other Expressions

* 〜から		from . . .
* ぜひ	是非	by all means
* ところで		by the way
* みんな		all
* もう		already

Numbers (used to count small items)

* ひとつ	一つ	one
* ふたつ	二つ	two
みっつ	三つ	three
よっつ	四つ	four
いつつ	五つ	five
むっつ	六つ	six
ななつ	七つ	seven
やっつ	八つ	eight
ここのつ	九つ	nine
とお	十	ten

文法 Grammar
ぶん ぼう

1 Past Tense Short Forms

We will now continue the discussion on short forms, which we started in the last lesson. Here we will learn the past tense paradigm of short forms.

Past tense, affirmative

		compare with:
verbs:	読んだ[a] よ	読んで よ
い-adjectives:	かわい<u>かった</u>[b]	かわい<u>かった</u>です
な-adjectives:	静か<u>だった</u>[c] しず	静か<u>でした</u> しず
noun ＋ です:	学生<u>だった</u>[c] がくせい	学生<u>でした</u> がくせい

Past tense, negative

verbs:	読まな<u>かった</u>[d]	読ま<u>ない</u>
い-adjectives:	かわいくな<u>かった</u>[b]	かわいくな<u>かった</u>です
な-adjectives:	静かじゃな<u>かった</u>[b] しず	静かじゃな<u>かった</u>です しず
noun ＋ です:	学生じゃな<u>かった</u>[b] がくせい	学生じゃな<u>かった</u>です がくせい

Below is a brief discussion on the formation of past tense short forms.

Verbs in the affirmative (**a** above)
→ replace て / で in *te*-forms with た / だ

Verbs in the negative (**d** above)
→ replace い in the present tense negative ない with かった

い-adjectives (both in the affirmative and negative) and
な-adjectives and noun＋です in the negative (**b** above)
→ drop the final です in the long forms

な-adjectives and noun＋です in the affirmative (**c** above)
→ replace でした in the long forms with だった

The two irregularities that we noted earlier are observed here once again. They are:

行く → 行った   いい → よかった よくなかった[1]
い   い

---

[1] See 行って in Lesson 6. See よかったです, よくないです, and よくなかったです in Lesson 5.
い

Short form predicates in the past tense can be used in the same way as the present tense forms, which we discussed in Lesson 8.

- In casual conversations

晩ご飯、食べた？ ── うん、食べた。

Have dinner yet? *Uh-huh, I did.*

- In represented, or quoted, speech

スーさんは、高校の時めがねをかけていたと言っていました。

Sue said that she wore (had worn) glasses in high school.

（私は）トムさんがやったと思います。

I think Tom did it.

Note that in Japanese the tense of the original utterance is preserved when it is reported. If you are reporting somebody's utterance in which the present tense is used, you must also use the present tense inside the quote. Thus, if your friend Sue said 今、日本語を勉強しています, using the present tense, your report will be:

スーさんは日本語を勉強していると言っていました。

Sue said that she <u>was</u> studying Japanese.

2　Qualifying Nouns with Verbs and Adjectives

The short forms of verbs can be used to qualify nouns, much like adjectives can. In the example below, the phrase あそこで本を読んでいる (reading a book over there) is used as a qualifier for the noun 学生.[2]

あそこで本を読んでいる 学生はみちこさんです。

The <u>student</u> who is reading a book over there is Michiko.

The following table shows various forms of noun qualification. The phrases in the boxes qualify the noun 人 (person) to their right. Example 1 is a straightforward adjectival example. Example 2 contains a phrase describing a person's attribute (Lesson 7), example 3 has a verb in the short form (Lesson 8), and example 4 has a な-adjective, which is relational (Lesson 5).

---

[2] A qualifying phrase like this, which has a sentence-like structure of its own, is technically known as a "relative clause."

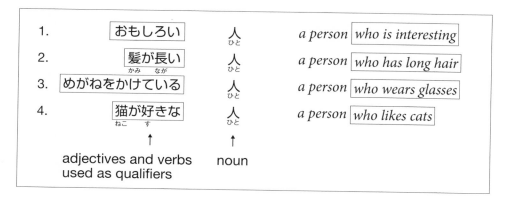

Here are more examples of verbs used in descriptions of people.

あそこで写真を撮っている 人 (はだれですか。)
(Who is) the person taking pictures over there?

毎日運動をする 人 (は元気です。)
People who do physical exercises every day (are healthy.)

たばこを吸わない 人 (が好きです。)
(I like) people who do not smoke.

去年結婚した 友だち (から手紙が来ました。)
(A letter came from) a friend who got married last year.

3 　まだ〜ていません

Consider first the following pair of sentences in English.

Zelda has lost her key.
Zelda lost her key.

These two sentences present the same fact, Zelda losing her key, in different ways. The first, "present perfect" example describes the event as something that is connected with the present: hearing the sentence, one will understand that Zelda is still without her key. On the other hand, the second "simple past" example describes the event as something that is independent of the situation at the present moment; we do not know whether Zelda is still looking for her key or has later retrieved it.

In Japanese, past tense forms do double duty on the affirmative end of polarity, but the past tense and the ている construction share the work on the negative end. Thus in the affirmative, the past tense is used both with words like きのう (disconnected from the present) and もう ("already," connected with the present).

私はきのう宿題を<u>しました</u>。 　　and　　 私はもう宿題を<u>しました</u>。
I did the homework yesterday. 　　　　　　*I have already done the homework.*

With the negative, the past is used to talk about a finished time period like きのう, but ている is used if your intention is to talk about how things stand now ("not yet").

私はきのう宿題を<u>しませんでした</u>。 　and　 私はまだ宿題を<u>していません</u>。
I did not do the homework yesterday. 　　　　 *I have not done the homework yet.*

> まだ〜ていません 　　　*have not ... yet*

This use of ている can be found both with verbs describing *changes* and with verbs describing *activities*, as defined in Lesson 7.

スーさんはまだ起きていません。 　　　(change)
Sue has not woken up yet.

私はまだ昼ご飯を食べていません。 　　(activity)
I haven't eaten lunch yet.

4　〜から

We learned in Lesson 6 that から added to a sentence means "because."

私は朝ご飯を食べませんでした。忙しかったですから。
I didn't have breakfast. (Because) I was busy.

In this lesson, we learn to incorporate the explanation clauses in the statements themselves, rather than adding them as separate sentences. You can simply transpose the "explanation＋から" sequence to the beginning of a sentence for which the explanation is offered.

> (explanation) から、(situation)。
> 　　　= (situation), *because* (explanation).
> 　　　= (explanation), *therefore*, (situation).

あした試験があるから、私は今晩勉強します。

I will study this evening, because we will have an exam tomorrow.

(= We will have an exam tomorrow, therefore, I will study this evening.)

寒かったから、出かけませんでした。

We didn't go out, because it was cold.

(= It was cold, therefore, we didn't go out.)

Note that the resulting order of elements resembles that of a "therefore" sentence more closely than that of a "because" clause in English.

Before the conjunction から, you find both the long and short forms. Thus the から clauses in the above examples can be rewritten as あした試験がありますから and 寒かったですから.[3] The long form before から is more polite, and is frequently found in request and suggestion sentences.

かぶきの切符がありますから、一緒に見に行きましょう。

Let's go to see Kabuki. I have tickets.

---

[3] The long form before から is inappropriate when the entire sentence ends in a short form, however. Thus it is inappropriate to say: × 寒かったですから、出かけなかった。

練習 P r a c t i c e
れん　しゅう

(I) Short Forms Past

A. Verbs

(a) Change the following verbs into the past affirmatives. ◾K09-08

Example:　かく　→　かいた

1. はなす	5. いく	9. あらう	13. いそぐ
2. しぬ	6. あそぶ	10. くる	14. もらう
3. のむ	7. つくる	11. ひく	15. おどる
4. かける	8. でる	12. まつ	16. せんたくする

(b) Change the following verbs into the past negatives. ◾K09-09

Example:　かく　→　かかなかった

1. みる	5. はく	9. あらう	13. おぼえる
2. すてる	6. はじまる	10. くる	14. うたう
3. しる	7. つくる	11. いう	15. せんたくする
4. かける	8. かえる	12. やすむ	16. うんどうする

B. Adjectives and Nouns

(a) Change the following into the past affirmatives. ◾K09-10

Example:　たかい　　→　たかかった
　　　　　げんきな　→　げんきだった
　　　　　がくせい　→　がくせいだった

1. ゆうめいな	4. かわいい	7. やすい	10. かっこいい
2. あめ	5. みじかい	8. きれいな	11. さびしい
3. あかい	6. しんせつな	9. いいてんき	12. ねむい (sleepy)

(b) Change the following into the past negatives. 🔊 K09-11

Example:　たかい　　→　たかくなかった

げんきな　→　げんきじゃなかった

がくせい　→　がくせいじゃなかった

1. いじわるな　　4. かわいい　　　7. あおい　　　10. かっこいい

2. びょうき　　　5. ながい　　　　8. しずかな　　11. おもしろい

3. わかい　　　　6. べんりな　　　9. いいてんき　12. さびしい

Ⅱ Informal Speech

A. Using the cues below, make questions about yesterday in informal speech. How do you answer those questions? 🔊 K09-12

Example:　テレビを見る

→　Q：きのうテレビを見た？

A：うん、見た。／ううん、見なかった。

1. ピザを食べる
2. 散歩する
3. 図書館で本を借りる
4. うちを掃除する
5. うちで料理する
6. 友だちに会う
7. 単語を覚える
8. 学校に来る
9. 家族に電話をかける
10. コンピューターを使う
11. 手紙をもらう
12. 遊びに行く
13. 運動する
14. クラブ (club) で踊る

B. Make questions about childhood in informal speech. How do you answer those questions?  K09-13

Example: 元気
→ Q：子供の時、元気だった？
A：うん、元気だった。／ううん、元気じゃなかった。

1. かわいい
2. 髪が長い
3. 背が高い
4. 勉強が好き
5. スキーが上手
6. さびしい

7. 楽しい
8. スポーツが好き
9. 宿題がきらい
10. 頭がいい
11. 先生はやさしい
12. いじわる

Ⅲ 元気だったと思います

A. Make a guess about what the following people were like when they were in high school.

Example: 元気でしたか。
→ Q：メアリーさんは高校の時、元気でしたか。
A：はい、元気だったと思います。／
いいえ、元気じゃなかったと思います。

(a) メアリーさんについて  K09-14

1. かわいかったですか。
2. 日本語が上手でしたか。
3. 人気がありましたか。

4. よく勉強しましたか。
5. 日本に住んでいましたか。

(b) 山下先生について  K09-15

1. 背が高かったですか。
2. よくデートをしましたか。
3. よくギターを弾きましたか。

4. 踊るのが上手でしたか。
5. かっこよかったですか。

B. Talk about your classmates' childhood using the following expressions.

Example: 頭がいい → ロバートさんは子供の時、頭がよかったと思います。

1. かわいい
2. 元気
3. いい子

4. 運動するのが好き
5. よく遊ぶ
6. 背が高い／低い

7. ピアノを弾くのが上手
8. 髪が長い／短い
9. たくさん本を読む

Ⅳ ロバートさんは病気だったと言っていました

A. Report what the following people said, using 〜と言っていました。 🔊 K09-16

Example: お父さんは、若い時マイケル・ジャクソンが好きだったと言っていました。

Ex. 若い時、マイケル・ジャクソンが好きでした。
1. 友だちとよく踊りに行きました。
2. 踊るのがあまり上手じゃなかったです。
3. マイケルの歌をたくさん覚えました。

4. 先月、かぶきを見に行きました。
5. かぶきは十二時に始まって、四時に終わりました。
6. かぶきは長かったです。
7. かぶきはおもしろかったです。

8. きのう、大学に行きませんでした。
9. 病気でした。
10. 薬を飲んで、寝ていました。

B. Pair Work—Ask your partner the following questions. Take notes and report to the class later, using ～と言っていました.

1. 先週、何をしましたか。どうでしたか。
   せんしゅう　なに

2. 子供の時、どんな子供でしたか。よく何をしましたか。
   こども　とき　　　　　　こども　　　　　　なに

3. 夏休み／冬休みにどこへ行きましたか。どうでしたか。
   なつやす　ふゆやす　　　　　　い

4. 高校の時、よく何をしましたか。
   こうこう　とき　　なに

Ⓥ めがねをかけている人です
ひと

A. Look at the picture below and answer the questions.

Example:　田中さん
　　　　　　　た なか
　　　　　→　Q：田中さんはどの人ですか。
　　　　　　　　　た なか　　　　　ひと
　　　　　　　　A：めがねをかけている人です。
　　　　　　　　　　　　　　　　　ひと

1. 中村さん　　　　　　　4. 森さん
   なかむら　　　　　　　　　もり

2. 山口さん　　　　　　　5. 大川さん
   やまぐち　　　　　　　　　おおかわ

3. 野村さん　　　　　　　6. 鈴木さん
   の むら　　　　　　　　　すず き

B. Pair Work—One of you looks at picture A below and the other looks at picture B (p. 225). Ask each other questions and identify all the people in the picture.

Example:　よしこ　→　Ａ：よしこさんはどの人ですか。
　　　　　　　　　　　Ｂ：テレビを見ている人です。

Picture A

えり

ゆたか

よしこ

じゅん

ちかこ

Ask which of the people are the following:

1. たろう
2. きょうこ
3. だいすけ
4. ようこ

C. Class Activity—Describe your classmates.
The class is divided into two groups, A and B. Each member of group A acts out something and freezes in the middle of doing so. Members of group B answer the teacher's questions, using ～ている人です. Take turns when finished.

Example:　Teacher:　マイクさんはどの人ですか。
　　　　　　Student:　車を運転している人です。

Ⓥ）まだ食べていません

A. Answer the following questions using まだ～ていません. 📻 K09-17

Example:　Ｑ：もう昼ご飯を食べましたか。
　　　　　　　Ａ：いいえ、まだ食べていません。

1. もう切符を買いましたか。
2. もう宿題をしましたか。
3. もう作文を書きましたか。

4. もう薬を飲みましたか。
5. もう晩ご飯を食べましたか。
6. もう新しい単語を覚えましたか。

B. Pair Work—Ask if your partner has done . . . yet. If the answer is no, ask your partner out, as in the example (1). If yes, ask your partner how it was, as in (2).

Examples: the name of a newly released movie → 『ワンピース』を見る

(1) A：もう 『ワンピース』を見ましたか。
B：<u>いいえ、まだ見ていません。</u>Aさんは？
A：私もまだ見ていません。よかったら、一緒に見ませんか。
B：ええ、いいですね。

(2) A：もう 『ワンピース』を見ましたか。
B：<u>ええ、もう見ました。</u>
A：そうですか。どうでしたか。
B：すごくおもしろかったですよ。

1. the name of a newly released movie ＿＿＿＿＿＿＿＿＿＿＿を見る

2. the name of a new game ＿＿＿＿＿＿＿＿＿＿＿をする

3. the name of a new restaurant/shop/place ＿＿＿＿＿＿＿＿＿＿＿に行く

4. the name of a newly released song/music ＿＿＿＿＿＿＿＿＿＿＿を聞く

Ⅶ 天気がいいから、遊びに行きます

A. Match up the phrases to make sense.

1. 魚がきらいだから ・ ・今はひまです。
2. 試験が終わったから ・ ・行きませんか。
3. 旅行に行ったから ・ ・すしを食べません。
4. コンサートの切符を二枚もらったから・ ・急ぎましょう。
5. 天気がよくなかったから ・ ・遊びに行きませんでした。
6. クラスが始まるから ・ ・お金がありません。

B. Complete the following sentences adding reasons.

1. _____から、お金がぜんぜんありません。

2. _____から、日本語を勉強しています。

3. _____から、先週の週末は忙しかったです。

4. _____から、きのう学校を休みました。

Ⅷ まとめの練習

A. Role Play—One of you is working at a fast-food restaurant. The other is a customer. Using Dialogue Ⅲ as a model, order some food and drinks from the menu below. Be sure to say how many you want.

B. Answer the following questions.

1. ピアノを弾きますか。

2. ギターを弾くのが上手ですか。

3. 踊るのが好きですか。

4. 病気の時、よく薬を飲みますか。

5. よく散歩しますか。

6. 去年の誕生日 (birthday) に何かもらいましたか。

   だれに何をもらいましたか。

7. 今日、クラスは何時に始まりましたか。何時に終わりますか。

8. 犬が好きですか。

9. 子供の時、よく友だちと遊びましたか。

10. どんな色のＴシャツを持っていますか。

11. 今度の試験は難しいと思いますか。

12. あなたの国では、どんなスポーツが人気がありますか。

13. どんな色が好きですか。

Pair Work Ⓥ B.

(→ p. 222)

Example:　　よしこ　→　Ａ：よしこさんはどの人ですか。
　　　　　　　　　　　　　Ｂ：テレビを見ている人です。

Picture B

Ask which of the people are the following:

1. ゆたか

2. じゅん

3. ちかこ

4. えり

Culture Note

日本の伝統文化 Japanese Traditional Culture
にほん　でんとう　ぶんか

歌舞伎
かぶき
Kabuki

文楽
ぶんらく
Puppet theater

落語
らくご
Humorous storytelling

能
のう
Masked musical drama

相撲
すもう
Sumo wrestling

柔道
じゅうどう
Judo

剣道
けんどう
Japanese fencing

お茶（茶道）
ちゃ　さどう
Tea ceremony

生け花（華道）
いけばな　かどう
Flower arrangement

書道
しょどう
Calligraphy

Useful Expressions

色
いろ

C o l o r s

There are two kinds of words for colors.

Group 1: い-adjectives

黒い くろ	——— black		白い しろ	——— white
赤い あか	——— red		青い あお	——— blue
黄色い き いろ	——— yellow		茶色い ちゃいろ	——— brown

These words become nouns without the い.

赤いかばん   *red bag*
あか

赤がいちばん好きです。   *I like red the best.*
あか   す

Group 2: nouns

緑／グリーン みどり	——— green		紫 むらさき	——— purple
灰色／グレー はいいろ	——— gray		水色 みずいろ	——— light blue
ピンク	——— pink		金色／ゴールド きんいろ	——— gold
銀色／シルバー ぎんいろ	——— silver			

These words need の in order to make noun phrases.

緑／グリーンのセーター   *green sweater*
みどり

Here are some words related to colors.

顔が青いですね。   *You look pale.*
かお あお

白黒の写真   *black and white picture*
しろくろ しゃしん

メアリーさんは金髪です。   *Mary has blonde hair.*
きんぱつ

第10課 | L E S S O N ·················· 10

冬休みの予定 Winter Vacation Plans
　ふゆ　やす　　　　　　よ　てい

会 話 D i a l o g u e
かい わ

Ⅰ Winter vacation is approaching. 🔊 K10-01/02

1 メアリー： 寒くなりましたね。
　　　　　　さむ

2 たけし： ええ。メアリーさん、冬休みはどうしますか。
　　　　　　　　　　　　　　　　ふゆやす

3 メアリー： 韓国か台湾に行くつもりですが、まだ決めていません。
　　　　　　かんこく たいわん い　　　　　　　　　　　き

4 たけし： いいですね。

5 メアリー： 韓国と台湾とどっちのほうがいいと思いますか。
　　　　　　かんこく たいわん　　　　　　　　　　おも

6 たけし： うーん、台湾のほうが暖かいと思います。でも、スーさんは韓国の
　　　　　　　　　　たいわん　　あたた　おも　　　　　　　　　　　　かんこく

7 　　　　　食べ物はおいしいと言っていましたよ。
　　　　　　た もの　　　　　　い

8 メアリー： そうですか。ところで、たけしさんはどこかに行きますか。
　　　　　　　　　　　　　　　　　　　　　　　　　　　い

9 たけし： どこにも行きません。お金がないから、ここにいます。
　　　　　　　　　　い　　　　　かね

10 メアリー： そうですか。じゃあ、たけしさんにおみやげを買ってきますよ。
　　　　　　　　　　　　　　　　　　　　　　　　　　　　　　か

11 たけし： わあ、ありがとう。

Ⅱ At a travel agency. 🔊 K10-03/04

1 メアリー： 大阪からソウルまで飛行機の予約をお願いします。
　　　　　　おおさか　　　　　　ひこうき　よやく　ねが

2 旅行会社の人： はい、いつですか。
　りょこうがいしゃ ひと

3 メアリー： 十二月十九日です。
　　　　　　じゅうに がつじゅうく にち

4 旅行会社の人： 午前と午後の便がありますが……。
　りょこうがいしゃ ひと　ごぜん ごご びん

5 メアリー： 午前のをお願いします。
　　　　　　ごぜん　　ねが

6 　　　　　クレジットカードで払ってもいいですか。
　　　　　　　　　　　　　　　はら

7 旅行会社の人： はい。
　りょこうがいしゃ ひと

8 メアリー： ソウルまでどのぐらいかかりますか。

9 旅行会社の人： 一時間半ぐらいです。
　りょこうがいしゃ ひと　いちじ かんはん

I

Mary: It is getting cold.

Takeshi: Yes. Mary, what will you do at winter break?

Mary: I am planning to go to Korea or Taiwan, but I haven't decided yet.

Takeshi: That's nice.

Mary: Which do you think is better, Korea or Taiwan?

Takeshi: Mm . . . I think it is warmer in Taiwan. But Sue said that the food was delicious in Korea.

Mary: I see. By the way, are you going somewhere, Takeshi?

Takeshi: I won't go anywhere. I don't have money, so I will stay here.

Mary: Is that so? Then I'll buy some souvenir for you.

Takeshi: Wow, thank you.

II

Mary: I'd like to reserve a plane ticket from Osaka to Seoul.

Travel agent: When is it?

Mary: December 19.

Travel agent: We have a morning flight and an afternoon flight.

Mary: A morning flight, please. Can I use a credit card?

Travel agent: Yes.

Mary: How long does it take to Seoul?

Travel agent: About one and a half hours.

単語
たん ご

 K10-05

Vocabulary

Nouns

あき	秋	fall
いしゃ	医者	doctor
えき	駅	station
おかねもち	お金持ち	rich person
かお	顔	face
きせつ	季節	season
ぎゅうにゅう	牛乳	milk
* クレジットカード		credit card
ケーキ		cake
ことし	今年	this year
サッカー		soccer
シャツ		shirt
しんかんせん	新幹線	Shinkansen; "Bullet Train"
すし		sushi
せいかつ	生活	life; living
せかい	世界	world
ちかてつ	地下鉄	subway
てぶくろ	手袋	gloves
てんぷら	天ぷら	tempura
とこや	床屋	barber's
はる	春	spring
パンツ		pants
びよういん	美容院	beauty parlor
* びん	便	flight
ふね	船	ship; boat
やきゅう	野球	baseball
ゆうめいじん	有名人	celebrity
* よやく	予約	reservation
らいがっき	来学期	next semester
りんご		apple

い-adjectives

* あたたかい	暖かい	warm

* Words that appear in the dialogue

おそい	遅い	slow; late
すずしい	涼しい	cool (weather—not used for things)
つめたい	冷たい	cold (things/people)
ねむい	眠い	sleepy

な-adjective

| かんたん（な） | 簡単 | easy; simple |

U-verbs

*かかる		to take (amount of time/money) (*no particle*)
とまる	泊まる	to stay (at a hotel, etc.) （〜に）
*なる		to become
*はらう	払う	to pay （〜を）

Ru-verb

| *きめる | 決める | to decide （〜を） |

Irregular Verbs

| りょこうする | 旅行する | to travel |
| れんしゅうする | 練習する | to practice （〜を） |

Adverbs and Other Expressions

あるいて	歩いて	on foot
いちばん	一番	best
*〜か〜		or
〜かげつ	〜か月	for . . . months
〜ご	〜後	in . . . time; after . . .
このごろ		these days
〜しゅうかん	〜週間	for . . . weeks
*〜で		by (means of transportation); with (a tool)
どうやって		how; by what means
どちら		which
*どっち		which
*どのぐらい		how much; how long
〜ねん	〜年	. . . years
はやく	早く／速く	(do something) early; fast

文法 Grammar
ぶん　ぼう

1 Comparison between Two Items

In Japanese, adjectives have the same shape in noncomparative and comparative sentences; there is no alteration as in "great/greater." The idea of comparison is expressed by adding something to the nouns that are compared.

| A <u>のほうが</u>　B <u>より</u>[1] (property)。 | = | A <u>is more</u> (property) <u>than</u> B. |

中国のほうが日本より大きいです。
ちゅうごく　　　　　　にほん　　おお
China is larger than Japan.

You can ask for another person's opinion on two things in comparative terms.

| AとBと　どちらのほう / どっちのほう[2] が　(property)。 |
| = *Between A and B, which is more (property)?* |

バスと電車とどっちのほうが安いですか。
　　　てんしゃ　　　　　　　　やす
Which is cheaper, (going by) bus or (by) train?

2 Comparison among Three or More Items

In comparison among three or more items, the degree qualifier いちばん is used.

| [(class of items) <u>の中で</u>]　A が<u>いちばん</u> (property)。 |
| なか |
| = A is <u>the most</u> (property) [<u>among</u> (a class of items)]. |

ロシアとフランスと日本の中で、どこがいちばん寒いですか。
　　　　　　　　　　にほん　なか　　　　　　　　　　さむ
Between Russia, France, and Japan, which country has the coldest climate?

---

[1] In real life, the phrases Aのほうが and Bより often appear in the reverse order, making it very easy to be misled into believing the opposite of what is actually said. Don't rely on the word order, therefore, to decide which item is claimed to be superior. Listen carefully for the words のほうが and より.

[2] In place of どちらのほう and どっちのほう, you can also use どちら and どっち. Any one of these can be used in question sentences seeking comparisons between two items. どっち and どっちのほう are slightly more colloquial than どちら and どちらのほう.

ロシアが<u>いちばん</u>寒いと思います。
Russia is the coldest, I think.

季節の<u>中</u>でいつが<u>いちばん</u>好きですか。
What season do you like best?

秋が<u>いちばん</u>好きです。
I like fall the most.

Note that the words のほう and どっち are not used in statements of comparison among three or more items. Normal question words like だれ, どれ, 何, いつ, and どこ are used instead.[3]

3 adjective/noun + の

When a noun follows an adjective, and when it is clear what you are referring to, you can replace the noun with the pronoun の, "one." You can use の to avoid repetition.

私は黒い<u>セーター</u>を持っています。赤い<u>の</u>も持っています。（の＝セーター）
I have a black sweater. I have a red one, too.

安い<u>辞書</u>を買いに行きました。でもいい<u>の</u>がありませんでした。（の＝辞書）
I went to buy an inexpensive dictionary, but there were no good ones.

| い-adjective な-adjective | + noun | → | い-adjective な-adjective | + の |

Similarly, a noun following another noun can be reduced. Here, a sequence of the form "noun₁ の noun₂" will be reduced to "noun₁ の." You simply omit the second noun.

これはスーさんの<u>かばん</u>ですか。

Is this Sue's bag?

いいえ、それはメアリーさんの＿＿です。

No, that is Mary's __.

---

[3] The tendency is to use どれ when a list of items is presented, and to use 何 when a group is referred to collectively. Compare:

りんごとみかんとさくらんぼの中で、どれがいちばん好きですか。
Which do you like best, apples, tangerines, or cherries?
くだものの中で、何がいちばん好きですか。
What fruit do you like best?

アメリカの<u>アイスクリーム</u>のほうが日本の＿＿＿よりおいしいです。
_{に ほん}
American ice cream is more delicious than Japanese one.

noun₁ の noun₂　　→　　noun₁ の ＿＿＿

4 〜つもりだ

つもり follows verbs in the present tense short forms to describe what a person is planning to do in the future. You can also use a verb in the negative plus つもり to describe what you are planning *not* to do, or what you do *not* intend to do.

verb (present, short) ＋ つもりだ　　　　*(I) intend to do . . .*

（私は）週末にたけしさんとテニスをする<u>つもりです</u>。
_{わたし}　_{しゅうまつ}
I intend to play tennis with Takeshi this weekend.

山下先生はあした大学に来<u>ない</u>つもりです。
_{やましたせんせい}　　_{だいがく}　_こ
Professor Yamashita does not intend to come to school tomorrow.

お寺を見に行く<u>つもりでした</u>が、天気がよくなかったから、行きませんでした。
_{て ら}　_み　_い　　　　　　　　　_{てん き}　　　　　　　　　　　_い
We were planning to visit a temple, but we didn't, because the weather was not good.

5 adjective ＋ なる

The verb なる means "to become," indicating a change. なる follows nouns and both types of adjectives.

い-adjectives:	暖かい	→	暖かくなる	*to become warm/warmer*
	_{あたた}		_{あたた}	
な-adjectives:	静か（な）	→	静かになる	*to become quiet/quieter*
	_{しず}		_{しず}	
nouns:	会社員	→	会社員になる	*to become a company*
	_{かいしゃいん}		_{かいしゃいん}	*employee*

日本語の勉強が楽しくなりました。
_{に ほん ご}　_{べんきょう}　_{たの}
Studying the Japanese language is fun now (though it was like torture before).

日本語の勉強が好きになりました。
_{に ほん ご}　_{べんきょう}　_す
I have grown fond of studying the Japanese language.

With い-adjectives, the final い is dropped and く is added, as in their negative conjugations. A common mistake is to expand the pattern of な-adjectives and nouns and use に with い-adjectives. It is wrong to say, for example, ×暖かいになる.

When an adjective is used with なる, a question arises whether the sentence describes an absolute change (e.g., "it has become warm, hence it is not cold any longer") or a relative change (e.g., "it has become warmer, but it is still cold"). なる sentences are ambiguous in isolation. If you want to make clear that you are talking in relative terms, you can use the pattern for comparison together with なる.

メアリーさんは前より日本語が上手になりました。
Mary has become better in Japanese than before.

6　どこかに/どこにも

In Lesson 8 we learned the Japanese expressions for "something" and "not . . . anything," 何か and 何も. As you must have noticed, these expressions are made up of the question word for things, 何, plus particles か and も. Other expressions for "some" and "any" in Japanese follow this pattern. Thus,

something	何か__	*someone*	だれか__	*somewhere*	どこか__
not anything	何__も	*not anyone*	だれ__も	*not anywhere*	どこ__も

As we noted in Lesson 8, these words are used by themselves, where particles は, が, or を would be expected. It is, then, interesting to observe how these expressions interact with other particles, such as に, へ, and で. These particles appear in the places shown with underscores above. Let us look at some examples.

どこかへ行きましたか。
Did you go anywhere?

いいえ、どこへも行きませんでした。
No, I didn't go anywhere.

だれかに会いましたか。
Did you see anybody?

いいえ、だれにも会いませんでした。
No, I didn't see anybody.

何かしましたか。
Did you do anything?

いいえ、何もしませんでした。
No, I didn't do anything.

7　で

You can use the particle で with nouns that describe the means of transportation and the instruments you use.

はしでご飯を食べます。   *We eat our meals with chopsticks.*

日本語で話しましょう。   *Let's talk in Japanese.*

バスで駅まで行きました。   *I went to the station by bus.*

テレビで映画を見ました。   *I saw a movie on TV.*

表現ノート……10
ひょう げん

Expression Notes 10

午前と午後の便がありますが……▶We sometimes use が and けど (but) at the end of a sentence when we want our partners to treat what we have just said as a given, common ground to build upon. These words often indicate the speaker's intention to give her partner a chance to react and speak up. By relegating the right to speak to one's partner, they also contribute to the politeness of one's utterance.

In the dialogue, the travel agent lays out the relevant information on the table; there are two flights, one leaving in the morning and another in the afternoon. が attached to her sentence indicates that she wants to build upon, and move forward with, these pieces of information. Instead of asking the obvious question, namely, どちらがいいですか, the agent chooses not to finish her sentence, and lets her customer come forward with an answer immediately.

練習 Practice
れん しゅう

① バスのほうが電車より速いです
でん しゃ　　　　　　　はや

A. Look at the pictures below and answer the following questions. 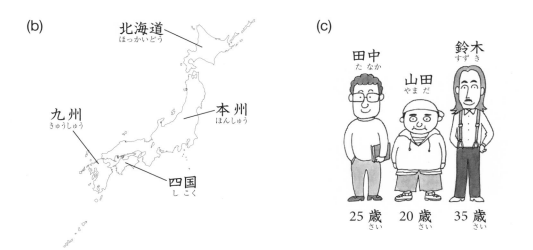 K10-06

Example:　Q：電車とバスとどちらのほうが速いですか。
　　　　　　　　てんしゃ　　　　　　　　　　　　　　はや
　　　　　　　A：バスのほうが電車より速いです。
　　　　　　　　　　　　　　てんしゃ　　はや

Picture (a)

1. 新幹線とバスとどちらのほうが速いですか。
　しんかんせん　　　　　　　　　　　　　はや
2. 新幹線と電車とどちらのほうが遅いですか。
　しんかんせん　てんしゃ　　　　　　　　おそ
3. 新幹線とバスとどちらのほうが安いですか。
　しんかんせん　　　　　　　　　　　　　やす
4. 電車とバスとどちらのほうが高いですか。
　てんしゃ　　　　　　　　　　　　たか

Picture (b)

5. 北海道と九州とどっちのほうが大きいですか。
　ほっかいどう　きゅうしゅう　　　　　　おお
6. 九州と四国とどっちのほうが小さいですか。
　きゅうしゅう　しこく　　　　　　　　ちい

Picture (c)

7. 田中さんと山田さんとどっちのほうが背が高いですか。
　たなか　　やまだ　　　　　　　　　　せ　たか
8. 山田さんと鈴木さんとどっちのほうが背が低いですか。
　やまだ　　すずき　　　　　　　　　　せ　ひく
9. 田中さんと鈴木さんとどっちのほうが若いですか。
　たなか　　すずき　　　　　　　　　わか
10. 山田さんと鈴木さんとどっちのほうが髪が短いですか。
　やまだ　　すずき　　　　　　　　　かみ　みじか

(a)

二時間半　￥14,000
に じ かんはん

七時間　￥6,000
しち じ かん

九時間　￥9,000
く じ かん

大阪
おおさか

東京
とうきょう

(b)

北海道
ほっかいどう

本州
ほんしゅう

九州
きゅうしゅう

四国
しこく

(c)

田中
たなか

山田
やまだ

鈴木
すずき

25 歳　20 歳　35 歳
さい　　さい　　さい

B. Pair Work—Make questions using the following cues and ask your partner. When you answer the questions, add reasons for your answers if possible.

Example:　夏／冬（好き）
　　　　　→　Ａ：夏と冬とどちら（のほう）が好きですか。
　　　　　　　Ｂ：夏のほうが（冬より）好きです。
　　　　　　　　　（or 夏も冬も好きです。／夏も冬もきらいです。）
　　　　　　　Ａ：どうしてですか。
　　　　　　　Ｂ：泳ぐのが好きですから。

1. すし／天ぷら（おいしい）
2. 頭がいい人／かっこいい人（好き）
3. 野球／サッカー（人気がある）
4. 中国料理／日本料理（好き）
5. 船／飛行機（好き）
6. 日本の車／ドイツ (Germany) の車（いい）
7. 漢字／カタカナ（かんたん）
8. 春／秋（好き）
9. 日本の冬／あなたの国の冬（暖かい）
10. 日本の生活／あなたの国の生活（大変 or 楽しい）

Ⅱ 新幹線がいちばん速いです

A. Look at the pictures on the previous page and answer the questions below.

🔊 K10-07

Example:　Ｑ：この中で、どれがいちばん速いですか。
　　　　　　Ａ：新幹線がいちばん速いです。

Picture (a)

1. この中で、どれがいちばん遅いですか。
2. この中で、どれがいちばん安いですか。

Picture (b)

3. この中で、どこがいちばん大きいですか。
   なか　　　　　　　　　　　　おお

4. この中で、どこがいちばん小さいですか。
   なか　　　　　　　　　　　　ちい

Picture (c)

5. この中で、だれがいちばん背が高いですか。
   なか　　　　　　　　　　　せ　たか

6. この中で、だれがいちばん若いですか。
   なか　　　　　　　　　　　わか

7. この中で、だれがいちばん髪が長いですか。
   なか　　　　　　　　　　　かみ　なが

B. Pair Work—Make questions using the following cues and ask your partner.

Example: 食べ物／好き
   た　もの　す
   → Q：食べ物の中で、何がいちばん好きですか。
   　　　 た　もの　なか　なに　　　　　　 す
   　　 A：すしがいちばん好きです。
   　　　　　　　　　　　　 す

1. 飲み物／好き
   の　もの　す

2. 世界の町／好き
   せ かい　まち　す

3. 有名人／好き
   ゆうめいじん　す

4. 日本料理／きらい
   に ほんりょう り

5. 音楽／好き
   おんがく　す

6. 季節／好き
   き せつ　す

7. クラス／いい学生
   がくせい

8. クラス／背が高い
   せ　たか

9. クラス／たくさん食べる
   た

C. Group Work—Make a group of three or four people. Ask each other questions and make as many superlative sentences as possible about the group.

Example: この中で、Aさんがいちばん若いです。
   なか　　　　　　　　　 わか
   Bさんがいちばん背が高いです。
   　　　　　　　　　 せ　たか
   Cさんがいちばんよく遅くクラスに来ます。
   　　　　　　　　　　　 おそ　　　　　 き

D. Class Activity—First form pairs and make comparative and superlative question sentences with your partner. (You should know the answers.) Then ask questions to the class. The rest of the class answer the questions.

Example: 富士山 (Mt. Fuji) とエベレスト (Mt. Everest) とどちらのほうが高いですか。
   ふ じ さん　　　　　　　　　　　　　　　　　　　　　　　　　　　　　 たか
   田中さんと山田さんとどちらのほうが若いですか。
   た なか　　　 やま だ　　　　　　　　　　　　 わか
   クラスの中で今日だれがいちばんお金を持っていますか。
   　　　　 なか きょう　　　　　　　　　　 かね　も
   世界の国の中でどこがいちばん小さいですか。
   せ かい　くに　なか　　　　　　　　　 ちい

⑩これは私のです
わたし

A. This is a refrigerator in a dormitory. Tell whose each thing is, using の. 🔊 K10-08

Example: このりんごはリーさんのです。

B. Pair Work—Ask your partner the following questions.

Example: A：どちらのコーヒーがいいですか。
B：熱いのがいいです。
あつ

熱い　　　　冷たい
あつ　　　　つめ

(1) どちらの手袋がいいですか。
て ぶくろ

(2) どちらのパンツがいいですか。

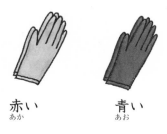

赤い　　　　青い
あか　　　　あお

長い　　　　短い
なが　　　　みじか

(3) どちらのシャツがいいですか。

白い
しろ

黒い
くろ

(4) どちらのかばんがいいですか。

きれい

安い
やす

(5) どちらのガイドブックを買いますか。
か

Guide
Book
Japan

英語
えいご

ガイドブック
日本

日本語
にほんご

(6) どちらの教科書がいいですか。
きょうかしょ

Easy
Japanese

かんたん

日本語
上級文法
と語彙

難しい
むずか

Ⅳ 見に行くつもりです
み　い

A. You are planning to do/not to do the following things next week. Tell what you will/will not do using ～つもりです。 K10-09

Example: 月曜日に本を読むつもりです。
げつよう び　ほん　よ

月曜日 げつよう び	Ex. to read books	1. to practice the piano
火曜日 か よう び	2. to do exercises	
水曜日 すいよう び	3. to do laundry	
木曜日 もくよう び	4. to write letters to friends	5. not to go out
金曜日 きんよう び	6. to eat dinner with friends	7. not to study Japanese
土曜日 ど よう び	8. to stay at a friend's	9. not to go home
日曜日 にちよう び	10. to clean a room	11. not to get up early

B. Answer the following questions.

Example:　Q：週末、映画を見に行きますか。
　　　　　　A：ええ、見に行くつもりです。／
　　　　　　　　いいえ、見に行かないつもりです。

1. 今日の午後、勉強しますか。
2. 今晩、テレビを見ますか。
3. あさって、買い物をしますか。
4. 週末、料理を作りますか。
5. 三年後、日本にいますか。
6. 来学期も日本語を勉強しますか。
7. 今度の休みに旅行しますか。

ⓥ きれいになりました

A. Describe the following pictures. 🔊 K10-10

Example:　きれい　→　きれいになりました。

Ex. きれい

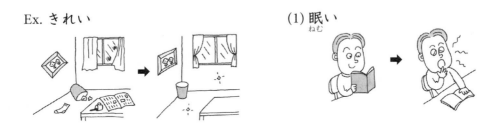

(1) 眠い

(2) 元気

(3) 大きい

(4) 髪が短い

(5) ひま (6) 暑い
あつ (7) 涼しい
すず

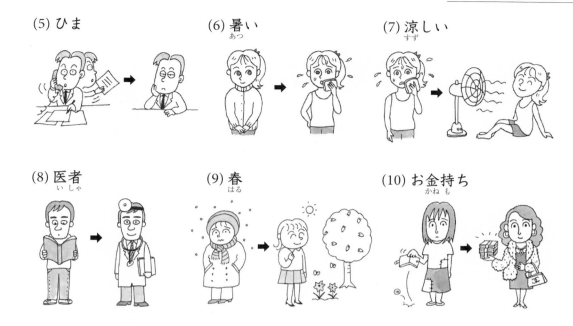

(8) 医者
い しゃ (9) 春
はる (10) お金持ち
かね も

B. Fill in the blanks with appropriate forms.

1. 掃除をしたから、部屋が＿＿＿＿＿＿＿なりました。
そうじ　　　　　　へ や

2. 美容院／床屋に行ったから、髪が＿＿＿＿＿＿＿なりました。
びょういん　とこ や　い　　　　　かみ

3. 子供の時、野菜がきらいでしたが、今、＿＿＿＿＿＿＿なりました。
こ ども　とき　や さい　　　　　　　　いま

4. 毎日ピアノを練習しているから、＿＿＿＿＿＿＿なりました。
まいにち　　　れんしゅう

5. お酒をたくさん飲んで、顔が＿＿＿＿＿＿＿なりました。
さけ　　　　　　の　　　かお

6. 十一月は暖かったですが、このごろ＿＿＿＿＿＿＿なりました。
じゅういちがつ　あたた

7. 教えるのが好きだから、＿＿＿＿＿＿＿なるつもりです。
おし　　　　　す

Ⅵ どこかに行きましたか

A. Takeshi was sick yesterday. Mary did a lot of things without him. Answer the questions based on the chart below. 🔊 K10-11

	Mary	**Takeshi**
(Ex.) eat	sushi and tempura	nothing
drink	green tea and coffee	nothing
go	Osaka	nowhere
meet	Robert	nobody
do	watch a movie	nothing

Example 1:　Q：きのう、メアリーさんは何か食べましたか。

　　　　　　A：はい、すしと天ぷらを食べました。

Example 2:　Q：きのう、たけしさんは何か食べましたか。

　　　　　　A：いいえ、何も食べませんでした。

1. きのう、メアリーさんは何か飲みましたか。
2. きのう、たけしさんは何か飲みましたか。
3. きのう、メアリーさんはどこかに行きましたか。
4. きのう、たけしさんはどこかに行きましたか。
5. きのう、メアリーさんはだれかに会いましたか。
6. きのう、たけしさんはだれかに会いましたか。
7. きのう、メアリーさんは何かしましたか。
8. きのう、たけしさんは何かしましたか。

B. Pair Work—Ask your partner the following questions.

Example:　Q：週末、何かしましたか。

　　　　　A：はい、映画を見ました。／いいえ、何もしませんでした。

1. 先週の週末、どこかに行きましたか。
2. 先週の週末、だれかに会いましたか。
3. 今日、何か食べましたか。
4. 今日、何か飲みましたか。
5. 今週の週末、どこかに行きますか。
6. 今週の週末、何かするつもりですか。

Ⅶ 自転車で行きます

A. Look at the pictures and answer each question as in the example below. K10-12

Example:　Q：うちから駅までどうやって行きますか。
　　　　　A：うちから駅まで自転車で行きます。

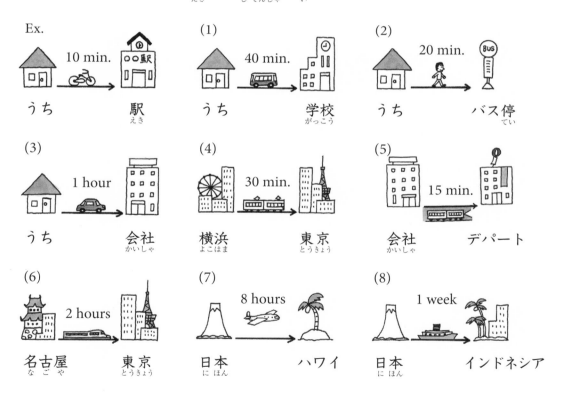

B. Use the same pictures and answer the questions as in the example below.
K10-13

Example:　Q：うちから駅までどのぐらいかかりますか。
　　　　　A：うちから駅まで十分かかります。

C. Ask three classmates how they get from their houses to school and fill in the chart.

Example: Q：うちから大学までどうやって来ますか。

A：自転車で来ます。

Q：どのぐらいかかりますか。

A：十五分ぐらいかかります。

名前	どうやって	どのぐらい

Ⅷ まとめの練習

A. The chart below shows winter vacation plans for Mary and her friends. First, answer the following questions about Mary's plan.

Mary	will go to Korea with Sue	by plane	3 weeks	will stay at Sue's house	will do shopping and eat Korean foods
Robert	will go back to London	by plane	2 weeks		will meet friends
Ken	will go to Tokyo with a friend	by bullet train	3 days	will stay at a hotel	will play at Tokyo Disneyland
Tom	will go to the south pole（南極）	by boat	2 months	doesn't know yet	will take pictures with penguins（ペンギン）
Takeshi	will go nowhere				

1. メアリーさんは今年の冬休みにどこかに行くつもりですか。

2. どうやって韓国へ行きますか。だれと行きますか。

3. どのぐらい行きますか。

4. どこに泊まりますか。

5. 韓国で何をするつもりですか。

How about the others' plans? Make pairs and ask questions.

B. Pair Work—Talk about your plans for the upcoming vacation.

C. Role Play—One of you works for a travel agency and the other is a customer. Using Dialogue II as a model, make reservations for the following tickets.

1. From Nagoya to Seoul（ソウル）	Jan. 1	1 person	morning flight
2. From Tokyo to Paris（パリ）	Feb. 14	1 person	window seat
3. From Osaka to Rome（ローマ）	Apr. 18	2 people	aisle seats
4. From Tokyo to Bangkok（バンコク）	Aug. 20	4 people	afternoon flight

window seat ＝窓側の席　　aisle seat ＝通路側の席
　　　　　　　まどがわ　せき　　　　　　　つうろがわ　せき

日本の交通機関 Public Transportation in Japan
にほん　こうつうきかん

Japan's public transportation system is highly developed, especially within metropolitan areas and between major cities. The most common forms of public transportation are trains, buses, and, in major cities, subways. The Japan Railways Group (JR Group) has a train network covering almost all areas of the country. Travel by public transportation is enjoyable, safe, and efficient. Here are some tips for you.

Shinkansen

Japan Rail Pass

If you are in Japan on a "Temporary Visitor" entry permit and want to travel to different regions, consider getting a **Japan Rail Pass**, which offers unlimited travel on almost all JR lines (including bullet trains, except Nozomi) for a certain number of days.

If you are planning a budget trip during vacation time, the **Seishun 18 Kippu**（青春18きっぷ）may be the best option. This seasonal discount
せいしゅん
ticket gives you five days of unlimited rides on local and rapid-service JR trains for only 11,500 yen.

Highway buses are another good way to travel between major cities. Compared with express rail services, highway bus travel usually takes longer hours but costs less. Also, if you travel on an overnight bus, you can save on accommodation costs.

Highway bus

写真提供：JR東日本／ジェイアールバス関東

Useful Expressions

駅で
えき

At the Station

Types of Trains

普通 ———————— local
ふつう

急行 ———————— express
きゅうこう

特急 ———————— super express
とっきゅう

Destination

〜行き ———————— bound for . . .
い

〜方面 ———————— serving . . . areas
ほうめん

Types of Tickets and Seats

乗車券 ———————— (boarding) ticket
じょうしゃけん

回数券 ———————— coupons
かいすうけん

定期券 ———————— commuter's pass
ていきけん

学割 ———————— student discount
がくわり

指定席 ———————— reserved seat
していせき

自由席 ———————— general admission seat
じゆうせき

禁煙車 ———————— nonsmoking car
きんえんしゃ

一号車 ———————— Car No. 1
いちごうしゃ

往復 ———————— round trip
おうふく

片道 ———————— one way
かたみち

Places in stations

〜番線 ———————— track number . . .
ばんせん

切符売り場 ———————— ticket vending area
きっぷうば

改札 ———————— gate
かいさつ

ホーム ———————— platform

売店 ———————— shop; stand
ばいてん

出口 ———————— exit
でぐち

入口 ———————— entrance
いりぐち

階段 ———————— stairs
かいだん

いちばん前 ——— first car; front end
まえ

いちばん後ろ ——— last car; tail end
うし

Miscellaneous Public Transportation Terms

乗り換え ———————— transfer
のか

次は〜 ———————— next (stop), . . .
つぎ

先発 ———————— departing first
せんぱつ

次発 ———————— departing second
じはつ

終電 ———————— last train
しゅうでん

Announcements

まもなく発車します。————————— We will be leaving soon.
<small>はっしゃ</small>

電車が参ります。————————— A train is arriving.
<small>でんしゃ まい</small>

次は〜に止まります。————————— Next (we'll stop at) . . .
<small>つぎ と</small>

ドアが閉まります。ご注意ください。—— The doors are closing. Please be
<small>し ちゅう い</small> careful.

Expressions

この電車は秋葉原に止まりますか。——— Does this train stop at Akihabara?
<small>でんしゃ あき は ばら と</small>

終電は何時ですか。————————— What time is the last train?
<small>しゅうでん なん じ</small>

東京までの指定席を一枚お願いします。—— One reserved ticket to Tokyo,
<small>とうきょう し てい せき いちまい ねが</small> please.

学割が使えますか。————————— Can I get a student discount?
<small>がくわり つか</small>

*　　　　*　　　　*

A：鎌倉行きの電車はどれですか。
<small>かまくら い てんしゃ</small>
Which one is the train bound for Kamakura?

B：二番線です。
<small>に ばんせん</small>
Track number two.

写真提供：共同通信社

第11課｜L E S S O N ·················11

休みのあと After the Vacation
やす

会 話 Dialogue
かい わ

Michiko and Mary meet after the vacation.

Ⅰ 🔊 K11-01/02

1 みちこ：　　メアリーさん、久しぶりですね。休みはどうでしたか。
　　　　　　　　　　　　　　　　ひさ　　　　　　　　やす

2 メアリー：　すごく楽しかったです。韓国で買い物をしたり、韓国料理を食べた
　　　　　　　　　　　たの　　　　　　かんこく　か　もの　　　　かんこくりょうり　た

3 　　　　　　りしました。

4 みちこ：　　いいですね。私も旅行したいです。
　　　　　　　　　　　　　わたし　りょこう

5 メアリー：　みちこさんの休みは楽しかったですか。
　　　　　　　　　　　　　　やす　　たの

6 みちこ：　　まあまあでした。一日だけドライブに行きましたが、毎日アルバイ
　　　　　　　　　　　　　　　いちにち　　　　　　　い　　　　　　　まいにち

7 　　　　　　トをしていました。

Ⅱ 🔊 K11-03/04

1 メアリー：　みちこさん、友だちを紹介します。こちらはジョンさんです。
　　　　　　　　　　　　　とも　　しょうかい

2 　　　　　　ジョンさんは先月、日本に来ました。
　　　　　　　　　　　　せんげつ　にほん　き

3 ジョン：　　初めまして。
　　　　　　　はじ

4 みちこ：　　初めまして、山川みちこです。
　　　　　　　はじ　　　　やまかわ

Ⅲ 🔊 K11-05/06

1 みちこ：　　ジョンさん、出身はどこですか。
　　　　　　　　　　　　しゅっしん

2 ジョン：　　オーストラリアのケアンズです。

3 みちこ：　　そうですか。

4 ジョン：　　みちこさんはケアンズに行ったことがありますか。
　　　　　　　　　　　　　　　　　い

5 みちこ：　　いいえ、ありません。

6 ジョン：　　山や海があって、きれいな所ですよ。グレートバリアリーフで有名です。
　　　　　　　やま　うみ　　　　　　　　　ところ　　　　　　　　　　　　　　　ゆうめい

7　　　　　　みちこさんはどこの出身ですか。

8 みちこ：　長野です。今度遊びに来てください。食べ物もおいしいですよ。

9 ジョン：　ぜひ、行きたいです。

Ⅰ

Michiko: Mary, I haven't seen you for a long time. How was your vacation?

Mary: It was really fun. I went shopping, ate Korean dishes, and things like that in Korea.

Michiko: Sounds good. I want to travel, too.

Mary: Did you have a fun vacation, Michiko?

Michiko: It was okay. I went for a drive just for one day, but I was working part-time every day.

Ⅱ

Mary: Michiko, I want to introduce you to a friend of mine. This is John. He came to Japan last month.

John: How do you do?

Michiko: How do you do? I am Michiko Yamakawa.

Ⅲ

Michiko: John, where are you from?

John: I am from Cairns, Australia.

Michiko: Is that so.

John: Have you been to Cairns?

Michiko: No, I haven't.

John: It has mountains and the ocean and is a beautiful place. It's famous for the Great Barrier Reef. Where are you from, Michiko?

Michiko: I am from Nagano. Please come to visit me sometime. The food is good, too.

John: By all means, I would love to.

単語
たん ご
V o c a b u l a r y

🔊 K11-07

N o u n s

* オーストラリア		Australia
おかし	お菓子	snack; sweets
おしょうがつ	お正月	New Year's
おとこのこ	男の子	boy
おまつり	お祭り	festival
おもちゃ		toy
おんせん	温泉	spa; hot spring
おんなのこ	女の子	girl
がいこく	外国	foreign country
かしゅ	歌手	singer
かわ	川	river
キャンプ		camp
* こちら		this person (polite)
こんがっき	今学期	this semester
しゃちょう	社長	president of a company
じゅぎょう	授業	class
しょうらい	将来	future
じんじゃ	神社	shrine
つり		fishing
* ドライブ		drive
ビール		beer
びじゅつかん	美術館	art museum
ホストファミリー		host family
みずうみ	湖	lake
* やま	山	mountain
ゆめ	夢	dream
ルームメート		roommate

U - v e r b s

うそをつく		to tell a lie
おなかがすく		to become hungry
かう	飼う	to own (a pet) （〜を）
サボる		to cut (classes) （〜を）

* Words that appear in the dialogue

とる	取る	to take (a class); to get (a grade) （〜を）
ならう	習う	to learn （〜を）
のぼる	登る	to climb （*place* に）
はたらく	働く	to work

Ru-verbs

| つかれる | 疲れる | to get tired |
| やめる | | to quit （〜を） |

Irregular Verbs

けんかする		to have a fight; to quarrel
* しょうかいする	紹介する	to introduce （*person* に *person* を）
ダイエットする		to go on a diet
ちこくする	遅刻する	to be late (for an appointment) （〜に）
りゅうがくする	留学する	to study abroad （*place* に）

Adverbs and Other Expressions

あと	後	after (an event) （*event* の）
* しゅっしん	出身	coming from （*place* の）
そして		and then
* 〜だけ		just . . . ; only . . .
〜てん	〜点	. . . points
* ひさしぶり	久しぶり	it has been a long time
* まあまあ		okay; so-so
もっと		more

ADDITIONAL VOCABULARY 🔊 K11-08

職業 (Occupations)
しょくぎょう

さっか（作家）	writer	じょゆう（女優）	actress
ジャーナリスト	journalist	かんごし（看護師）	nurse
けいさつかん（警察官）	police officer	しょうぼうし（消防士）	firefighter
はいゆう（俳優）	actor; actress	まんがか（漫画家）	cartoonist
うちゅうひこうし（宇宙飛行士）	astronaut		
やきゅうせんしゅ（野球選手）	baseball player		
だいとうりょう（大統領）	president of a country		

文法 Grammar
ぶん ぽう

1 ～たい

You can use a verb stem (the verb form that goes before ます)＋たいです to describe your hope or aspiration.

今度の週末は、映画を見たいです。 or 映画が見たいです。
こんど しゅうまつ えいが み えいが み
I want to see a film this weekend.

いつか中国に行きたいです。
ちゅうごく い
I want to go to China someday.

> verb stem ＋ たいです　　　*I want to do . . .*

As you can see in the first example above, having たい attached to a verb slightly affects the composition of the sentence. A verb that takes the particle を can have either the particle を or が when it is followed by たい. Particles other than を remain the same.

The combination of a verb and たい conjugates as an い-adjective. Here are examples of negative and past tense たい sentences.

あの人には会いたくないです。
ひと あ
I don't want to see that person.

セーターが買いたかったから、デパートに行きました。
か い
I went to a department store, because I wanted to buy a sweater.

If your wish is one you have entertained for some time, that is, if you "have wanted to," you can use たいと思っています instead of たいです。
おも

たいです sentences are not usually used to describe wishes held by others. Somebody else's wishes are usually reported in Japanese either as quotations, observations, or guesses. To quote somebody, saying that she wants to do something, you can use と言っていました with たい.
い

メアリーさんはチベットに行きたいと言っていました。
い い
Mary said she wanted to go to Tibet.

To describe your observation to the effect that somebody wants to do something, you must use a special verb たがっている instead of たい. If a verb takes the particle を, the derived verb たがっている will retain the を, unlike たい, with which we had a choice between the particles が and を.

メアリーさんは着物を着たがっています。
<ruby>着物<rt>き もの</rt></ruby> <ruby>着<rt>き</rt></ruby>

(It seems) Mary wants to wear a kimono.

The verb たがっている, which comes from the dictionary form たがる, indicates "I think that she wants to, because of the way she is behaving." We will have more to say about this type of sentence in Lesson 14.

I want to . . . /Do you want to . . . ?	They want to . . .
・verb stem + たいです	・verb stem + たがっています
・たい conjugates as an い-adjective	・たがる conjugates as an *u*-verb
・が or を	・を only

2　〜たり〜たりする

You already know that you can connect two clauses with the *te*-form of predicates, as in:

大阪で買い物をして、晩ご飯を食べます。
<ruby>大阪<rt>おおさか</rt></ruby> <ruby>買<rt>か</rt></ruby>い<ruby>物<rt>もの</rt></ruby> <ruby>晩<rt>ばん</rt></ruby><ruby>飯<rt>はん</rt></ruby> <ruby>食<rt>た</rt></ruby>

In Osaka, I will do some shopping and eat dinner.

This sentence, however, tends to suggest that shopping and dining are *the only* activities you plan to perform in Osaka and that those two activities will be done in that order. If you want to avoid such implications and want to mention activities or events just *as examples*, and *in no set order*, you can use a special predicate form 〜たり〜たりする.

大阪で買い物をしたり、晩ご飯を食べたりします。
<ruby>大阪<rt>おおさか</rt></ruby> <ruby>買<rt>か</rt></ruby>い<ruby>物<rt>もの</rt></ruby> <ruby>晩<rt>ばん</rt></ruby><ruby>飯<rt>はん</rt></ruby> <ruby>食<rt>た</rt></ruby>

In Osaka, I will do such things as shopping, and eating dinner.

(activity A) たり　(activity B) たりする	*do such things as A and B*

To get the たり form of a predicate, you just add り to the past tense short form of a predicate. (Thus we have したり for the verb する, whose past tense is した, and 食べたり for 食べる, past tense 食べた.) Note that the helping verb する at the end of the sentence indicates the tense of the sentence. You can change a 〜たり〜たりする sentence into the past tense, or incorporate it in a bigger sentence, by working on the helping verb part.

週末は、勉強したり、友だちと話したり<u>しました</u>。
I studied and talked with my friends, among other things, over the weekend.

踊ったり、音楽を聞いたり<u>する</u>のが好きです。
I like dancing, listening to music, and so forth.

3 〜ことがある

The past tense short form of a verb ＋ ことがある describes that you did something, or something happened, in earlier times.

富士山に登った<u>ことがあります</u>。
I have had the experience of climbing Mt. Fuji.

たけしさんは授業を休んだ<u>ことがありません</u>。
Takeshi has never been absent from classes (in his life).

verb (short, past, affirmative) ＋ ことがある	*have the experience of . . .*

If somebody asks you a question using ことがありますか, you can just say あります/ありません or repeat the whole verbal complex (行ったことがあります/行ったことがありません).

ヨーロッパに行った<u>ことがあります</u>か。
Have you ever been to Europe?

　　—　　はい、行ったことがあります。
　　　　はい、あります。
　　　　（× はい、ことがあります。）
　　　　Yes, I have.

4 noun A や noun B

や connects two nouns, as does と. や suggests that the things referred to are proposed as examples, and that you are not citing an exhaustive list.

A や B	*A and B, for example*

京都や奈良に行きました。
I went to Kyoto and Nara (for example, and may have visited other places as well).

表現ノート……11
ひょう げん

は in negative sentences ▶ In negative sentences, you often find the particle は where you expect が or を. Observe the reply sentences in the dialogues below:

Q：山下先生はテレビを見ますか。 *Do you watch TV, Prof. Yamashita?*
やましたせんせい み

A：いいえ、テレビ<u>は</u>見ません。 *No, I don't.*
み

Q：コーヒーが好きですか。 *Do you like coffee?*
す

A：いいえ、コーヒー<u>は</u>好きじゃないです。 *No, I don't.*
す

を and が, respectively, would not be ungrammatical in the above examples. Many Japanese speakers, however, find the は versions more natural.

The rule of thumb is that negative Japanese sentences tend to contain at least one は phrase. If you add 私は to the sentences above, therefore, the need for は
わたし
is already fulfilled, and Japanese speakers feel much less compelled to use は after テレビ and コーヒー.

は may also follow particles like で and に.

英語で<u>は</u>話したくないです。 *I don't want to speak in English.*
えい ご はな

広島に<u>は</u>行ったことがありません。 *I have never been to Hiroshima.*
ひろしま い

だけ ▶ You can add だけ to numbers to talk about having just that many items. だけ implies that you have something up to the amount needed, but not more than that.

私はその人に一回<u>だけ</u>会ったことがあります。
わたし ひと いっかい あ

I have met that person <u>just</u> once.

一つ<u>だけ</u>質問があります。 *I have <u>just</u> one question.*
ひと しつもん

三十分<u>だけ</u>寝ました。 *I slept for <u>just</u> thirty minutes.*
さんじゅっぷん ね

だけ suggests that you can live with that few, though the number admittedly could have been higher. We will learn another word in Lesson 14, namely, しか, which means "only" in the sense that you do not have enough of.

に ▶ You can use the particle に to indicate the occasion on which you do something.

晩ご飯<u>に</u>サラダを食べました。 *I ate salad <u>at</u> dinner.*
ばん はん た

に can also indicate the role you want something to play.

おみやげに絵葉書を買いました。　　*I bought a postcard <u>as</u> a souvenir.*

ドライブ▶ドライブ is used when you go somewhere by car for pleasure. To say "to have a drive" or "to go for a drive," use ドライブに行く or ドライブする.

湖までドライブに行きました／ドライブしました。
I went for a drive to the lake.

When you simply want to say "to drive a car" (not necessarily for pleasure), use 運転する instead.

日本で車を運転したことがありますか。
Have you ever driven a car in Japan?

夢▶夢, like the English word "dream," has two meanings. One is the dream you have while sleeping; the others the dream that you wish would come true. To say "I have a dream," in Japanese, you use the verb 見る for sleeping dreams, and 持っている or ある for your visions.

ゆうべこわい夢を見ました。　　*I had a scary dream last night.*
夢を持っています／夢があります。　*I have a dream.*
あなたの将来の夢は何ですか。　*What is your future dream?*

には▶The particle は often follows the particle に in sentences describing a place in terms of the things that are found there.

(1) 東京にはデパートがたくさんあります。
(2) 東京にデパートがたくさんあります。
There are many department stores in Tokyo.

There is a subtle difference between the two sentences. The first sentence is about the places: they answer questions (either explicitly asked, or implicitly) like "What is Tokyo like?" The second sentence, on the other hand, is an answer to a question like "Where do you find many department stores?"

　　See the grammar note discussing the difference between が and は in Lesson 8. In the case of the particle に, the contrast is between the simple に and the combination には. (See also the grammar note on counting people in Lesson 7.)

練習 Practice

① ハンバーガーを食べたいです

A. Change the following phrases into 〜たい sentences. 🔊 K11-09

Example: ハンバーガーを食べる

(はい) → ハンバーガーを食べたいです。

(いいえ) → ハンバーガーを食べたくないです。

1. 湖に行く （はい）
2. 日本語を練習する （はい）
3. 温泉に行く （はい）
4. ゆっくり休む （いいえ）
5. 会社の社長になる （いいえ）
6. 日本で働く （はい）
7. 車を買う （はい）
8. 日本に住む （いいえ）
9. 留学する （はい）
10. 山に登る （いいえ）

B. Pair Work—Ask if your partner wants to do the things above. When you answer, give reasons as in the example.

Example: A：ハンバーガーを食べたいですか。

B：はい、食べたいです。おなかがすいていますから。／

いいえ、食べたくないです。さっき食べましたから。

C. Change the following phrases into 〜たい sentences in the past tense. 🔊 K11-10

Example: おもちゃの電車で遊ぶ

(はい) → 子供の時、おもちゃの電車で遊びたかったです。

(いいえ) → 子供の時、おもちゃの電車で遊びたくなかったです。

1. テレビを見る （はい）
2. 飛行機に乗る （はい）
3. ゲームをする （いいえ）
4. 犬を飼う （はい）
5. 学校をやめる （いいえ）
6. お祭りに行く （はい）
7. ピアノを習う （いいえ）
8. 車を運転する （はい）
9. 有名になる （はい）
10. ミッキー・マウスに会う （はい）

D. Pair Work—Ask if your partner wanted to do the things above during their childhood.

E. Pair Work—Ask your partner the following questions and report the answers as in the example. See p. 253 for occupation vocabulary.

Example:　　A：けんさんは何が食べたいですか。

　　　　　　B：ピザが食べたいです。

　　　→　　A：けんさんはピザが食べたいと言っていました。

　　　　　　（けんさんはピザを食べたがっています。）

1. 昼ご飯に何が食べたいですか。
2. 何がいちばん買いたいですか。
3. どこにいちばん行きたいですか。
4. だれにいちばん会いたいですか。
5. 何を習いたいですか。
6. 今週の週末、何がしたいですか。
7. 今、何をしたくないですか。
8. 子供の時、何になりたかったですか。
9. 将来、何になりたいですか。
10. 今学期の後、何がしたいですか。

F. Complete the following sentences.

1. 今日はいい天気だから、＿＿＿＿＿＿＿＿＿＿＿＿＿＿＿たいです。
2. あしたは休みだから、＿＿＿＿＿＿＿＿＿＿＿＿＿＿たいです。
3. 疲れたから、＿＿＿＿＿＿＿＿＿＿＿＿＿＿たくないです。
4. 田中さんはいじわるだから、一緒に＿＿＿＿＿＿＿＿＿＿たくないです。
5. 高校の時、もっと＿＿＿＿＿＿＿＿＿＿＿＿＿＿＿たかったです。

Ⅱ 掃除したり、洗濯したりします
そうじ　　　　せんたく

A. Tell what the following people did on the weekend using 〜たり〜たりする. 🔊 K11-11

Example:　ジョン : saw temples in Kyoto, went to a museum, etc.

→ ジョンさんはお寺を見たり、美術館に行ったりしました。
　　　　　　　てら　み　　びじゅつかん　い

1. たけし : went camping, went for a drive, etc.
2. きょうこ : made sweets, played games at home, etc.
3. スー : went to Osaka to have fun, went to eat, etc.
4. けん : cleaned his room, did laundry, etc.
5. ロバート : met friends, watched movies, etc.
6. 山下先生 : went to a hot spring, rested, etc.
　やましたせんせい

B. Look at the pictures and make your own sentences using 〜たり〜たりする.

C. Pair Work—Ask your partner the following questions. When you answer, use 〜たり〜たりする as in the example.

Example:　A : 日本で何をしましたか。
　　　　　　　にほん　なに
　　　　　　B : 日本のお菓子を食べたり、富士山 (Mt. Fuji) に登ったりしました。
　　　　　　　にほん　　かし　た　　ふじさん　　　　　　　　のぼ

1. 週末よく何をしますか。
　しゅうまつ　　なに
2. デートの時、何をしますか。
　　　　とき　なに
3. あなたの国ではお正月に何をしますか。
　　　　くに　　しょうがつ　なに
4. 子供の時、よく何をしましたか。
　こども　とき　　なに
5. 日本で何をしたいですか。
　にほん　なに

6. 冬休み／夏休みに何をしましたか。
   <small>ふゆやす なつやす なに</small>

7. クラスで何をしてはいけませんか。
   <small>なに</small>

8. 今度の週末、何をするつもりですか。
   <small>こん ど しゅうまつ なに</small>

9. 何をするのが好きですか／きらいですか。
   <small>なに す</small>

Ⅲ 有名人に会ったことがありますか
<small>ゆう めい じん あ</small>

A. The following are what John has or hasn't done. Make the sentences using
～ことがある.  K11-12

Example:　　○ eat tempura　→　天ぷらを食べたことがあります。
<small>てん た</small>

　　　　　　×　go to Tokyo　→　東京に行ったことがありません。
<small>とうきょう い</small>

1. ○ eat sushi
2. ○ study French
3. ○ work at a restaurant
4. × go to Hiroshima
5. × write a love letter（ラブレター）
6. ○ sleep in class
7. ○ climb Mt. Fuji
8. × drive a car in Japan
9. × see Japanese movies
10. × go to shrine

B. Pair Work—Make questions using ～ことがある and ask your partner.

Example:　　日本のお酒を飲む
<small>に ほん さけ の</small>

　　　→　　A：日本のお酒を飲んだことがありますか。
<small>に ほん さけ の</small>

　　　　　　B：はい、あります。

　　　　　　A：どうでしたか。

　　　　　　B：おいしかったです。

1. ダイエットをする
2. テストで０点を取る
   <small>れいてん と</small>
3. 英語を教える
   <small>えい ご おし</small>
4. 有名人に会う
   <small>ゆうめいじん あ</small>
5. カラオケに行く
   <small>い</small>
6. ふぐ (blowfish) を食べる
   <small>た</small>
7. 中国語を勉強する
   <small>ちゅうごく ご べんきょう</small>
8. 新幹線に乗る
   <small>しんかんせん の</small>
9. うそをつく
10. 日本料理を作る
    <small>に ほんりょう り つく</small>
11. 遅刻する
    <small>ち こく</small>
12. 授業をサボる
    <small>じゅぎょう</small>
13. 友だち／ルームメート／
    <small>とも</small>
    ホストファミリーとけんかする
14. 留学する
    <small>りゅうがく</small>
15. 川でつりをする
    <small>かわ</small>

Ⅳ すしや天ぷらをよく食べます

Pair Work—Ask your partner the following questions. When you answer, use 〜や〜 as in the example.

Example: A：どんな日本料理をよく食べますか。
B：すしや天ぷらをよく食べます。

1. どんなスポーツをよく見ますか。
2. どんな音楽が好きですか。
3. どんな料理をよく作りますか。
4. あなたの大学の食堂には、どんな食べ物がありますか。
5. あなたの大学には、どこの国の人がいますか。
6. 外国に行ったことがありますか。どこですか。
7. 今、どんな授業を取っていますか。
8. 俳優 (actors) の中で、だれが好きですか。
9. 歌手の中で、だれが好きですか。

Ⅴ まとめの練習

A. Talk about your dream for the future or what it was when you were a child.

1. あなたの夢は何ですか。
   Example: 私は将来、お金持ちになりたいです。そして、いろいろな国に行きたいです。

2. 子供の時の夢は何でしたか。
   Example: 子供の時、歌手になりたかったです。

B. Class Activity—Find someone who . . .

1. has seen celebrities _____
2. has never used chopsticks _____
3. wants to live in Japan in the future _____
4. wanted to be a star (スター) as a child _____
5. wants to cut classes tomorrow _____

C. Class Activity—Bring pictures of your hometown and describe it.

Example:

私 はニューヨークの 出身です。ニューヨークはとても 大きくてにぎやかです。
きれいな 公園 や 有名 な 美術館 やたくさんの 劇場 (theater) があります。
よくミュージカルを 見たり、散歩 したりしました。
夏休み に 帰って、友だち に 会いたいです。

Culture Note

お正月 New Year's

お正月 (New Year's) is the biggest homecoming holiday in Japan. Japanese celebrate New Year's Day on January 1, unlike most other Asians, who go by the lunar calendar. Most businesses are closed on and around New Year's Day.

New Year's Eve is called 大晦日, and people try to finish their seasonal chores—cleaning the house thoroughly, writing greeting cards (年賀状), and so on—by this date. Dinner for New Year's Eve often includes 年越しそば (buckwheat noodles), as the long noodles symbolize the desire for longevity.

When saying good-bye to someone whom you do not expect to see again until the new year, the traditional parting phrase is よいお年を (Have a happy New Year!). When you meet somebody for the first time in the new year, you say あけましておめでとうございます (Happy New Year!).

Many people go to 神社 (Shinto shrines) and お寺 (Buddhist temples) for 初詣 or the "first worship of the year," which is likely to be their only visit to shrines and temples for the year, since Japan is a largely secular society.

Special dishes called お節料理 are eaten for New Year's. Each dish is said to signify a particular wish—black beans (黒豆) for diligence and health (a pun on the word まめ), herring roe (数の子) for having many offspring, and so forth. The staple food for New Year's is おもち (rice cake), which is toasted or served in 雑煮 (New Year's soup).

Children expect to receive お年玉, which are gifts of money from their parents, grandparents, aunts, uncles, and even family guests.

写真提供：共同通信社

Useful Expressions

日本語のクラスで
に ほん ご

In the Japanese Class

Expressions

どちらでもいいです。——Both are fine.

同じです。————Same thing.
おな

だいたい同じです。———More or less the same.
おな

ちょっと違います。———A little different.
ちが

使えません。————Can't use it.
つか

だめです。————No good.

手をあげてください。——Raise your hand.
て

読んできてください。————Read it before coming to class.
よ

宿題を出してください。————Hand in the homework.
しゅくだい だ

教科書を閉じてください。——— Close the textbook.
きょう か しょ と

となりの人に聞いてください。——Ask the person sitting next to you.
ひと き

やめてください。——————Please stop.

今日はこれで終わります。———That's it for today.
きょう お

Vocabulary

宿題————homework
しゅくだい

しめきり——deadline

練習————exercise
れんしゅう

意味————meaning
い み

発音————pronunciation
はつおん

文法————grammar
ぶんぽう

質問————question
しつもん

答————answer
こたえ

例————example
れい

かっこ———（　）(parenthesis)

まる———○ (correct)

ばつ———✕ (wrong)

くだけた言い方——colloquial expression
い かた

かたい言い方——bookish expression
い かた

ていねいな言い方——polite expression
い かた

方言————dialect
ほうげん

標準語————standard Japanese
ひょうじゅん ご

たとえば————for example

ほかに————anything else

〜番————number . . .
ばん

〜ページ————page number . . .

〜行目————line number . . .
ぎょうめ

二人ずつ————two people each
ふたり

第12課 | L E S S O N ⋯⋯⋯⋯⋯⋯ 12

病 気 Feeling III
びょう き

会 話 D i a l o g u e
かい わ

Ⅰ Mary and Michiko are talking at school. 🔊 K12-01/02

1 みちこ： メアリーさん、元気がありませんね。
げんき

2 メアリー： うーん。ちょっとおなかが痛いんです。
いた

3 みちこ： どうしたんですか。

4 メアリー： きのう友だちと晩ご飯を食べに行ったんです。たぶん食べすぎたん
とも ばん はん た い た

5 　　　　　　だと思います。
おも

6 みちこ： 大丈夫ですか。
だいじょうぶ

7 メアリー： ええ。心配しないでください。……ああ、痛い。
しんぱい いた

8 みちこ： 病院に行ったほうがいいですよ。
びょういん い

Ⅱ At a hospital. 🔊 K12-03/04

1 メアリー： 先生、のどが痛いんです。きのうはおなかが痛かったんです。
せんせい いた いた

2 医　者： ああ、そうですか。熱もありますね。かぜですね。
い しゃ ねつ

3 メアリー： あの、もうすぐテニスの試合があるので、練習しなきゃいけないん
しあい れんしゅう

4 　　　　　　ですが……。

5 医　者： 二三日、運動しないほうがいいでしょう。
い しゃ に さんにち うんどう

6 メアリー： わかりました。

7 医　者： 今日は薬を飲んで、早く寝てください。
い しゃ きょう くすり の はや ね

8 メアリー： はい、ありがとうございました。

9 医　者： お大事に。
い しゃ だいじ

I

Michiko: You don't look well, Mary.

Mary: Um . . . I have a little stomachache.

Michiko: What's the matter?

Mary: I went out to have dinner with my friend yesterday. I think maybe I ate too much.

Michiko: Are you all right?

Mary: Yes. Don't worry about it. Oh, it hurts.

Michiko: You had better go to a hospital.

Ⅱ

Mary: Doctor, I have a sore throat. I had a stomachache yesterday.

Doctor: I see. You have a fever, too. It is just a cold.

Mary: Well, I will have a tennis tournament soon, so I have to practice, though . . .

Doctor: You had better not exercise for a couple of days.

Mary: I understand.

Doctor: Take medicine and go to bed early tonight.

Mary: Yes. Thank you so much.

Doctor: Take care.

単語
たんご
V o c a b u l a r y

 K12-05

N o u n s

あし	足	leg; foot
いみ	意味	meaning
おてあらい	お手洗い	restroom
* おなか		stomach
* かぜ	風邪	cold
かのじょ	彼女	girlfriend; she
かれ	彼	boyfriend; he
きおん	気温	temperature (weather—not used for things)
くもり	曇り	cloudy weather
* しあい	試合	match; game
ジュース		juice
せいじ	政治	politics
せいせき	成績	grade (on a test, etc.)
せき		cough
* のど		throat
は	歯	tooth
はな	花	flower
はれ	晴れ	sunny weather
ふく	服	clothes
ふつかよい	二日酔い	hangover
プレゼント		present
ホームシック		homesickness
マイナス		minus
もの	物	thing (concrete object)
ゆき	雪	snow
ようじ	用事	business to take care of

い - a d j e c t i v e s

あまい	甘い	sweet
* いたい	痛い	hurt; painful
おおい	多い	there are many . . .
せまい	狭い	narrow; not spacious

* Words that appear in the dialogue

| つごうがわるい | 都合が悪い | inconvenient; to have a scheduling conflict |
| わるい | 悪い | bad |

な-adjective

| すてき（な） | 素敵 | nice |

U-verbs

あるく	歩く	to walk
かぜをひく	風邪をひく	to catch a cold
きょうみがある	興味がある	to be interested (in . . .) (*topic* に)
なくす		to lose （〜を）
* ねつがある	熱がある	to have a fever
のどがかわく	のどが渇く	to become thirsty

Ru-verbs

| せきがでる | せきが出る | to cough |
| わかれる | 別れる | to break up; to separate (*person* と) |

Irregular Verbs

| きんちょうする | 緊張する | to get nervous |
| * しんぱいする | 心配する | to worry |

Adverbs and Other Expressions

* おだいじに	お大事に	Get well soon.
* げんきがない	元気がない	don't look well
* たぶん	多分	probably; maybe
できるだけ		as much as possible
* 〜でしょう		probably; . . . , right?
〜ど	〜度	. . . degrees (temperature)
* にさんにち	二三日	for two to three days
* 〜ので		because . . .
はじめて	初めて	for the first time
* もうすぐ		very soon; in a few moments/days

文法 Grammar
ぶん　ぽう

1 〜んです

There are two distinct ways to make a statement in Japanese. One way is to simply report the facts as they are observed. This is the mode of speech that we have learned so far. In this lesson, we will learn a new way: the mode of *explaining* things.

A *report* is an isolated description of a fact. When you are late for an appointment, you can already report in Japanese what has happened, バスが来ませんでした. This sentence, however, does not have the right apologetic tone, because it is not offered as an explanation for anything. If you want to mention the busses failing to run on time as an excuse for being late, you will need to use the *explanation* mode of speech, and say:

バスが来なかった<u>んです</u>。　*(As it happens,) the bus didn't come.*
き

An explanation has two components, one that is explicitly described in the sentence (the bus not coming), and another, which is implied, or explained, by it (you being late for the appointment). The sentence-final expression んです serves as the link between what the sentence says and what it accounts for. Compare:

あしたテストがあります。　*I have an exam tomorrow. (a simple observation)*
あしたテストがある<u>んです</u>。　*I have an exam tomorrow. (So I can't go out tonight.)*

トイレに行きたいです。　*I want to go to the bathroom. (declaration of one's wish)*
い
トイレに行きたい<u>んです</u>。　*I want to go to the bathroom. (So tell me where it is.)*
い

んです goes after the short form of a predicate. The predicate can be either in the affirmative or in the negative, either in the present tense or in the past tense. んです itself is invariant and does not usually appear in the negative or the past tense forms.[1] In writing, it is more common to find のです instead of んです.

成績がよくない<u>んです</u>。　(in response to the question "Why do you look so upset?")
せいせき
(As a matter of fact) My grade is not good.

---

[1] In casual exchanges, んです appears in its short form, んだ. In casual questions, んですか is replaced by の. We will examine these further in Lesson 15.

試験が終わった<u>ん</u>です。 (explaining to a person who has caught you smiling)
The exam is over. (That's why I'm smiling.)

When it follows a noun or a な-adjective, な comes in between.

	report sentences	explanation sentences
な-adjective:	静かです	静か<u>な</u>んです
noun:	学生です	学生<u>な</u>んです

You can use んです in questions to invite explications and further clarifications from the person you are talking to. It is very often used together with question words, such as どうして (why) and どうした (what has happened).

Q：どうして彼と別れた<u>ん</u>ですか。
Why did you break up with your boyfriend? (You've got to tell me.)

A：彼、ぜんぜんお風呂に入らない<u>ん</u>です。
Oh, him. He never takes a bath. (That's a good enough reason, isn't it?)

Q：どうした<u>ん</u>ですか。
What happened? (You look shattered.)

A：猫が死んだ<u>ん</u>です。[2]
My cat died. (That should explain how I look today.)

You can also use んです to provide an additional comment on what has just been said.

A：とてもいい教科書ですね。
That's a great textbook that you are using.

B：ええ。私の大学の先生が書いた<u>ん</u>です。
You bet. The professors at my university wrote it (for your information).

In the written language, you see のです instead of んです. It has the same functions but is stylistically more formal.

---

[2] A どうしたんですか question is best answered by a んです sentence with the subject marked with the particle が rather than は, as in this example. See Lesson 8 for a related discussion.

2 ～すぎる

Verb stems may be followed by the helping verb すぎる, which means "too much," or "to excess." すぎる conjugates as a regular *ru*-verb.

早く起きすぎました。	*I got up too early.*
食べすぎてはいけません。	*You must not eat too much.*

すぎる can also follow い- and な-adjective bases (the parts which do not change in conjugations); you drop the い and な at the end of the adjectives and then add すぎる.

（高い）　この本は高すぎます。	*This book is too expensive.*
（静かな）　この町は静かすぎます。	*This town is too quiet.*

You use すぎる when something is beyond normal or proper, suggesting that you do not welcome it. Thus 親切すぎます (too kind) for example is not a straightforward compliment. Use modifiers like とても and すごく if you simply want to say that something is in a high degree.

3 ～ほうがいいです

ほうがいいです "it is better (for you) to do . . ." is a sentence-final expression which you can use to give advice. When you suggest an activity with ほうがいいです, you are giving a very specific piece of advice; namely, that it is advisable to do it, and if one does not follow the advice, there is a danger or a problem.

ほうがいいです is peculiar in that it follows different tense forms, depending on whether the advice given is in the affirmative or the negative. When the advice is in the affirmative, ほうがいいです generally follows the past tense short form of a verb. When the advice is in the negative, however, the verb is in the *present* tense short form.

もっと野菜を食べたほうがいいですよ。	*You'd better eat more vegetables.*
授業を休まないほうがいいですよ。	*It is better not to skip classes.*

4   〜ので

You can use ので to give the reason for the situation described in the balance of the sentence. Semantically, ので is just like から. Stylistically, ので sounds slightly more formal than から.

> (reason) ので   (situation)。   (situation), *because* (reason).

いつも日本語で話す<u>ので</u>、日本語が上手になりました。
My Japanese has improved, because I always speak Japanese.

宿題がたくさんあった<u>ので</u>、きのうの夜、寝ませんでした。
I did not sleep last night, because I had a lot of homework.

The reason part of a sentence ends in a short form predicate as above. When ので follows a な-adjective or a noun, な comes in between, as it did with the explanatory predicate んです。

その人はいじわる<u>な</u>ので、きらいです。
I do not like that person, because he is mean.

今日は日曜日<u>な</u>ので、銀行は休みです。
Banks are closed, because today is a Sunday.

5   〜なければいけません／〜なきゃいけません

We use なければいけません and なきゃいけません[3] to say that it is necessary to do something, or "must." The なきゃ variant is very colloquial and is mainly found in the spoken language, while the more formal なければ variant is often seen in the written language.

試験があるから、勉強し<u>なければいけません</u>／<u>なきゃいけません</u>。
I have to study, because there will be an exam.

なければ and なきゃ mean "if you do not do . . ." and いけません roughly means "you cannot go"; なければいけません and なきゃいけません therefore literally mean "you cannot

---

[3] There are more varieties for "must" sentences: なく<u>ちゃ</u>いけません, なく<u>ては</u>いけません, and <u>ないと</u>いけません. You can also substitute なりません for いけません in the なければ and なきゃ combinations, like なければなりません, なきゃなりません. In casual speech, you can also leave out いけません and end the sentence like: 食べなきゃ。／食べなくちゃ。／食べないと。

go not doing . . ." with the double negatives giving rise to the affirmative sense of the mandate. な in なければ and なきゃ comes from the negative ない. Just drop the last い and replace it with ければ or きゃ.

verb	short negative	"must"
食べる	食べない	食べなければいけません / 食べなきゃいけません
言う	言わない	言わなければいけません / 言わなきゃいけません
する	しない	しなければいけません / しなきゃいけません
くる	こない	こなければいけません / こなきゃいけません

You can change いけません to いけませんでした to say you *had to*, and to なきゃいけない (the short form, present tense) in casual speech and to なければいけない in the written language.

けさは、六時に起きなきゃいけませんでした。　　(long form, past)
I had to get up at six this morning.

毎日、練習しなきゃいけないんです。　　(short form, present)
(The truth is,) I must practice every day.

6　～でしょう

We use the sentence-final expression でしょう (probably) when we are making a guess or a prediction. でしょう follows verbs and い-adjectives in short forms, in the affirmative and in the negative.[4]

(verb)
あしたは雨が降るでしょう。　　　　　　　*It will probably rain tomorrow.*
　　　　　降らないでしょう。　　　　　　　*It will probably not rain tomorrow.*

(い-adjective)
北海道は寒いでしょう。　　　　　　　　　*It is probably cold in Hokkaido.*
　　　　寒くないでしょう。　　　　　　　　*It is probably not cold in Hokkaido.*

でしょう may also follow な-adjective bases and nouns. Note that でしょう goes directly after these elements; we do not use ×～なでしょう, ×～のでしょう, or ×～だでしょう.

---

[4] でしょう may also follow predicates in the past tense. We will, however, concentrate on the present tense examples in this lesson.

(な-adjective)

山下先生は魚が好きでしょう。
やましたせんせい　さかな　す

Professor Yamashita probably likes fish.

　　　　　好きじゃないでしょう。
　　　　　す

Professor Yamashita probably doesn't
like fish.

(noun)

あの人はオーストラリア人でしょう。
ひと　　　　　　　　　じん

That person is probably an Australian.

　　　オーストラリア人じゃないでしょう。
　　　　　　　　　　　じん

That person is probably not an
Australian.

でしょう sentences can be turned into questions (〜でしょうか), which can be used to in-vite another person's opinion or guess.

日本語と韓国語と、どっちのほうが難しいでしょうか。
にほんご　かんこくご　　　　　　　　　むずか

Which would you say is more difficult, Japanese or Korean?

The short form of でしょう is だろう. You can use it to cautiously phrase a prediction or an analysis.

たけしさんは興味があるだろうと思います。
きょうみ　　　　　　　おも

I think Takeshi would be interested in it.

In casual exchanges, you can use でしょう (with the question intonation, and most often pronounced as somewhat shorter でしょ) when you want to check if your partner agrees that you have the correct understanding about what you have just said.

ジョン、中国語がわかるでしょ？ これ、読んで。
ちゅうごくご　　　　　　　　　　よ

John, you understand Chinese, right? Can you read this for me?

練習 P r a c t i c e
れん　しゅう

① どうしたんですか

A. You are in the following situations. Explain them using 〜んです. 📶 K12-06

Example: 頭が痛いです
あたま　いた

→　Q：どうしたんですか。

　　A：頭が痛いんです。
　　　　あたま　いた

(1) 彼から電話が
かれ　　　でんわ
ありました

(2) プレゼントを
もらいました

(3) あしたは休みです
やす

(4) きのうは
誕生日でした
たんじょうび

(5) テストが難しく
むずか
なかったです

(6) のどが痛いです
いた

(7) かぜをひきました

(8) 切符をなくしました
きっぷ

ticket

(9) あしたテストが
あります

(10) せきが出ます
て

(11) 彼女と別れました
かのじょ　　わか

(12) お手洗いに行きたい
です
て あら　　い

B.　Respond to the comments using 〜んです. 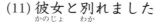 K12-07

Example:

すてきな車ですね。
くるま

My father's　→　父のなんです。
ちち

(1)　きれいな花ですね。
はな

I received them
from my friend.

(2)　新しい靴ですね。
あたら　　くつ

Italian ones
（イタリア）

(3)　かわいい服ですね。
ふく

I made it.

(4)　いいかばんですね。

It was cheap.

(5)　かっこいい彼ですね。
かれ

kind

C. Pair Work—Your partner has said something nice about what you have.
   Respond using 〜んです.

   Example:　B：すてきな時計ですね。
   　　　　　　A：友だちにもらったんです。

D. Pair Work—Make up dialogues asking for reasons.

   Example:　I went to Tokyo last week.

   →　A：先週東京に行きました。
   　　　B：どうして東京に行ったんですか。
   　　　A：母がアメリカから来たんです。

1. I am very tired.
2. I have no money.
3. It is not convenient today.（都合が悪い）
4. I want to marry my boyfriend/girlfriend.
5. I am going to Japan to study.
6. He speaks Chinese very well.（中国語が上手です）
7. I don't want to watch that movie.

Ⅱ 食べすぎました

A. Describe the following pictures using 〜すぎる. Use "verb ＋ すぎる" for (1)
   through (4) and "adjective ＋ すぎる" for (5) through (10). 🔊 K12-08

   Example:

→　作りすぎました。

→　この部屋はせますぎます。

B. Look at the verbs below. Think about the results of over doing these things and make sentences as in the example.

Example: 食べる → 食べすぎたから、おなかが痛いんです。
　　　　　た　　　　　　た

1. 飲む
　の
2. 勉強する
　べんきょう
3. パソコンを使う
　　　　　　つか

4. 本を読む
　ほん　よ
5. テニスをする
6. 甘い物を食べる
　あま　もの　た

7. 歌を歌う
　うた　うた
8. 緊張する
　きんちょう

Ⅲ 薬を飲んだほうがいいです
くすり の

A. Using the cues below, give advice to a friend who has a headache. Decide if you should use the affirmative or the negative. 🔊 K12-09

Example: 薬を飲む → B：頭が痛いんです。
　　　　　くすり の　　　　　あたま いた

　　　　　　　　　　　　A：薬を飲んだほうがいいですよ。
　　　　　　　　　　　　　　くすり の

1. 早く寝る　　　　　3. 病院に行く　　　　　5. うちに帰る
　はや ね　　　　　　 びょういん い　　　　　　　 かえ

2. 遊びに行く　　　　4. 仕事を休む　　　　　6. 運動する
　あそ い　　　　　　　しごと やす　　　　　　　うんどう

B. Pair Work—Give advice to your partner in the following situations, using ～ほうがいい。

Example: 日本語が上手になりたい
　　　　　にほんご じょうず

　　　　→ B：日本語が上手になりたいんです。
　　　　　　　にほんご じょうず

　　　　　　A：日本人の友だちを作ったほうがいいですよ。／
　　　　　　　 にほんじん とも　　　 つく

　　　　　　できるだけ英語を話さないほうがいいですよ。
　　　　　　　　　　　えいご はな

1. ホームシックだ　　　4. お金がない　　　　7. 歯が痛い
　　　　　　　　　　　　　 かね　　　　　　　　は いた

2. やせたい　　　　　　5. 成績が悪い　　　　8. 教科書をなくした
　　　　　　　　　　　　 せいせき わる　　　　きょうかしょ

3. 友だちとけんかした　6. 二日酔いだ　　　　9. いつも授業に遅刻する
　とも　　　　　　　　　 ふつか よ　　　　　　じゅぎょう ちこく

C. Pair Work—You are a health counselor. Someone who hasn't been feeling well is at your office. Ask the following questions. Complete this form first, then give your advice using ～ほうがいい。

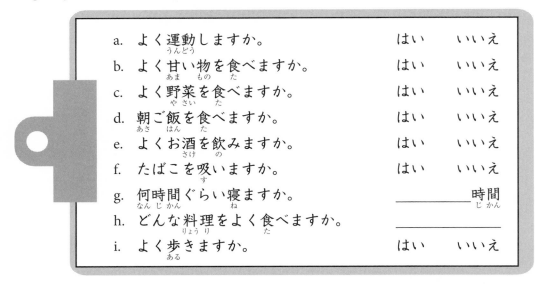

a.	よく運動しますか。 うんどう	はい　　いいえ
b.	よく甘い物を食べますか。 あま もの た	はい　　いいえ
c.	よく野菜を食べますか。 やさい た	はい　　いいえ
d.	朝ご飯を食べますか。 あさ はん た	はい　　いいえ
e.	よくお酒を飲みますか。 さけ の	はい　　いいえ
f.	たばこを吸いますか。 す	はい　　いいえ
g.	何時間ぐらい寝ますか。 なんじかん ね	＿＿＿＿時間 じかん
h.	どんな料理をよく食べますか。 りょうり た	＿＿＿＿
i.	よく歩きますか。 ある	はい　　いいえ

Ⅳ いい天気なので、散歩します

A. Connect the two sentences using 〜ので. (((•))) K12-10

Example: いい天気です／散歩します
→ いい天気なので、散歩します。

1. 安いです／買います
2. あの映画はおもしろくないです／見たくないです
3. 今週は忙しかったです／疲れています
4. 病気でした／授業を休みました
5. 彼女はいつも親切です／人気があります
6. 政治に興味がありません／新聞を読みません
7. あしたテストがあります／勉強します
8. のどがかわきました／ジュースが飲みたいです
9. 歩きすぎました／足が痛いです

B. Make sentences using the cues below as reasons, according to the example.

Example: かぜをひきました → かぜをひいたので、授業を休みました。

1. お金がありません
2. おなかがすいています
3. ホームシックです
4. 用事があります
5. 単語の意味がわかりません
6. 疲れました

C. Fill in the blanks with appropriate words.

1. _____ので、中国に行きたいです。
2. _____ので、人気があります。
3. _____ので、かぜをひきました
4. _____ので、別れました。
5. _____ので、日本に住みたくないです。
6. _____ので、遅刻しました
7. _____ので、緊張しています。

Ⓥ 七時に起きなければいけません/起きなきゃいけません
しち じ　お　　　　　　　　　　　　　　　　　　　お

A. The following is your schedule for tomorrow. Make sentences according to the example. 🔊 K12-11

Example:　7:00 A.M. ／起きる　→　七時に起きなければいけません。
　　　　　　　　　　　　お　　　　しち じ　お

Ex.	7:00 A.M.	起きる
1.	8:00 A.M.	うちを出る
2.	9:00 A.M.	授業に出る
3.	1:00 P.M.	山下先生に会う
4.	2:00 P.M.	英語を教える
5.	3:00 P.M.	図書館に行って、本を借りる
6.	5:00 P.M.	うちに帰る
7.	6:00 P.M.	ホストファミリーと晩ご飯を食べる
8.	8:00 P.M.	宿題をする
9.	9:00 P.M.	シャワーを浴びる
10.	10:00 P.M.	薬を飲む
11.	11:00 P.M.	家族に電話をかける

B. Answer the following questions.

1. 日本語の授業で何をしなければいけませんか。
2. かっこよくなりたいんです。何をしなければいけませんか。
3. 友だちが遊びに来ます。何をしなければいけませんか。
4. あしたは初めてのデートです。何をしなければいけませんか。
5. 子供の時、何をしなければいけませんでしたか。

C. Using the cues in A, tell your friend what you must do tomorrow. 🔊 K12-12

Example:　7:00 A.M. ／起きる　→　七時に起きなきゃいけない。
　　　　　　　　　　　　お　　　　しち じ　お

D. Pair Work—Invite the partner to do the following things together on a specific time. Turn down the invitation and give explanation using 〜なきゃいけない.

Example: play tennis

→ A：あしたの朝、一緒にテニスをしませんか。

B：すみません。ちょっと都合が悪いんです。
あしたはうちにいなきゃいけないんです。

1. do homework
2. eat lunch
3. drink coffee
4. study in the library
5. go to karaoke
6. travel

Ⅵ あしたは晴れでしょう

A. Here is tomorrow's weather forecast (天気予報). Look at the map and play the role of a meteorologist and tell the weather forecasts for each city. 🔊 K12-13

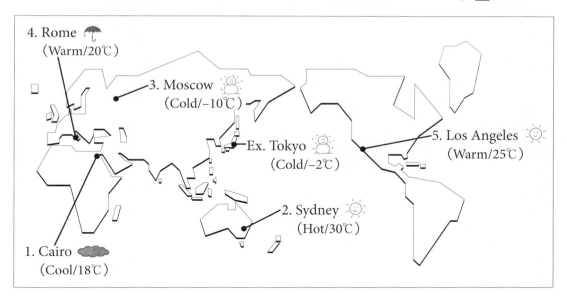

Example: Tokyo → 東京はあした雪でしょう。寒いでしょう。
気温はマイナス二度ぐらいでしょう。

1. Cairo（カイロ）
2. Sydney（シドニー）
3. Moscow（モスクワ）
4. Rome（ローマ）
5. Los Angeles（ロサンゼルス）

B. Pair Work—Play the role of a meteorologist. Predict the weather for your favorite city. The other person fills in the blanks. Switch roles and do the same thing.

city	weather	temperature

Ⅶ まとめの練習
れんしゅう

A. Using Dialogue Ⅰ as a model, make skits in the following situations.

—Your friend looks sad.

—Your friend looks happy.

B. Pair Work—A and B are deciding when they can play tennis together. Play the role of A and B. Discuss your schedules and find the day on which both of you are available. Refer to the next page for B's schedule.

Example: 　A：来週の月曜日に一緒にテニスをしませんか。
　　　　　　　らいしゅう　げつようび　いっしょ

　　　　　　B：来週の月曜日はちょっと都合が悪いんです。英語を教えなきゃ
　　　　　　　らいしゅう　げつようび　　　　　　つごう　わる　　　　えいご　おし

　　　　　　いけないんです。日曜日はどうですか。
　　　　　　　　　　　　　にちようび

A's schedule

Sunday	go shopping
Monday	
Tuesday	read books
Wednesday	
Thursday	
Friday	meet friends
Saturday	

C. Role Play—Visiting a Doctor's Office

Using Dialogue Ⅱ as a model, act the role of a doctor or a patient.

Doctor—Fill out the medical report below and give advice to the patient.

Patient—Describe the symptoms you have and answer the doctor's questions.

Name: _____		**Age:** _____
Symptoms: ☐ Sore throat		☐ Cough
☐ Headache		☐ Fever
☐ Stomachache		☐ Allergy（アレルギー）
☐ Any other pain		☐ Others

Pair Work Ⅶ B.

(→ p. 284)

Example:　A：来週の月曜日に一緒にテニスをしませんか。

　　　　　B：来週の月曜日はちょっと都合が悪いんです。英語を教えなきゃ
いけないんです。日曜日はどうですか。

B's schedule

Sunday	
Monday	teach English
Tuesday	
Wednesday	clean rooms, do laundry, etc.
Thursday	
Friday	
Saturday	practice karate（空手）

日本の気候　The Japanese Climate
にほん　きこう

The seasons in Japan can be very different depending on where you go.

	Naha	Tokyo	Sapporo
Cherry trees blossom	Mid-January	Late March	Early May
Rainy season starts	Early May	Mid-June	No rainy season
First snowfall	No snow	January	October
January temperatures	High: 19.1 Low: 14.3	High: 9.8 Low: 2.1	High: −0.9 Low: −7.7
August temperatures	High: 30.9 Low: 26.1	High: 30.8 Low: 24.2	High: 26.1 Low: 18.5
Annual precipitation	2036.7 mm	1466.8 mm	1127.6 mm

Winter is sunny and dry on the Pacific coast, but cloudy and snowy on the Sea of Japan coast. Spring is rather short because daily temperatures rise quickly and the season is cut short by the arrival of the rainy season (梅雨), which lasts for about a month and a half. Summer in つゆ most parts of Japan is hot and very humid, and almost tropical in some places. Typhoons (台風) make occasional landfalls in summer and early fall. たいふう

Temperature, including body temperature, is measured in Celsius. Here is a conversion scale for those of you who are more used to the Fahrenheit system.

Useful Expressions
健康と病気
けん こう びょう き

H e a l t h   a n d   I l l n e s s

At the Reception of the Clinic

Patient: すみません。初めてなんですが。
はじ
Excuse me. This is my first visit.

Receptionist: はい、保険証を見せてください。
ほ けんしょう み
Okay. Please show me your health insurance certificate.

この紙に名前と住所を書いてください。
かみ なまえ じゅうしょ か
Please fill in your name and address on this paper.

*   *   *

Patient: これは何の薬ですか。
なん くすり
What kind of medicine are these?

Receptionist: 痛み止めです。食後に飲んでください。
いた ど しょくご の
These are painkillers. Please take one after meals.

Patient: わかりました。
I see.

Receptionist: お大事に。
だい じ
Please take care.

Expressions for Illness（病気）and Injuries（けが）
びょう き

下痢です。——————————————— I have diarrhea.
げ り

便秘です。——————————————— I am constipated.
べん ぴ

生理です。——————————————— I have my period.
せい り

花粉症です。————————————— I have hay fever.
か ふんしょう

（〜に）アレルギーがあります。———— I have an allergy to . . .

虫歯があります。———————————— I have a bad tooth.
むし ば

くしゃみが出ます。——————————— I sneeze.
て

鼻水が出ます。————————————— I have a runny nose.
はなみず て

背中がかゆいです。——————————— My back itches.
せ なか

発疹があります。——————————— I have rashes.
はっしん

めまいがします。——————————— I feel dizzy.

吐きました。——————————————— I threw up.
は

気分が悪いです。——————————— I am not feeling well.
き ぶん　わる

やけどをしました。————————— I burned myself.

足の骨を折りました。——————— I broke my leg.
あし ほね　お

けがをしました。——————————— I hurt myself.

Vocabulary

● 医者 (Doctor's office)
　　いしゃ

内科——————————— physician
ないか

皮膚科 ————————— dermatologist
ひ ふ か

外科——————————— surgeon
げ か

産婦人科————————— obstetrician and gynecologist
さん ふ じん か

整形外科————————— orthopedic surgeon
せいけい げ か

眼科——————————— ophthalmologist
がん か

歯科——————————— dentist
し か

耳鼻科 ————————— otorhinolaryngologist; ENT doctor
じ び か

● その他 (Miscellaneous)
　　た

抗生物質———————— antibiotic
こうせいぶっしつ

レントゲン ————— X-ray

手術 ————————— operation
しゅじゅつ

注射 ————————— injection
ちゅうしゃ

体温計 ———————— thermometer
たいおんけい

読み書き編
よ　か　へん
Reading and Writing Section

第1課 L E S S O N ·······················1
だい いっ か

ひらがな Hiragana

① Hiragana Practice

A. Choose the correct *hiragana*.

1. *yo*　ま　よ　　　　4. *su*　む　す　　　　7. *ta*　た　に

2. *ho*　は　ほ　　　　5. *ki*　さ　き　　　　8. *ro*　ろ　る

3. *me*　ぬ　め　　　　6. *chi*　さ　ち　　　　9. *e*　え　ん

B. Match the words.

Person's name			Place name	
1. たなか ・	・ Sakuma	6. くまもと・	・ Morioka
2. やまもと・	・ Tanaka	7. おかやま・	・ Yokohama
3. さくま ・	・ Morikawa	8. もりおか・	・ Mito
4. たかはし・	・ Takahashi	9. よこはま・	・ Okayama
5. もりかわ・	・ Yamamoto	10. みと ・	・ Kumamoto

C. What's wrong with the *hiragana* below? Rewrite the correct *hiragana*.

1.　　　　2.　　　　3.　　　　4.　　　　5.

ほ　　む　　き　　Ｊ　　あ

D. Write as many *hiragana* as possible which contain the following parts.

1.
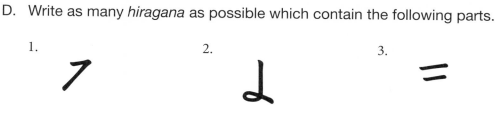

2.

3.

4.

5.

E. Pay attention to the pronunciation and add diacritical marks ﹅ and ﹆ to appropriate *hiragana*.  Y01-1

1. いちこ　　　*ichigo* (strawberry)

4. かいこくしん　　*gaikokujin* (foreigner)

2. たんこ　　　*dango* (dumpling)

5. たんほほ　　　*tanpopo* (dandelion)

3. さふとん　　*zabuton* (cushon)

6. かんへき　　　*ganpeki* (cliff)

F. Pay attention to the pronunciation of each word, and mark with ○ for the correct one. Y01-2

1. *shashin* (photograph)　　　(しやしん ・ しゃしん)

2. *dokusho* (reading)　　　(どくしょ ・ どくしよ)

3. *kyori* (distance)　　　(きょり ・ きより)

4. *hiyasu* (to chill)　　　(ひゃす ・ ひやす)

5. *chairo* (brown)　　　(ちゃいろ ・ ちやいろ)

6. *onna no hito* (woman)　　　(おんなのひと ・ おっなのひと)

7. *kitte* (stamp)　　　(きて ・ きって)

8. *motto* (more)　　　(もつと ・ もっと)

G. Read the following pairs paying attention to the long vowels. 📢 Y01-3

1. おばさん ― おばあさん
   (aunt)　　　　　　(grandmother)

2. おじいさん ― おじさん
   (grandfather)　　　　(uncle)

3. しゅじん ― しゅうじん
   (husband)　　　　(prisoner)

4. おや ― おおや
   (parent)　　　(landlord)

5. せいき ― せき
   (century)　　(seat)

H. Put the *hiragana* in the right order to make sense.

Example:　だともち　→　と も だ ち

1. わんで　＿＿ ＿＿ ＿＿

2. ごいえ　＿＿ ＿＿ ＿＿

3. んほに　＿＿ ＿＿ ＿＿

4. えなま　＿＿ ＿＿ ＿＿

5. んせせい　＿＿ ＿＿ ＿＿ ＿＿

6. がだいく　＿＿ ＿＿ ＿＿ ＿＿

Ⅱ Reading Practice

Read the following people's self-introduction and answer the questions. Refer to vocabulary list on p. 41. 📢 Y01-4

1.

たなか ゆうこです。
かいしゃいんです。

2.

はらだ りょうです。
だいがくせいです。
せんこうは れきしです。

3.

かとう やすおです。
だいがくいんせいです。
せんこうは けいざいです。

4.

わたしの なまえは きたの ひろみです。
こうこうの さんねんせいです。

やまだ まことです。
だいがくせいです。
せんこうは にほんごです。

5.

1. Who is an office worker? _____

2. Whose major is Japanese? _____

3. Who is a high school student? _____

4. What is Harada's major? _____

Ⅲ Writing Practice

You received a letter from a Japanese friend. Read it and write a letter introducing yourself.

> はじめまして、まえかわ みちこです。
> にほんじんです。
> わたしは だいがくの いちねんせいです。
> せんこうは えいごです。
> よろしくおねがいします。

第2課 L E S S O N ⋯⋯⋯2
だい に か

カタカナ Katakana

①Katakana Practice

A. Choose the correct *katakana*.

1. *o* オ ア
2. *nu* ヌ メ
3. *sa* テ サ

4. *shi* シ ツ
5. *ku* ワ ク
6. *ma* マ ム

7. *ru* レ ル
8. *ho* モ ホ
9. *yu* エ ユ

B. Match the following words and pictures.

1. ( ) オレンジジュース
2. ( ) フライドポテト
3. ( ) ケーキ
4. ( ) サラダ
5. ( ) チョコレートパフェ
6. ( ) コーヒー

7. ( ) サンドイッチ
8. ( ) ステーキ
9. ( ) スパゲッティ
10. ( ) ピザ
11. ( ) トースト
12. ( ) レモンティー

(a)

(b)

(c)

(d)

(e)

(f)

(g)

(h)

(i)

(j)

(k)

(l)

C. Match each country with its capital city.

<table>
<tr><td>Countries</td><td></td><td>Capital cities</td></tr>
<tr><td>1. マレーシア</td><td>・</td><td>・オタワ</td></tr>
<tr><td>2. オランダ</td><td>・</td><td>・ワシントンＤＣ</td></tr>
<tr><td>3. アメリカ</td><td>・</td><td>・ニューデリー</td></tr>
<tr><td>4. エジプト</td><td>・</td><td>・アムステルダム</td></tr>
<tr><td>5. オーストラリア</td><td>・</td><td>・クアラルンプール</td></tr>
<tr><td>6. スウェーデン</td><td>・</td><td>・ブエノスアイレス</td></tr>
<tr><td>7. インド</td><td>・</td><td>・キャンベラ</td></tr>
<tr><td>8. アルゼンチン</td><td>・</td><td>・カイロ</td></tr>
<tr><td>9. カナダ</td><td>・</td><td>・ストックホルム</td></tr>
</table>

D. Word Search—Find the following country names in the box of *katakana*.

Example:　ベトナム (Vietnam)

シンガポール (Singapore)
チェコ (Czech)
アメリカ (America)
スウェーデン (Sweden)
エクアドル (Ecuador)
メキシコ (Mexico)
ブラジル (Brazil)
スペイン (Spain)
オランダ (Holland)
インドネシア (Indonesia)
カナダ (Canada)
ルワンダ (Rwanda)
タイ (Thailand)
オーストラリア (Australia)

<table>
<tr><td>イ</td><td>ン</td><td>ド</td><td>ネ</td><td>シ</td><td>ア</td><td>イ</td><td>ル</td><td>ワ</td><td>ン</td><td>ダ</td></tr>
<tr><td>コ</td><td>ウ</td><td>モ</td><td>リ</td><td>ブ</td><td>ク</td><td>ロ</td><td>ク</td><td>マ</td><td>チ</td><td>コ</td></tr>
<tr><td>オ</td><td>ー</td><td>ス</td><td>ト</td><td>ラ</td><td>リ</td><td>ア</td><td>ネ</td><td>コ</td><td>エ</td><td>イ</td></tr>
<tr><td>ラ</td><td>タ</td><td>ウ</td><td>ナ</td><td>ジ</td><td>ア</td><td>メ</td><td>キ</td><td>シ</td><td>コ</td><td>ヌ</td></tr>
<tr><td>ン</td><td>ヌ</td><td>ェ</td><td>メ</td><td>ル</td><td>ヒ</td><td>リ</td><td>ネ</td><td>ズ</td><td>ミ</td><td>ベ</td></tr>
<tr><td>ダ</td><td>キ</td><td>ー</td><td>ク</td><td>ヘ</td><td>ル</td><td>カ</td><td>ナ</td><td>ダ</td><td>ラ</td><td>ト</td></tr>
<tr><td>カ</td><td>モ</td><td>デ</td><td>ジ</td><td>ビ</td><td>ス</td><td>ペ</td><td>イ</td><td>ン</td><td>ク</td><td>ナ</td></tr>
<tr><td>ワ</td><td>シ</td><td>ン</td><td>ガ</td><td>ポ</td><td>ー</td><td>ル</td><td>パ</td><td>ン</td><td>ダ</td><td>ム</td></tr>
<tr><td>タ</td><td>イ</td><td>ゴ</td><td>リ</td><td>ラ</td><td>エ</td><td>ク</td><td>ア</td><td>ド</td><td>ル</td><td>メ</td></tr>
</table>

E. Put the *katakana* in the right order to make sense.

Example: キ ケ ー → <u>ケ ー キ</u>

1. ト ノ ー ___ ___ ___

2. ン ペ ___ ___

3. ニ ュ メ ー ___ ___ ___ ___

4. ン ジ ー ズ ___ ___ ___ ___

Ⓘ Name Tags

Write your name[1] in the box below and make your own name tag.

Example: メ ア リ ー ・ ハ ー ト

メアリー・ハート

---

[1] **Your name in Japanese**

Japanese have only one given name and one surname, which is placed first, as in:

たなか たけし [last—first]

Foreign names are normally written in *katakana* and in its native order. A dot " ・ " or a space is often used between first name and last name.

Mary Hart → メ ア リ ー ・ ハ ー ト or メ ア リ ー ハ ー ト [first—last]

East Asian names such as Korean or Chinese, can be written in kanji.

Yao Ming → ヨ ウ メ イ or 姚 明 [last—first]

Ⅲ Reading Practice

Mary wrote about the things below. Find out which item she wrote about.  Y02

1. (　　)　これは わたしの ぼうしじゃないです。
　　　　　 キャシーさんの ぼうしです。
　　　　　 ニューヨークヤンキースの ぼうしです。

2. (　　)　これは わたしの じてんしゃです。
　　　　　 オーストラリアの じてんしゃです。
　　　　　 たかいです。

3. (　　)　これは ミシェルさんの じしょです。
　　　　　 スペインごの じしょじゃないです。
　　　　　 フランスごの じしょです。

4. (　　)　これは ジャクソンさんの くつです。
　　　　　 イタリアの くつじゃないです。
　　　　　 アメリカの くつです。

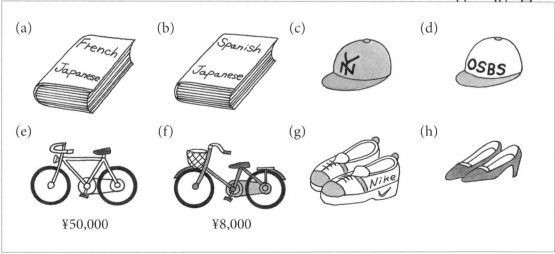

(a)　French Japanese　(b)　Spanish Japanese　(c)　NY　(d)　OSBS

(e)　¥50,000　(f)　¥8,000　(g)　Nike　(h)

Ⅳ Writing Practice

Write about the things you or your classmates own. Use Mary's sentences in Ⅲ as a model.

第3課 L E S S O N ················3
まいにちのせいかつ Daily Life

		読み	用例
001	一 (one)	▶いち　いっ ▷ひと	一(いち) one　一時(いちじ) one o'clock 一年生(いちねんせい) first-year student 一分(いっぷん) one minute　一つ(ひとつ) one (1) 一
002	二 (two)	▶に ▷ふた	二(に) two　二時(にじ) two o'clock 二年生(にねんせい) second-year student　二つ(ふたつ) two 二日間(ふつかかん) two days (2) 一　二
003	三 (three)	▶さん ▷みっ	三(さん) three　三時(さんじ) three o'clock 三年生(さんねんせい) third-year student 三月(さんがつ) March　三つ(みっつ) three (3) 一　二　三
004	四 (four)	▶し ▷よん　よ 　よっ	四(よん) four　四時(よじ) four o'clock 四年生(よねんせい) fourth-year student 四月(しがつ) April　四つ(よっつ) four (5) 1　冂　冃　四　四
005	五 (five)	▶ご ▷いつ	五(ご) five　五時(ごじ) five o'clock 五月(ごがつ) May　五歳(ごさい) five years old 五つ(いつつ) five (4) 一　丁　万　五
006	六 (six)	▶ろく　ろっ ▷むっ	六(ろく) six　六時(ろくじ) six o'clock 六百(ろっぴゃく) six hundred 六分(ろっぷん) six minutes　六つ(むっつ) six (4) 亠　宀　六
007	七 (seven)	▶しち ▷なな	七(しち／なな) seven　七時(しちじ) seven o'clock 七月(しちがつ) July　七つ(ななつ) seven 七人(ななにん／しちにん) seven people (2) 一　七
008	八 (eight)	▶はち　はっ ▷やっ	八(はち) eight　八時(はちじ) eight o'clock 八百(はっぴゃく) eight hundred 八歳(はっさい) eight years old　八つ(やっつ) eight (2) ノ　八

009	九 (nine)	▶きゅう　く ▷ここの	九(きゅう) nine　九時(くじ) nine o'clock 九月(くがつ) September　九歳(きゅうさい) nine years old 九つ(ここのつ) nine
			(2) ノ　九
010	十 (ten)	▶じゅう 　じゅっ　じっ ▷とお	十(じゅう) ten　十時(じゅうじ) ten o'clock 十月(じゅうがつ) October 十歳(じゅっさい／じっさい) ten years old　十(とお) ten
			(2) 一　十
011	百 (hundred)	▶ひゃく 　びゃく 　ぴゃく	百(ひゃく) hundred　三百(さんびゃく) three hundred 六百(ろっぴゃく) six hundred　八百(はっぴゃく) eight hundred
			(6) 一　ア　ア　百　百　百
012	千 (thousand)	▶せん　ぜん	千(せん) thousand　三千(さんぜん) three thousand 八千(はっせん) eight thousand 千円(せんえん) one thousand yen
			(3) ノ　二　千
013	万 (ten thousand)	▶まん	一万(いちまん) ten thousand 十万(じゅうまん) one hundred thousand 百万(ひゃくまん) one million
			(3) 一　ア　万
014	円 (yen; circle)	▶えん ▷まる	百円(ひゃくえん) one hundred yen 円(えん) circle　円高(えんだか) strong yen 円い(まるい) round
			(4) 丨　冂　冃　円
015	時 (time)	▶じ ▷とき	一時(いちじ) one o'clock 子どもの時(こどものとき) in one's childhood 時々(ときどき) sometimes　時計(とけい) watch; clock
			(10) 丨　冂　日　日　日ー　日十　昉　昁　時　時

(▶ indicates the *on-yomi* [pronunciation originally borrowed from Chinese] and ▷ indicates the *kun-yomi* [native Japanese reading].)

① 漢字の練習 (Kanji Practice)
かん じ　れんしゅう

A. Read the price of the following items in kanji and write it in numbers.

Example: チョコレート

百五十円

（¥ 150 ）

1. ハンカチ

六百五十円

（¥　　　）

2. せんす

千八百円

（¥　　　）

3. きもの

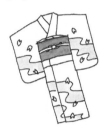

七十一万四千円

（¥　　　　　）

4. テレビ

十二万三千円

（¥　　　　　）

5. いえ

三千九百万円

（¥　　　　　　）

B. Write the following prices in kanji.

Example:　¥5,420　→　　五千四百二十円

1. ¥30　＿＿＿＿＿＿＿＿

2. ¥140　＿＿＿＿＿＿＿＿

3. ¥251　＿＿＿＿＿＿＿＿

4. ¥6,070　＿＿＿＿＿＿＿＿

5. ¥8,190　＿＿＿＿＿＿＿＿

6. ¥42,500　＿＿＿＿＿＿＿＿＿＿

7. ¥168,000　＿＿＿＿＿＿＿＿＿＿

8. ¥3,200,000　＿＿＿＿＿＿＿＿＿＿

9. ¥57,000,000　＿＿＿＿＿＿＿＿＿＿

Ⅱ まいにちのせいかつ

A student writes about his daily routine. Read the passage and find out about his schedule and fill in the blanks below. 🔊 Y03

わたしはまいにち七時におきます。うちであさごはんをたべます。八時にだいがくへいきます。九時ににほんごをべんきょうします。十二時半にだいがくでひるごはんをたべます。ときどきコーヒーをのみます。四時にとしょかんでほんをよみます。六時ごろうちへかえります。十時にテレビをみます。十二時ごろねます。

7:00 _____

(   ) go to the university

9:00 _____

(   ) eat lunch

4:00 _____

6:00 _____

(   ) watch TV

(   ) _____

Ⅲ 書く練習 (Writing Practice)

Write about your daily routine. Use the above passage as a model.

第4課 L E S S O N ⋯⋯⋯4
メアリーさんのしゅうまつ Mary's Weekend

016	日 (day; sun)	▶に にち にっ ▷び ひ か	日本(にほん) Japan　日曜日(にちようび) Sunday 毎日(まいにち) every day　母の日(ははのひ) Mother's Day 日記(にっき) diary　三日(みっか) three days (4) 丨 冂 日 日
017	本 (book; basis)	▶ほん ▷もと	本(ほん) book　日本(にほん) Japan 日本語(にほんご) Japanese language 山本さん(やまもとさん) Mr./Ms. Yamamoto (5) 一 十 オ 木 本
018	人 (person)	▶じん にん ▷ひと	日本人(にほんじん) Japanese people 一人で(ひとりで) alone　この人(このひと) this person 三人(さんにん) three people (2) ノ 人
019	月 (moon; month)	▶げつ がつ ▷つき	月曜日(げつようび) Monday　一月(いちがつ) January 月(つき) moon　今月(こんげつ) this month 一か月(いっかげつ) one month (4) 丿 刀 月 月
020	火 (fire)	▶か ▷ひ び	火曜日(かようび) Tuesday 火(ひ) fire　火山(かざん) volcano　花火(はなび) fireworks 火星(かせい) Mars (4) 丶 丷 少 火
021	水 (water)	▶すい ▷みず	水曜日(すいようび) Wednesday　水(みず) water 水泳(すいえい) swimming　水道(すいどう) water supply 水着(みずぎ) bathing suit (4) 亅 オ 가 水
022	木 (tree)	▶もく ▷き	木曜日(もくようび) Thursday 木(き) tree　木村さん(きむらさん) Mr./Ms. Kimura (4) 一 十 オ 木
023	金 (gold; money)	▶きん ▷かね	金曜日(きんようび) Friday お金(おかね) money　料金(りょうきん) charge お金持ち(おかねもち) rich person (8) ノ 人 ᐱ 仐 仐 全 余 金

No.	Kanji	Readings	Examples / Stroke order
024	土	▶ど　と ▷つち (soil)	土曜日（どようび）Saturday 土（つち）soil　土地（とち）land　粘土（ねんど）clay (3) 一　十　土
025	曜	▶よう (weekday)	日曜日（にちようび）Sunday 曜日（ようび）day of the week (18) 丨 冂 冃 日 日ᄀ 日ᄏ 日ᄏ 日ᄏᄀ 日ᄏᄏ 日羽 日羽 日羽 日羽 日羽 日羽 曜 曜 曜
026	上	▶じょう ▷うえ　のぼ (up)	上（うえ）top; above 上手な（じょうずな）good at　屋上（おくじょう）rooftop 上る（のぼる）to go up (3) 丨　⺊　上
027	下	▶か ▷した　くだ (down)	下（した）under 地下鉄（ちかてつ）subway　下手な（へたな）poor at 下さい（ください）Please give/do . . . (3) 一　丅　下
028	中	▶ちゅう 　じゅう ▷なか (middle)	中（なか）inside 中国（ちゅうごく）China　中学（ちゅうがく）junior high school 一年中（いちねんじゅう）all year around (4) 丨　冂　口　中
029	半	▶はん (half)	三時半（さんじはん）half past three 半分（はんぶん）half　半年（はんとし）half a year 半額（はんがく）half price (5) ヽ　ソ　䒑　兰　半

(▶ indicates the *on-yomi* and ▷ indicates the *kun-yomi*.)

Ⅰ 漢字の練習 (Kanji Practice)
かん じ れんしゅう

A. Match the kanji with the English equivalents.

1. 水曜日・   ・Sunday

2. 金曜日・   ・Monday

3. 日曜日・   ・Tuesday

4. 月曜日・   ・Wednesday

5. 土曜日・   ・Thursday

6. 木曜日・   ・Friday

7. 火曜日・   ・Saturday

B. Look at the picture and choose the appropriate kanji for the blanks.

上　下　中

1. レストランはビルの＿＿＿＿＿＿です。
(building)

2. 日本語学校はレストランの＿＿＿＿＿＿です。
ご がっこう

3. スーパーはレストランの＿＿＿＿＿＿です。

Ⅱ おかあさんへのメモ

メアリーさんはおかあさんにメモをかきました。
Read the memo and answer the questions.

1. メアリーさんはきょうなにをしますか。

2. うちでばんごはんをたべますか。

3. 何時ごろかえりますか。
なん

おかあさんへ
きょうは ともだちと だい
がくで べんきょうします。
うちで ばんごはんを
たべません。
九時半ごろ かえります。

十月二十一日
メアリー

Ⅲ メアリーさんのしゅうまつ

Read the following passage about Mary's weekend. 🔊 Y04

金曜日に日本人のともだちとこうえんにいきました。こうえんでともだちとはなしました。それから、レストランへいきました。たくさんたべました。

土曜日は一人でおてらへいきました。たくさんみせがありました。みせでおまんじゅうをかいました。

日曜日はおそくおきました。おかあさんもおそくおきました。わたしはあさテレビをみました。それから、おかあさんとひるごはんをたべました。ごごは日本語をべんきょうしました。本もよみました。

みせ　　　shop; store
おまんじゅう　sweet bun
おそく　(do something) late

Answer the following activities in the order Mary did them.

(　　) → (　　) → (　　) → (　　) → (　　)

(a) studied Japanese　　(b) went to a restaurant　　(c) went to a park
(d) bought sweet buns　(e) watched TV

Ⅳ 書く練習 (Writing Practice)

A. You are going out. Write a memo to someone in your house, telling when you will be back and whether you will have dinner at home.

B. Write about your weekend.

第5課 ｜ L E S S O N ⋯⋯⋯⋯⋯⋯5
りょこう Travel

030	山	▶さん ▷やま (mountain)	山 (やま) mountain 山川さん (やまかわさん) Mr./Ms. Yamakawa 富士山 (ふじさん) Mt. Fuji (3) 丨 山 山
031	川	▷かわ がわ (river)	川 (かわ) river　山川さん (やまかわさん) Mr./Ms. Yamakawa 小川さん (おがわさん) Mr./Ms. Ogawa (3) ノ 川 川
032	元	▶げん がん ▷もと (origin)	元気な (げんきな) fine 元日 (がんじつ) the first day of the year　地元 (じもと) local (4) 一 二 テ 元
033	気	▶き (spirit)	元気な (げんきな) fine　天気 (てんき) weather 電気 (でんき) electricity　気持ち (きもち) feeling 人気 (にんき) popularity (6) ノ 一 气 气 気 気
034	天	▶てん (heaven)	天気 (てんき) weather 天国 (てんごく) heaven　天皇 (てんのう) Japanese emperor 天才 (てんさい) genius (4) 一 二 チ 天
035	私	▶し ▷わたし (I; private)	私 (わたし) I 私立大学 (しりつだいがく) private university 私鉄 (してつ) private railroad (7) 一 二 千 禾 禾 私 私
036	今	▶こん ▷いま (now)	今 (いま) now　今日 (きょう) today 今晩 (こんばん) tonight　今月 (こんげつ) this month 今年 (ことし) this year (4) ノ 人 今 今
037	田	▷た だ (rice field)	田中さん (たなかさん) Mr./Ms. Tanaka 山田さん (やまださん) Mr./Ms. Yamada 田んぼ (たんぼ) rice field (5) 丨 冂 冂 田 田

038	女 (woman)	▶じょ ▷おんな	女の人(おんなのひと) woman 女性(じょせい) woman　女の子(おんなのこ) girl 長女(ちょうじょ) the eldest daughter
			(3) く　夕　女
039	男 (man)	▶だん ▷おとこ	男の人(おとこのひと) man 男性(だんせい) man　男の子(おとこのこ) boy 男子学生(だんしがくせい) male student
			(7) 一　冂　冂　田　田　男　男
040	見 (to see)	▶けん ▷み	見る(みる) to see 見物(けんぶつ) sightseeing　花見(はなみ) flower viewing 意見(いけん) opinion
			(7) 丨　冂　冂　目　目　目　見
041	行 (to go)	▶こう　ぎょう ▷い	行く(いく) to go 銀行(ぎんこう) bank　一行目(いちぎょうめ) first line 旅行(りょこう) travel
			(6) ノ　ク　イ　行　行　行
042	食 (to eat)	▶しょく ▷た	食べる(たべる) to eat 食べ物(たべもの) food　食堂(しょくどう) cafeteria 食事(しょくじ) meal　朝食(ちょうしょく) breakfast
			(9) ノ　人　人　今　今　今　食　食　食
043	飲 (to drink)	▶いん ▷の	飲む(のむ) to drink 飲み物(のみもの) drink 飲酒運転(いんしゅうんてん) drunken driving
			(12) ノ　人　人　今　今　今　食　食　食　飲　飲　飲

(▶ indicates the *on-yomi* and ▷ indicates the *kun-yomi*.)

Ⅰ 漢字の練習 (Kanji Practice)

A. Using the parts below, make up the correct kanji.

Example: 目 → 見

1. 艮   3. ム   5. カ   7. ハ   9. メ

2. 欠   4. 二   6. 气   8. 良   10. 田

B. Match the following sentences with the pictures.

1. (　　) えいがを見ます。
2. (　　) コーヒーを飲みます。
3. (　　) ハンバーガーを食べます。
4. (　　) 男の人と女の人がいます。
5. (　　) 山と川があります。
6. (　　) 今日はいい天気です。
7. (　　) 銀行に行きます。
   ぎんこう

C. Match the kanji with the reading.

1. (　　) 一日   4. (　　) 四日   7. (　　) 七日   10. (　　) 十日
2. (　　) 二日   5. (　　) 五日   8. (　　) 八日   11. (　　) 二十日
3. (　　) 三日   6. (　　) 六日   9. (　　) 九日

(a) いつか　(b) ここのか　(c) ついたち　(d) とおか　(e) なのか　(f) はつか
(g) ふつか　(h) みっか　(i) むいか　(j) ようか　(k) よっか

Ⅱ りょこうのはがき

A. Match the following *katakana* words with the English equivalents.

1. コーヒー　・ 　　　　　　・ cake
2. コンサート・ 　　　　　　・ coffee
3. ウィーン　・ 　　　　　　・ cafe
4. カフェ　　・ 　　　　　　・ classical music
5. クラシック・ 　　　　　　・ concert
6. ケーキ　　・ 　　　　　　・ Vienna

B. ようこさんはみちこさんにはがきをかきました。

Read the postcard below. Write ○ for the things she did or does and write ×
for the things she didn't or doesn't do in Vienna. 🔊 Y05-1

1. (　　) see an old castle
2. (　　) go to see a ballet
3. (　　) take pictures

4. (　　) drink beer at the cafe
5. (　　) enjoy sweets
6. (　　) eat at McDonald's

みちこさんへ
　元気ですか。私は今ウィーンにいます。ここは
ちょっとさむいです。ウィーンはとてもきれいな
まちです。
　きのうはおしろを見ました。ふるかった
ですが、とてもきれいでした。たくさんしゃしんを
とりました。よるはクラシックのコンサートに
行きました。よかったです。
　ウィーンにはカフェがたくさんあります。
まいにちカフェでコーヒーを飲みます。ケーキも
食べます。すごくおいしいです。四日にかえります。
また日本であいましょうね。
　　　　　　　　　山田 ようこ

〒305-0836

つくば市山中42-5

山川 みちこさま

Japan

～さま　Mr./Ms. (used in letter writing)　　おしろ　castle
　　　～が　…, but　　　よる　night　　　また　again

C. ロバートさんもともだちにはがきをかきました。
Read the postcard below and answer the following questions in Japanese.

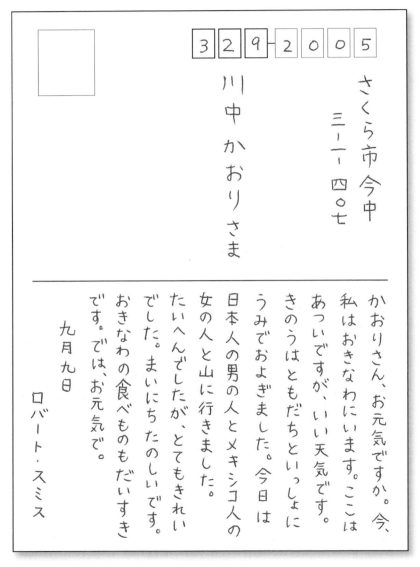 Y05-2

1. ロバートさんは今どこにいますか。

2. どんな天気ですか。

3. きのうは なにをしましたか。

4. 今日は なにをしましたか。だれとしましたか。

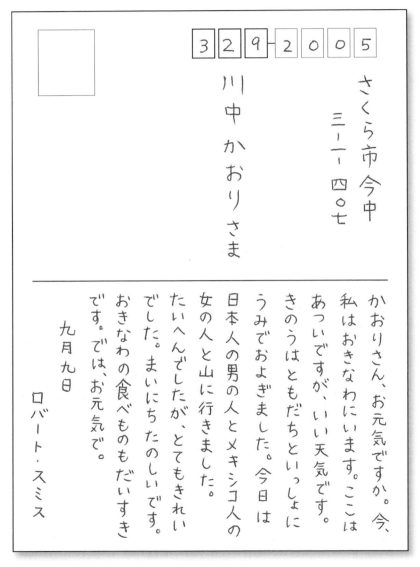

メキシコ　Mexico　　山　mountain
たいへん（な）　tough　　では、お元気で　Take care.

(Ⅲ)書く練習 (Writing Practice)
か れんしゅう

The following are your Japanese friends' addresses in your pocket notebook.
Copy their addresses on the postcards and write about your vacation.

名　前 な　まえ	住　　所 じゅう　しょ
今中ゆみ いまなか	〒753-0041　山口県山口市東山 36-8 やまぐちけんやまぐち し ひがしやま
上田一男 うえ だ かず お	〒112-0002　東京都文京区小石川 7-7 とうきょう と ぶんきょうく こ いしかわ

Japanese addresses

Japanese addresses start with the postal code followed by the prefecture, city, and neighborhoods as follows:

(1) 〒 (2) 753－0041
(3) 山口県 (4) 山口市 (5) 東山 (6) 36－8
やまぐちけん　やまぐち し　ひがしやま
(7) 今中ゆみ (8) 様
いまなか　　　さま

(1) postal symbol　　(4) city, village, etc.　　(7) name
(2) postal code　　(5) neighborhoods　　(8) "Mr./Ms."
(3) prefecture　　(6) block number and house number

Note that, like all Japanese texts, addresses can be written vertically as well as horizontally.

第6課 | L E S S O N ·················· 6
私のすきなレストラン My Favorite Restaurant

044	東 (east)	▶とう ▷ひがし	東(ひがし) east　東口(ひがしぐち) east exit 東京(とうきょう) Tokyo　関東(かんとう) Kanto area 東洋(とうよう) the East
			(8) 一 ㇒ 戸 両 亘 車 東 東
045	西 (west)	▶せい　さい ▷にし	西(にし) west　西口(にしぐち) west exit 北西(ほくせい) northwest　関西(かんさい) Kansai area 西洋(せいよう) the West
			(6) 一 ㇒ 両 两 西 西
046	南 (south)	▶なん ▷みなみ	南(みなみ) south　南口(みなみぐち) south exit 南東(なんとう) southeast　南極(なんきょく) Antarctica 東南アジア(とうなんアジア) Southeast Asia
			(9) 一 十 广 声 内 两 南 南 南
047	北 (north)	▶ほく　ほっ ▷きた	北(きた) north　北口(きたぐち) north exit 東北(とうほく) Tohoku area　北極(ほっきょく) North Pole 北海道(ほっかいどう) Hokkaido
			(5) ㇀ 十 圠 北 北
048	口 (mouth)	▶こう ▷ぐち　くち	北口(きたぐち) north exit 口(くち) mouth　人口(じんこう) population 入り口／入口(いりぐち) entrance
			(3) 丨 冂 口
049	出 (to exit)	▶しゅっ 　しゅつ ▷で　だ	出る(でる) to exit　出口(でぐち) exit 出す(だす) to take something out　出席(しゅっせき) attendance 輸出(ゆしゅつ) export
			(5) 丨 屮 屮 出 出
050	右 (right)	▶う　ゆう ▷みぎ	右(みぎ) right 右折(うせつ) right turn　左右(さゆう) right and left 右手(みぎて) right hand　右側(みぎがわ) right side
			(5) ノ ナ 才 右 右
051	左 (left)	▶さ ▷ひだり	左(ひだり) left 左折(させつ) left turn　左手(ひだりて) left hand 左利き(ひだりきき) left-handed
			(5) 一 ナ 左 左 左

052	分	▶ぶん ぷん ぶん ▷わ (minute; to divide)	五分(ごふん) five minutes
			十分(じゅっぷん／じっぷん) ten minutes
			自分(じぶん) oneself　分ける(わける) to divide
			(4) ノ 八 分 分
053	先	▶せん ▷さき (ahead)	先生(せんせい) teacher
			先週(せんしゅう) last week　先に(さきに) ahead
			先月(せんげつ) last month　先輩(せんぱい) senior member
			(6) ノ ⺧ ⺧ 生 先 先
054	生	▶せい しょう ▷う (birth)	学生(がくせい) student　先生(せんせい) teacher
			生まれる(うまれる) to be born
			一生に一度(いっしょうにいちど) once in a life time
			(5) ノ ⺧ 牛 生 生
055	大	▶だい たい ▷おお (big)	大学生(だいがくせい) college student　大きい(おおきい) big
			大変な(たいへんな) tough　大人(おとな) adult
			大使館(たいしかん) embassy
			(3) 一 ナ 大
056	学	▶がく がっ ▷まな (learning)	大学(だいがく) university　学生(がくせい) student
			学校(がっこう) school　学ぶ(まなぶ) to study
			学部(がくぶ) department; faculty
			(8) ⺀ ⺀ ⺍ ⺍ ⺍ 学 学 学
057	外	▶がい ▷そと (outside)	外国(がいこく) foreign country
			外国人(がいこくじん) foreigner
			外(そと) outside　海外(かいがい) overseas
			(5) ノ ク タ 外 外
058	国	▶こく ごく こっ ▷くに (country)	外国(がいこく) foreign country　中国(ちゅうごく) China
			国(くに) country　韓国(かんこく) South Korea
			国会(こっかい) the Diet
			(8) 丨 冂 冂 冂 囝 国 国 国

(▶ indicates the *on-yomi* and ▷ indicates the *kun-yomi*.)

① 漢字の練習 (Kanji Practice)

A. Combine the following kanji and make compound words. You can use the same kanji more than once.

Example: 外 + 国 → 外国

気　生　外　先　学　天　日　国　今　大

B. Indicate where each place is located on the map.

1. (　　) レストラン・アルデンテ：えきの中にあります。南口の近くです。

2. (　　) ロイヤルホテル：えきの東口を出て、まっすぐ五分ぐらいです。

3. (　　) 山下先生のうち：北口を出て、右へ十分ぐらいです。

4. (　　) こうえん：西口をまっすぐ十五分ぐらい行ってください。

5. (　　) 大学：北口を出て、左へ十分ぐらい行ってください。

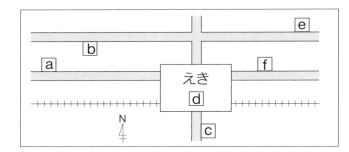

えき　　　station
出る　　　to exit
まっすぐ　straight

② でんごんばん (Bulletin Board)

Look at the bulletin board on the next page and answer the questions.

1. If you want to buy a bicycle, who are you going to contact?

2. Where will the party be held? Are you going to bring anything?

3. How do you get to the concert hall?

4. What can you do for the winter break (from December to January)?

ホームステイ
プログラム

東北のまちでホームステイをしませんか。
とうほく
十二月二十八日（日）〜 一月三日（土）
きれいな山と川の近くです。
　　　　　　　　　ちか

えいごをおしえてください。
日本人の大学生です。
９３１−２６８２
　　　　　　ようこ

セール!!
じてんしゃ
¥8,000

あたらしいです。
でんわしてください。
（よる7時〜11時）

　山田　597-1651

ハロウィーン パーティー

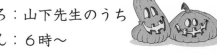

ところ：山下先生のうち
じかん：6時〜
ともだちをつれてきてもいいですよ！
飲みものをもってきてください。

イタリアンレストラン
マンジャーレ

ランチ 1,200 円
Ａセット（サラダ・コーヒー）
Ｂセット（パン・コーヒー）

ギターコンサート

11月12日（金）
6：30〜

西コンサートホール
（西駅3出口を出て左へ3分）
　えき

Ⅲ 私のすきなレストラン

Chiaki writes about her favorite restaurant. Read the passage and answer the questions. 🔊 Y06

私のすきなレストラン

　私のすきなレストランは、イタリアりょうりのマンジャーレです。えきの南口を出て、右へ五分ぐらいです。ちいさいレストランです。シェフはイタリア人のアントニオさんです。アントニオさんはとてもおもしろい人です。アントニオさんのりょうりはとてもおいしいです。私はよくマンジャーレに行きます。マンジャーレでワインを飲んで、ピザを食べます。アイスクリームもおいしいです。ここでいつもたくさん食べます。りょうりはやすいですから。外国人もたくさんきます。みなさんもきてください。

イタリア	Italy	ピザ	pizza
りょうり	cooking; dish	いつも	always
シェフ	chef	みなさん	everyone
ワイン	wine		

A. Where is the restaurant?

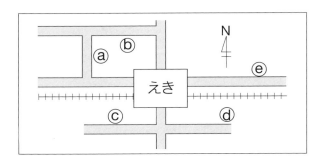

B. Circle the food or drink the writer has at the restaurant.

> ピザ　　スパゲッティ　　アイスクリーム
>
> ワイン　　ビール　　ステーキ

C. Choose the correct answer.

1. マンジャーレは $\left\{ \begin{array}{l} 大きい \\ ちいさい \end{array} \right\}$ レストランです。

2. マンジャーレは $\left\{ \begin{array}{l} たかい \\ やすい \end{array} \right\}$ です。

3. アントニオさんは $\left\{ \begin{array}{l} おもしろい \\ つまらない \end{array} \right\}$ 人です。

4. マンジャーレに外国人が $\left\{ \begin{array}{l} きます。 \\ きません。 \end{array} \right\}$

Ⅳ 書く練習 (Writing Practice)
か　　れんしゅう

A. You are organizing a party. Write a flyer about the party. Be sure to include: what kind of party it is, what time it starts, where it is held, what to bring, how to get there, and so on.

B. Write about your favorite restaurant.

第7課｜L E S S O N ·······7
メアリーさんのてがみ Mary's Letter

059	京 (capital)	▶きょう	東京(とうきょう) Tokyo　京子(きょうこ) Kyoko 京都(きょうと) Kyoto 上京する(じょうきょうする) to go to the capital
			(8) ’ 一 十 古 古 京 京 京
060	子 (child)	▶し ▷こ	子ども(こども) child　京子(きょうこ) Kyoko 女の子(おんなのこ) girl　男の子(おとこのこ) boy 電子辞書(でんしじしょ) electronic dictionary
			(3) ⁊ 了 子
061	小 (small)	▶しょう ▷ちい	小さい(ちいさい) small 小学校(しょうがっこう) elementary school 小学生(しょうがくせい) elementary school student
			(3) 亅 小 小
062	会 (to meet)	▶かい ▷あ	会う(あう) to meet　会社(かいしゃ) company 会社員(かいしゃいん) office worker 会議(かいぎ) meeting　教会(きょうかい) church
			(6) ノ 人 人 ム 会 会
063	社 (company)	▶しゃ じゃ	会社(かいしゃ) company 神社(じんじゃ) shrine　社会(しゃかい) society 入社(にゅうしゃ) entry to a company
			(7) ` ⁊ ネ ネ ネ 社 社
064	父 (father)	▶ふ ▷ちち とう	父(ちち) father　お父さん(おとうさん) father 父母(ふぼ) father and mother　祖父(そふ) grandfather
			(4) ⺍ ハ 父 父
065	母 (mother)	▶ぼ ▷はは かあ	母(はは) mother　お母さん(おかあさん) mother 母語(ほご) mother tongue　祖母(そぼ) grandmother
			(5) ㇄ 凵 母 母 母
066	高 (high)	▶こう ▷たか	高い(たかい) expensive; high　高校(こうこう) high school 高校生(こうこうせい) high school student 最高(さいこう) the best
			(10) ’ 一 十 古 古 亭 高 高 高 高

067	校 (school)	▸こう	学校（がっこう）school　高校（こうこう）high school 高校生（こうこうせい）high school student 中学校（ちゅうがっこう）junior high school
			⑽ 一 十 才 木 术 朽 柞 柊 校 校
068	毎 (every)	▸まい	毎日（まいにち）every day 毎週（まいしゅう）every week　毎晩（まいばん）every night 毎年（まいねん／まいとし）every year
			⑹ 丿 𠂉 仁 乞 每 毎
069	語 (word)	▸ご	日本語（にほんご）Japanese language 英語（えいご）English language 敬語（けいご）honorific expressions
			⒁ 丶 亠 亍 言 言 言 訂 訝 語 語 語 語
070	文 (sentence)	▸ぶん	文学（ぶんがく）literature 作文（さくぶん）composition　文字（もじ）letter; character 文化（ぶんか）culture　文法（ぶんぽう）grammar
			⑷ 丶 亠 ナ 文
071	帰 (to return)	▸き ▷かえ	帰る（かえる）to return 帰国（きこく）going home　帰宅（きたく）returning home 帰り（かえり）return
			⑽ 丿 刂 刂 刂 刂 归 帰 帰 帰 帰
072	入 (to enter)	▸にゅう ▷はい い いり	入る（はいる）to enter 入り口／入口（いりぐち）entrance 入れる（いれる）to put something in　輸入（ゆにゅう）import
			⑵ 丿 入

(▶ indicates the *on-yomi* and ▷ indicates the *kun-yomi*.)

① 漢字の練習
かんじ　れんしゅう

A. Fill in the blanks with the appropriate kanji.

1. 日本 _____ 学　　高 _____ 三年生
ねん　　　　　_____ と母
父　文　校

2. _____ 日、_____ は六時におきます。
母　毎

3. 日本 _____ はよくおふろに _____ ります。
人　入

4. 東 _____ に行きました。食べものは _____ かったです。
京　高

B. Which new kanji from this lesson include the *katakana* below?

Example: エ → 左

1. ヨ →　　　　2. ネ →　　　　3. ム →　　　　4. ロ →

C. Word Search—Find seven kanji compounds from this lesson and six review compounds.

Example: 先生

帰	父	文	学	山	西
行	食	高	校	女	田
東	会	出	口	毎	日
京	社	母	天	時	本
右	中	元	気	先	語
外	国	人	左	生	男

Ⅱ メアリーさんのてがみ

京子さんは今アリゾナにすんでいます。メアリーさんは京子さんにてがみをかきました。🔊 Y07

京子さんへ

京子さん、お元気ですか。アリゾナはあついですか。日本はすこしさむいです。今、私は日本のかぞくと大学のちかくにすんでいます。ここは小さくて、しずかなまちです。

私のかぞくは四人です。みんなとてもしんせつで、たのしいです。お父さんは会社につとめています。いそがしくて、毎日おそく帰ります。お母さんはとてもおもしろい人です。いっしょによくはなします。いもうとは高校生です。らいねん大学ですから、よくべんきょうします。毎日学校から帰って、すぐじゅくへ行きます。日本の高校生は

たいへんですね。おにいさんは東京の大学に行っていますから、あまり会いません。

私は今、日本語と日本文学のクラスをとっています。テニスサークルにも入っています。とてもおもしろいです。

京子さんはいつ日本に帰りますか。日本で会いましょうね。たのしみにしています。

からだに気をつけてください。

十一月三日

メアリー・ハート

すこし	a little
みんな	all
～から	from ...
じゅく	cram school
文学	literature
とる	to take (a class)
(～を)たのしみにする	to look forward (to)
からだに気をつける	to take care of oneself

Summarize what Mary wrote about the following topics in Japanese.

    1. Japan: _____

    2. Her town: _____

    3. Father: _____

    4. Mother: _____

    5. Sister: _____

    6. Brother: _____

    7. School: _____

Ⅲ 書く練習
か　　れんしゅう

A. Write about the following topics.

    1. 日本は／私の国は_____

    _____

    2. 私のまちは_____

    _____

    3. かぞくは_____

    _____

    4. ともだちは_____

    _____

B. Write a letter to a Japanese friend. Describe your town, host family, friends, and so on.

第8課 LESSON 8
日本の会社員 Japanese Office Workers

073	員	▶いん (member)	会社員 (かいしゃいん) office worker 店員 (てんいん) store clerk　会員 (かいいん) member 駅員 (えきいん) station attendant
			(10) ` 丨 冂 冂 員 員 員 員 員 員 員
074	新	▶しん ▷あたら (new)	新しい (あたらしい) new　新聞 (しんぶん) newspaper 新幹線 (しんかんせん) Bullet Train 新鮮な (しんせんな) fresh
			(13) ` 亠 䒑 立 立 辛 辛 亲 新 新 新
075	聞	▶ぶん ▷き (to listen)	聞く (きく) to listen　新聞 (しんぶん) newspaper 聞こえる (きこえる) can be heard
			(14) 丨 冂 冃 冃 門 門 門 門 門 問 問 問 聞 聞
076	作	▶さく ▷つく (to make)	作る (つくる) to make 作文 (さくぶん) composition　作品 (さくひん) artistic piece 作者 (さくしゃ) author
			(7) ノ 亻 亻 亿 作 作 作
077	仕	▶し ▷つか (to serve)	仕事 (しごと) job 仕返し (しかえし) revenge 仕える (つかえる) to serve; to work under
			(5) ノ 亻 仁 什 仕
078	事	▶じ ▷ごと　こと (thing)	仕事 (しごと) job 事 (こと) thing　火事 (かじ) fire　食事 (しょくじ) meal 返事 (へんじ) reply
			(8) 一 亠 亖 亖 写 写 事 事
079	電	▶でん (electricity)	電車 (でんしゃ) train　電気 (でんき) electricity 電話 (でんわ) telephone　電池 (でんち) battery 電子辞書 (でんしじしょ) electronic dictionary
			(13) 一 冖 戸 币 币 币 雨 雨 雨 雪 雪 雷 電
080	車	▶しゃ ▷くるま (car)	車 (くるま) car　電車 (でんしゃ) train 自転車 (じてんしゃ) bicycle　車いす (くるまいす) wheel chair 駐車場 (ちゅうしゃじょう) parking lot
			(7) 一 厂 厅 戸 百 亘 車

081	休 (to rest)	▶きゅう ▷やす	休む (やすむ) to be absent; to rest 休み (やすみ) holiday; absence 休日 (きゅうじつ) holiday
			(6) ノ イ 仁 什 休 休
082	言 (to say)	▶げん ▷い こと	言う (いう) to say 言語学 (げんごがく) linguistics　方言 (ほうげん) dialect 言葉 (ことば) word; language
			(7) 、 二 亠 三 言 言 言
083	読 (to read)	▶どく ▷よ	読む (よむ) to read 読書 (どくしょ) reading books 読み物 (よみもの) reading matter
			(14) 、 ユ 亠 言 言 言 訂 訂 詰 詰 誄 読 読
084	思 (to think)	▶し ▷おも	思う (おもう) to think 不思議な (ふしぎな) mysterious 思い出す (おもいだす) to recall; to remember
			(9) 丨 冂 冊 田 田 甲 思 思 思
085	次 (next)	▶じ ▷つぎ	次 (つぎ) next 次女 (じじょ) second daughter 目次 (もくじ) table of contents　次回 (じかい) next time
			(6) 、 冫 冫 ア 次 次
086	何 (what)	▷なに なん	何 (なに) what　何時 (なんじ) what time 何人 (なんにん) how many people 何か (なにか) something
			(7) ノ イ 仁 仃 佢 佢 何

(▶ indicates the *on-yomi* and ▷ indicates the *kun-yomi*.)

Ⅰ 漢字の練習
かん じ れんしゅう

A. Using the parts below, make up as many kanji as possible.

Example: 乂 → 文 父

1. 言   2. 木   3. 日   4. 田   5. イ   6. 口

B. Match the following phrases with an appropriate verb.

1. 新聞を　・　　　　　　　・作る
2. 音楽を　・　　　　　　　・休む
　 おんがく
3. 仕事を　・　　　　　　　・読む
4. 日本語はおもしろいと・　　・する
5. ハンバーガーを・　　　　・思う
6. 電車に　・　　　　　　　・聞く
7. クラスを・　　　　　　　・のる

Ⅱ 日本の会社員

A. 留学生のウデイさんはアンケートを作って、日本人の会社員に聞きました。
　 りゅう
Read the following questionnaire.

アンケート

1. 仕事のストレスがありますか。

□ はい　　　　□ いいえ

2. よく残業をしますか。
　 ざんぎょう
□ よくする　　□ ときどきする

□ ぜんぜんしない

3. 仕事の後、何をしますか。
　 あと
4. 休みはたいてい何をしますか。

アンケート	questionnaire
ストレス	stress
残業（ざんぎょう）	overtime work
〜の後（〜のあと）	after ...

B. How would you answer the above questions?

C. ウデイさんはアンケートについてレポートを書きました。
Read the report below and answer the questions. 🕪 Y08

日本の会社員

ウデイ・クマール

　日本人の会社員は、電車の中で、ときどき新聞を読んでいますが、たいていみんな寝ています。みんなとても疲れていると思います。私はアンケートを作って、会社員十人に聞きました。

　まず、「仕事のストレスがありますか」と聞きました。九人は「はい」と答えました。「仕事が大変で、休みがあまりない」と言っていました。次に、「よく残業をしますか」と聞きました。三人は「よく残業をする」と言っていました。五人は「ときどき残業をする」と言っていました。次に「仕事の後、何をしますか」と聞きました。六人は「お酒を飲みに行く」と言っていました。二人は「カラオケに行く」と言っていました。最後に「休みはたいてい何をしますか」と聞きました。七人は「疲れているから、家にいる」と言っていました。

　日本の会社員はたくさん仕事をして、ストレスもあります。だから、休みは何もしません。アンケートをして、日本の会社員はとても大変だと思いました。

疲れている（つかれている）	to be tired	次に	secondly
まず	first of all	最後に（さいごに）	lastly
答える（こたえる）	to answer		

1. どうしてウデイさんはアンケートをしましたか。

2. 何人いましたか。

    (a) 仕事のストレスがある。 …… ＿＿＿＿＿人

    (b) よく残業をする。　　　 …… ＿＿＿＿＿人

    (c) ときどき残業をする。 …… ＿＿＿＿＿人

    (d) 仕事の後、お酒を飲む。 …… ＿＿＿＿＿人

    (e) 休みの日は出かけない。 …… ＿＿＿＿＿人

Ⅲ 書く練習

Make a questionnaire and ask several people the questions. Then, write a report based on the result.

第9課 L E S S O N 9

スーさんの日記 Sue's Diary
にっき

087	午 (noon)	▶ご	午前（ごぜん）A.M.　午後（ごご）P.M.; in the afternoon 午前中（ごぜんちゅう）in the morning 正午（しょうご）noon
			(4) ノ ⺒ ニ 午
088	後 (after)	▶ご ▷あと　うし	午後（ごご）P.M.; in the afternoon　〜の後（のあと）after … 後で（あとで）later　後ろ（うしろ）back; behind 最後に（さいごに）lastly
			(9) ノ ク イ 㣚 彳 徉 徉 移 後
089	前 (before)	▶ぜん ▷まえ	前（まえ）before; front　午前（ごぜん）A.M. 名前（なまえ）name 前売り（まえうり）advance sale
			(9) 丶 丷 广 广 芇 甪 前 前 前
090	名 (name)	▶めい ▷な	名前（なまえ）name 有名な（ゆうめいな）famous　名刺（めいし）name card 氏名（しめい）full name　地名（ちめい）place name
			(6) ノ ク タ 夕 名 名
091	白 (white)	▶はく ▷しろ	白い（しろい）white 白紙（はくし）blank sheet　白（しろ）white color 白鳥（はくちょう）swan
			(5) ノ 亻 白 白 白
092	雨 (rain)	▶う ▷あめ	雨（あめ）rain 雨期（うき）rainy season　梅雨（つゆ）rainy season
			(8) 一 厂 冂 币 雨 雨 雨 雨
093	書 (to write)	▶しょ ▷か	書く（かく）to write 辞書（じしょ）dictionary　教科書（きょうかしょ）textbook 図書館（としょかん）library
			(10) 一 ヲ ヲ ヨ 彐 聿 聿 書 書 書
094	友 (friend)	▶ゆう ▷とも	友だち（ともだち）friend 親友（しんゆう）best friend　友人（ゆうじん）friend 友情（ゆうじょう）friendship
			(4) 一 ナ 方 友

095	間	▶かん げん ▷あいだ (between)	時間(じかん) time　二時間(にじかん) two hours 間(あいだ) between　人間(にんげん) human being 一週間(いっしゅうかん) one week
			(12) 丨 冂 冂 冂 冃 門 門 門 間 間 間 間
096	家	▶か ▷いえ (house)	家(いえ) house 家族(かぞく) family　家(うち) house; home 家内(かない) my wife　作家(さっか) author
			(10) 丶 丷 宀 宀 宁 宁 㝉 宇 家 家
097	話	▶わ ▷はな はなし (to speak)	話す(はなす) to speak　話(はなし) talk; story 電話(でんわ) telephone 会話(かいわ) conversation
			(13) 丶 二 三 言 言 言 言 訐 訐 訐 訏 話 話
098	少	▶しょう ▷すこ すく (little)	少し(すこし) little 少ない(すくない) few　少々(しょうしょう) a little 少女(しょうじょ) girl　少年(しょうねん) boy
			(4) 丿 丿 小 少
099	古	▶こ ▷ふる (old)	古い(ふるい) old (for things) 中古(ちゅうこ) secondhand　古代(こだい) ancient times
			(5) 一 十 十 古 古
100	知	▶ち ▷し (to know)	知る(しる) to know 知人(ちじん) acquaintance 知り合い(しりあい) acquaintance
			(8) 丿 ㇏ 느 乍 矢 知 知 知
101	来	▶らい ▷く き こ (to come)	来る(くる) to come　来ます(きます) to come 来ない(こない) not to come 来週(らいしゅう) next week　来日(らいにち) visit to Japan
			(7) 一 ㇐ 冖 平 平 来 来

(▶ indicates the *on-yomi* and ▷ indicates the *kun-yomi*.)

①漢字の練習
かんじ れんしゅう

A. Fill in the blanks with the appropriate kanji.

1. この＿＿＿＿＿いＴシャツは五＿＿＿＿円でした。　｜ 百　白 ｜

2. ＿＿＿＿＿さいケーキを＿＿＿＿し食べました。　｜ 小　少 ｜

3. 一時＿＿＿＿テープを＿＿＿＿きました。　｜ 聞　間 ｜

4. 日本＿＿＿＿を＿＿＿＿します。　｜ 話　語 ｜

B. Choose the most appropriate word for each blank.

1. はじめまして。私の＿＿＿＿＿＿はキムです。　｜ 名前　午前 ｜

2. 毎日たいてい＿＿＿＿＿＿＿七時ごろおきます。　｜ 午後　午前 ｜

3. このかさは古いから、＿＿＿＿＿＿かさをかいます。

｜ 大きい　新しい ｜

4. 今日はいい＿＿＿＿＿だった。でも、あしたは＿＿＿＿＿がふると思う。

｜ 元気　天気　白　雨 ｜

5. メアリーのお父さんを＿＿＿＿＿いますか。　｜ 帰って　知って ｜

②スーさんの日記
にっき

スーさんは日記を書きました。　🔊 Y09-1
にっき

十一月二十五日（土）　雨

　今日は朝から雨がふっていた。午前中は友だちにメールを書い
　　　あさ
て、一時間ぐらい音楽を聞いた。昼ごろメアリーの家へ行った。
　　　　　　　おんがく　　　ひる
白くて、大きい家だった。メアリーのホストファミリーの山本さ
　　　　　　　　　　　　　　　　　　　　　　　　　　やまもと

んに会った。お父さんはせが高くて、やせている人だった。家で
晩ご飯を食べた。お母さんは「何もありませんが」と言っていたが、
たくさんごちそうがあった。晩ご飯はとてもおいしかった。お母
さんは料理がすごく上手だと思う。晩ご飯の後、いろいろな話を
した。そして、きれいな着物をもらった。お母さんは少し古いと
言っていたが、すごくきれいだ。メアリーのホストファミリーは
とてもしんせつで楽しかった。

日記（にっき）	diary	いろいろ（な）	various
午前中（ごぜんちゅう）	in the morning	話をする	to have a talk
昼（ひる）	noon	そして	and then
ホストファミリー	host family	着物（きもの）	kimono; Japanese
ごちそう	excellent food		traditional dress

A. Put the following pictures in the right order according to Sue's diary.

（　　）→（　　）→（　　）→（　　）→（　　）

B. Mark ○ if the following statements are true. Mark × if not true.

1. (　　　) スーさんは古い着物をもらった。
2. (　　　) お父さんはせがひくくて、やせている。
3. (　　　) 晩ご飯は何もなかった。
4. (　　　) スーさんはお母さんの料理が好きだ。
5. (　　　) 天気がよくなかった。
6. (　　　) メアリーさんのホストファミリーの名前は山田だ。

C. スーさんはメアリーさんのホストファミリーにメールを書きました。
Read the following mail. 🔊 Y09-2

山本さま
やまもと

きのうはどうもありがとうございました。
とてもたのしかったです。

りょうではあまり日本のりょうりを食べませんが、
お母さんのりょうりはとてもおいしかったです。
それから、きものをありがとうございました。
とてもきれいなきものですね。

かんこくにもあそびに来てください。
私はソウルのおもしろいところを知っていますから、
あんないします。

スー・キム
sue@genkinihongo.com

りょう	dormitory
あんないする	to show someone around

Ⅲ 書く練習
れんしゅう

A.   What did you do yesterday? Write a journal.

B.   Write a thank-you letter to someone.

Useful Expressions:

いろいろおせわになりました。(Thank you for everything.)

体 に気をつけてください。(Please take care of yourself.)
からだ

お会いできるのを楽しみにしています。(I am looking forward to seeing you.)
　　　　　　　たの

～おめでとう（ございます）。(Congratulations on . . .)

（お）たんじょうびおめでとう。(Happy Birthday)

第10課 | L E S S O N 10
かさじぞう The Folktale *Kasajizo*

102	住 (to live)	▶じゅう ▷す	住む（すむ）to live 住所（じゅうしょ）address 移住する（いじゅうする）to immigrate
			(7) ノ イ イ 仁 伫 住 住
103	正 (right)	▶しょう ▷ただ	お正月（おしょうがつ）New Year 正しい（ただしい）right　正午（しょうご）noon
			(5) 一 丁 下 下 正
104	年 (year)	▶ねん ▷とし	三年生（さんねんせい）third-year student 来年（らいねん）next year　今年（ことし）this year 年（とし）year
			(6) ノ ヒ ヒ 仁 厈 年
105	売 (to sell)	▶ばい ▷う	売る（うる）to sell 売店（ばいてん）stand; stall 自動販売機（じどうはんばいき）vending machine
			(7) 一 十 士 声 声 売 売
106	買 (to buy)	▶ばい ▷か	買う（かう）to buy 買い物（かいもの）shopping　売買（ばいばい）selling and buying
			(12) 丶 冖 冊 冊 四 四 罒 買 買 買 買 買
107	町 (town)	▶ちょう ▷まち	町（まち）town　北山町（きたやまちょう）Kitayama town 町長（ちょうちょう）mayor of a town
			(7) 丨 冂 冊 用 田 田 町
108	長 (long)	▶ちょう ▷なが	長い（ながい）long 長男（ちょうなん）the eldest son 社長（しゃちょう）company president
			(8) 丨 厂 F F 巨 長 長 長
109	道 (way)	▶どう ▷みち	道（みち）way; road 書道（しょどう）calligraphy　柔道（じゅうどう）judo 北海道（ほっかいどう）Hokkaido
			(12) 丶 丷 丷 屵 屵 产 首 首 首 首 道 道

110	雪 (snow)	▶せつ ▷ゆき	雪(ゆき) snow 新雪(しんせつ) new snow　雪だるま(ゆきだるま) snowman
			(11) 一 戸 戸 雨 雨 雪 雪 雪 雪 雪 雪
111	立 (to stand)	▶りつ ▷た	立つ(たつ) to stand 国立大学(こくりつだいがく) national university 私立高校(しりつこうこう) private high school
			(5) ` 一 一 ナ 立 立
112	自 (self)	▶じ	自分(じぶん) oneself 自動車(じどうしゃ) automobile　自転車(じてんしゃ) bicycle 自由(じゆう) freedom
			(6) ` 亻 亣 白 自 自
113	夜 (night)	▶や ▷よる　よ	夜(よる) night 夜中(よなか) middle of night　今夜(こんや) tonight 夜明け(よあけ) dawn
			(8) ` 一 广 广 产 夜 夜 夜
114	朝 (morning)	▶ちょう ▷あさ	朝(あさ) morning　今朝(けさ) this morning 朝食(ちょうしょく) breakfast　毎朝(まいあさ) every morning
			(12) 一 十 十 古 吉 直 車 朝 朝 朝 朝
115	持 (to hold)	▶じ ▷も	持つ(もつ) to hold　持ってくる(もってくる) to bring 所持品(しょじひん) belongings 気持ち(きもち) feeling
			(9) 一 十 オ 扌 扩 扩 拌 持 持

(▶ indicates the *on-yomi* and ▷ indicates the *kun-yomi*.)

Ⅰ 漢字の練習
かんじ　れんしゅう

A. Add strokes to the kanji below and turn them into new kanji from this lesson.

Example: 二 → 立

1. 上 →　　3. 雨 →　　5. 白 →　　7. 貝 →

2. 田 →　　4. 月 →　　6. 土 →　　8. 自 →

B. Write each antonym in kanji.

1. 買う　　⇔ _____　　3. みじかい ⇔ _____

2. すわる　⇔ _____　　4. 夜　　　　⇔ _____

C. Fill in the blanks with the appropriate kanji from the list, and add *hiragana* where necessary.

売　雪　住　買　長　立　持

1. 町で_____をしました。
　　　　shopping

2. かさを_____ていますか。
　　　　have

3. 本屋では本を_____ています。
　や　　　　　　(are) sell(ing)

4. よく_____がふります。
　　　　snow

5. おじいさんの話は_____。
　　　　　　　　　was long

6. アパートに_____でいます。
　　　　live

7. 私の後ろに女の人が_____。
　　　　　　　　　was standing

Ⅱ かさじぞう

A. Answer the following questions.

1. 日本ではお正月に何をすると思いますか。

2. (Picture 1) これはおじぞうさんです。何だと思いますか。

3. (Picture 2) このおじいさんとおばあさんがこの話の主人公 (main characters)
   です。どんな人だと思いますか。どんな生活をしていると思いますか。

写真提供：共同通信社

B. Read the Japanese folktale "かさじぞう" on pp. 338-9. Y10

C. Put the following pictures in the right order.

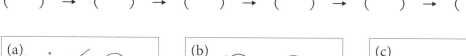

( ) → ( ) → ( ) → ( ) → ( ) → ( )

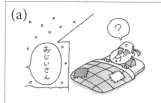

むかしむかし	once upon a time
かさ	bamboo hat
お正月	New Year's
年	year
おもち	rice cake
売る	to sell
かなしい	sad
山道（やまみち）	mountain road
じぞう／おじぞうさん	guardian deity of children
雪	snow
かぶせる	to put (a hat) on a person's head (*person* に *a hat* を)
自分	oneself
とる	to take off
いいこと	good deed
声（こえ）	voice
戸（と）	door
びっくりする	to be surprised
しあわせ（な）	happy

「このかさは古いですが、どうぞ。」と言って、おじいさんはおじぞうさんにかぶせました。

うちに帰って、おじいさんはおばあさんにおじぞうさんの話をしました。

おばあさんは「おじいさん、いいことをしましたね。」と言いました。

その夜おそく、おじいさんはだれかの声を聞きました。

「おじいさん、おじいさん。」

おじいさんは戸を開けて、びっくりしました。六人のおじぞうさんが立っていました。おじぞうさんはお正月のおもちをたくさん持っていました。

お正月の朝になりました。おじいさんとおばあさんはおもちをたくさん食べました。二人はとてもしあわせでした。

D. Mark ○ if the following statements are true. Mark × if not true.

1. （　　）おじいさんとおばあさんはお金持ちだった。
2. （　　）だれもおじいさんのかさを買わなかった。
3. （　　）おじいさんはおじぞうさんにかさを売った。
4. （　　）雪の中でおじいさんはおじぞうさんを六つ見た。
5. （　　）おじいさんは新しいかさを六つ持っていた。
6. （　　）おばあさんはおじいさんの話を聞いて、かなしくなった。
7. （　　）おじぞうさんはお金をたくさん持ってきた。
8. （　　）おじいさんとおばあさんのお正月はとてもよかった。

かさじぞう

むかしむかし、山の中におじいさんとおばあさんが住んでいました。おじいさんとおばあさんはうちでかさを作っていました。あしたはお正月です。新しい年がはじまります。でも、おじいさんとおばあさんはお金（かね）がなかったから、お正月のおもちもありませんでした。二人はかさを売って、おもちを買うつもりでした。

おじいさんはかさを持って、町に売りに行きました。でも、だれもかさを買いませんでした。おじいさんはかなしくなりました。

おじいさんは長い山道を歩いて（ある）帰りました。雪がたくさんふっていました。

「あっ！ おじぞうさんだ！」

雪の中におじぞうさんが六つ立っていました。

おじいさんは「おじぞうさん、さむくないですか。」と聞きました。

おじぞうさんは何も言いませんでした。

「どうぞかさを使って（つか）ください。」

おじいさんはおじぞうさんのあたまの上にかさをかぶせました。

「一つ、二つ、三つ、四つ、五つ。」

かさは五つでした。一人のおじぞうさんはかさがありませんでした。

おじいさんは自分のかさをとりました。

Ⅲ 書く練習（れんしゅう）

Choose one topic from the list below and write what you do/did on these days.

お正月　　クリスマス (Christmas)　　ハロウィーン (Halloween)

誕生日（たんじょうび）(Birthday)　　バレンタインデー (St. Valentaine's Day)

ラマダン (Ramadan)　　ハヌカー (Chanukkah)

ディーワーリー (Diwali)　　Others

第11課 LESSON·······················11

友だち募集 Looking for Friends
ぼ しゅう

#	漢字	読み	語例	筆順
116	手 (hand)	▶しゅ ▷て	手紙(てがみ) letter　歌手(かしゅ) singer 手(て) hand　手話(しゅわ) sign language 上手な(じょうずな) good at	(4) ー 二 三 手
117	紙 (paper)	▶し ▷がみ　かみ	手紙(てがみ) letter 紙(かみ) paper　和紙(わし) Japanese paper 表紙(ひょうし) cover page	(10) ⟨ ⟨ ⟨ ⟨ ⟨ ⟨ ⟨ ⟨ ⟨ 紙
118	好 (favorite; to like)	▶こう ▷す　この	好きな(すきな) to like　大好きな(だいすきな) to love 好意(こうい) good will　好み(このみ) liking; taste 好物(こうぶつ) favorite food	(6) ⟨ 女 女 好 好 好
119	近 (near)	▶きん ▷ちか	近く(ちかく) near; nearby　近所(きんじょ) neighborhood 最近(さいきん) recently 中近東(ちゅうきんとう) the Middle and Near East	(7) ′ ′ ′ 斤 斤 近 近
120	明 (bright)	▶めい ▷あか	明るい(あかるい) cheerful; bright 明日(あした) tomorrow　説明(せつめい) explanation 発明(はつめい) invention　文明(ぶんめい) civilization	(8) ⎮ 冂 日 日 日 明 明 明
121	病 (ill; sick)	▶びょう	病院(びょういん) hospital　病気(びょうき) illness 重病(じゅうびょう) serious illness 急病(きゅうびょう) sudden illness	(10) ′ 亠 广 广 疒 疒 疒 病 病 病
122	院 (institution)	▶いん	病院(びょういん) hospital 大学院(だいがくいん) graduate school 美容院(びよういん) beauty parlor	(10) ′ ⻖ ⻖ ⻖′ ⻖′ 阡 阥 陟 陟 院
123	映 (to reflect)	▶えい ▷うつ	映画(えいが) movie 映画館(えいがかん) movie theater 映る(うつる) to be reflected	(9) ⎮ 冂 日 日 日′ 旳 映 映

124	画	▶が　かく （picture）	映画（えいが）movie 画家（がか）painter　計画（けいかく）plan 漫画（まんが）comic (8) 一 一 一 丙 丙 丙 面 画 画
125	歌	▶か ▷うた （to sing）	歌う（うたう）to sing　歌（うた）song　歌手（かしゅ）singer 国歌（こっか）national anthem　歌舞伎（かぶき）Kabuki 歌詞（かし）lyrics (14) 一 一 一 一 可 可 可 哥 哥 哥 哥 歌 歌 歌
126	市	▶し ▷いち （city）	川口市（かわぐちし）Kawaguchi City 市役所（しやくしょ）city hall　市長（しちょう）mayor 市場（いちば）market (5) ` 一 亠 市 市
127	所	▶じょ　しょ ▷ところ 　どころ （place）	いろいろな所（ところ）various places 近所（きんじょ）neighborhood 台所（だいどころ）kitchen　住所（じゅうしょ）address (8) 一 一 一 戸 戸 所 所 所
128	勉	▶べん ▷つと （to make efforts）	勉強する（べんきょうする）to study 勉める（つとめる）to try hard　勤勉な（きんべんな）diligent (10) ノ ク 午 午 角 角 免 免 勉 勉
129	強	▶きょう　ごう ▷つよ （strong）	勉強する（べんきょうする）to study　強い（つよい）strong 強情な（ごうじょうな）obstinate　強盗（ごうとう）robbery 強力な（きょうりょくな）powerful (11) ` 그 弓 弓 弓 弓 弘 弘 弦 強 強
130	有	▶ゆう ▷あ （to exist）	有名な（ゆうめいな）famous 有料（ゆうりょう）toll; fee　有る（ある）to exist 有能な（ゆうのうな）talented (6) ノ ナ オ 有 有 有
131	旅	▶りょ ▷たび （travel）	旅行（りょこう）travel　旅館（りょかん）Japanese inn 一人旅（ひとりたび）traveling alone　旅券（りょけん）passport (10) ` 亠 亣 方 扩 扩 扩 旅 旅 旅

（ ▶ indicates the *on-yomi* and ▷ indicates the *kun-yomi*.）

Ⅰ 漢字の練習
かんじ れんしゅう

A. Combine the parts below to form the new kanji from this lesson.

B. Put one kanji in each box to make compounds.

(1) 歌 ☐
☐ 紙

(2) ☐ く
所

(3) 有 ☐
前

(4) ☐ 院
気 ☐

Ⅱ 友だち募集
ぼ しゅう

A. 質問に答えてください。(Answer the following questions.)
しつもん こた

1. あなたはインターネットや雑誌で友だちを募集したことがありますか。
ざっし ぼ しゅう

2. 友だちを募集している人にメールや手紙を書いたことがありますか。
ぼ しゅう

B. 「友だち募集」を読みましょう。 Y11-1
ぼ しゅう

友だちになってください

大学三年生です。専攻はフランス文
せんこう
学です。スポーツが大好きで、休み
の日には、テニスをしたり、サッカー
をしたりしています。カラオケにも
よく行きます。今度いっしょに遊び
こん ど あそ
ませんか。

裕子（20歳／女）
ゆう こ はたち

手紙ください！

会社員です。川口市に住んでいます。
アウトドアが好きで、休みの日は車
で近くの山や川に行きます。将来は
しょうらい
外国の山に登りたいと思っていま
のぼ
す。山に登るのが好きな人、手紙く
のぼ
ださい。

松本　明（23歳／男）
まつもと あきら さい

彼女募集！

20歳から25歳ぐらいで、明るくて、やさしくて、たばこを吸わない人。髪が長い人が好きです。ぼくは病院に勤めています。趣味はドライブと映画です。会って、いろいろ話しましょう。

ひろし（26歳／男）

いっしょにバンドをやりませんか

ロックが好きな女の子です。ギターをひくのが好きで、将来は歌手になりたいと思っています。私といっしょにバンドをやりませんか。それからコンサートもいっしょに行きましょう！

香（18歳／女）

〜募集（ぼしゅう）	looking for . . .	彼女（かのじょ）	girlfriend
女（おんな）	woman	明るい	cheerful
アウトドア	outdoor activities	趣味（しゅみ）	hobby
男（おとこ）	man	バンド	band

C. 次の人はだれですか。その人の名前を書いてください。

1. The person who is 18 years old 　　　　（　　　　　　　　）さん

2. The person who is a college student 　　（　　　　　　　　）さん

3. The person who likes movies 　　　　　（　　　　　　　　）さん

4. The person who likes climbing mountains （　　　　　　　　）さん

5. The person who is looking for a girlfriend （　　　　　　　　）さん

D. 質問に答えてください。

1. 裕子さんはどんなスポーツをしますか。

2. 裕子さんの専攻は何ですか。

3. ひろしさんはどんな人が好きですか。

4. 松本さんは車を運転しますか。

5. 香さんは何になりたいと思っていますか。
　　かおり

6. あなたはどの人と友だちになりたいですか。どうしてですか。

E. 「友だち募集」を見て、エバさんは松本さんに手紙を書きました。手紙を読んで、質問に
　　ぼしゅう　　　　　　　　　　　　　　　まつもと　　　　　　　　　　　　　　　　　　しつもん
　　答えてください。 📢 Y11-2
　　こた

松本　明　様
まつもと　あきら　さま
　　はじめまして。「友だち募集」を見ました。私も川口市に住んで
　　　　　　　　　　ぼしゅう
います。近所ですね。私はメキシコ人の留学生です。一月に日本
　　　　　　　　　　　　　　　　　　りゅう
に来ました。今、日本語や日本文化を勉強しています。私もアウ
　　　　　　　　　　　　　ぶんか
トドアが大好きで、山に登ったり、つりをしたりするのが好きです。
　　　　　　　　のぼ
旅行も好きです。外国は、アメリカや韓国に行ったことがあります。
　　　　　　　　　　　　　　かんこく
日本では、まだあまり旅行していませんが、これからいろいろな
所に行くつもりです。古いお寺や神社を見たいと思っています。
　　　　　　　　　　てら　じんじゃ
日本の有名な祭りも見たいです。スポーツはサッカーが好きです。
　　　　　　まつ
日本人の友だちをたくさん作って、日本語でいろいろなことを話
したいと思っています。よかったら、お返事ください。
　　　　　　　　　　　　　　　　　　　　へんじ

　三月二十一日

　　　　　　　　　　　　　　　　　　エバ・フェルナンデス

近所	neighborhood
文化（ぶんか）	culture
これから	from now on
こと	things; matters
お返事（おへんじ）	reply

1. エバさんはいつ日本に来ましたか。

2. エバさんは何をするのが好きですか。

3. エバさんは日本でどこに行きたいと思っていますか。

Ⅲ 書く練習
れんしゅう

A. 「友だち募集」を書きましょう。
ぼ しゅう

B. Ⅱ-B のどの人と友だちになりたいですか。その人に手紙を書きましょう。

第12課 | L E S S O N 12

七夕 Tanabata Festival
たな ばた

132	昔	▷むかし (ancient times)	昔（むかし）old times 昔話（むかしばなし）old tale　大昔（おおむかし）ancient times
			(8) 一 十 サ 出 芒 芒 昔 昔
133	々	 (symbol of repetition of a kanji)	昔々（むかしむかし）once upon a time 人々（ひとびと）people 時々（ときどき）sometimes　色々な（いろいろな）various
			(3) ノ 夂 々
134	神	▶じん しん こう ▷かみ (God)	神さま（かみさま）God　神社（じんじゃ）shrine 神道（しんとう）Shinto religion 神戸市（こうべし）Kobe City
			(9) ` ラ ネ ネ ネ 初 初 神 神
135	早	▶そう ▷はや (early)	早い（はやい）early 早起きする（はやおきする）to get up early 早朝（そうちょう）early morning
			(6) ノ 口 日 日 旦 早
136	起	▶き ▷お (to get up)	起きる（おきる）to get up 起こす（おこす）to wake someone up 起立する（きりつする）to stand up
			(10) 一 十 土 キ キ 走 走 起 起 起
137	牛	▶ぎゅう ▷うし (cow)	牛（うし）cow 牛乳（ぎゅうにゅう）milk　牛肉（ぎゅうにく）beef 子牛（こうし）calf; veal
			(4) ノ ヒ 二 牛
138	使	▶し ▷つか (to use)	使う（つかう）to use 大使（たいし）ambassador　使用中（しようちゅう）"Occupied" お使い（おつかい）errand
			(8) ノ イ イ 仁 仁 佢 使 使
139	働	▶どう ▷はたら ばたら (to work)	働く（はたらく）to work 共働き（ともばたらき）both husband and wife working 労働（ろうどう）labor
			(13) ノ イ イ 仁 仁 佢 佢 佰 佰 俥 俥 働 働

140	連 (to link)	▶れん ▷つ	連れて帰る (つれてかえる) to bring (a person) back 国連 (こくれん) United Nations 連休 (れんきゅう) consecutive holidays
			(10) 一 厂 厂 戸 甪 亘 車 車 連 連
141	別 (to separate)	▶べつ ▷わか	別れる (わかれる) to separate 別に (べつに) not in particular 特別な (とくべつな) special 差別 (さべつ) discrimination 別々に (べつべつに) separately
			(7) 丶 口 口 旦 另 別 別
142	度 (time; degrees)	▶ど	一度 (いちど) once 今度 (こんど) near future 温度 (おんど) temperature 三十度 (さんじゅうど) 30 degrees 態度 (たいど) attitude
			(9) 丶 一 广 广 庐 庐 庐 度 度
143	赤 (red)	▶せき ▷あか	赤 (あか) red color 赤い (あかい) red 赤ちゃん (あかちゃん) baby 赤道 (せきどう) the equator 赤十字 (せきじゅうじ) the Red Cross
			(7) 一 十 土 于 亦 赤 赤
144	青 (blue)	▶せい ▷あお	青 (あお) blue color 青い (あおい) blue 青年 (せいねん) youth 青空 (あおぞら) blue sky 青信号 (あおしんごう) green light
			(8) 一 十 キ 主 丰 青 青 青
145	色 (color)	▶しき　しょく ▷いろ	色 (いろ) color 色々な (いろいろな) various 景色 (けしき) scenery 特色 (とくしょく) characteristic
			(6) 丿 ク 匂 各 各 色

(▶ indicates the *on-yomi* and ▷ indicates the *kun-yomi*.)

① 漢字の練習
かんじ　　れんしゅう

A. Match the reading, kanji, and translation.

Example: むかし	・早・	・ to use
1. はや(い)	・青・	・ cow
2. お(きる)	・昔・	・ to get up
3. つか(う)	・牛・	・ early
4. わか(れる)	・色・	・ color
5. あか	・赤・	・ ancient times
6. あお	・起・	・ to separate
7. いろ	・別・	・ blue
8. うし	・使・	・ red

B. Which new kanji from this lesson include the *katakana* below?

1. マ →　　　2. ネ →　　　3. カ →　　　4. ヌ →

C. Which new kanji from this lesson shares the same component as each pair of kanji below?

Example: 朝　前 → 青

1. 住　仕　　　　2. 道　近　　　　3. 万　旅

② 七夕
たな　ばた

A. 絵 (picture) を見てください。これは何だと思いますか。七夕の日に作ります。
え　　　　　　　　　　　　　　　　　　　　　　　たなばた

B. 七夕の話を読みましょう。 🔊 Y12

七月七日は七夕です。これは七夕の話です。

昔々、天に神さまが住んでいました。娘が一人いて、名前はおりひめでした。おりひめはとてもまじめで、毎日、朝早く起きてはたを織っていました。

ある日、神さまは思いました。「おりひめはもう大人だ。結婚したほうがいいだろう。」

神さまはまじめな男の人を見つけました。天の川の向こうに住んでいる人で、名前はひこぼしでした。ひこぼしは牛を使って、畑で働いていました。

おりひめとひこぼしは結婚しました。二人はとても好きになりました。いつもいっしょにいて、ぜんぜん働きませんでした。神さまは怒りました。でも二人は仕事をしませんでした。

神さまはとても怒って、おりひめを家に連れて帰りました。二人は別れなければいけま

せんでした。おりひめはひこぼしに会いたくて、毎日泣いていました。

神さまは二人がかわいそうだと思って、言いました。

「おりひめ、ひこぼし、あなたたちは一年に一度だけ会ってもいい。それは七月七日の夜だ。おりひめ、あなたはその日、天の川の向こうに行ってもいい。でも、朝までに帰らなければいけない。」

一年に一度、七夕の夜におりひめとひこぼしは会います。二人の願いはかなうのです。

この日、私たちは赤や青などいろいろな色のたんざくに願いを書きます。七夕の日の願いはかなうと人々は言います。ある子供は「いい成績を取りたい」と書きます。ある人は「すてきな人に会いたい」と書きます。あなたは七夕の日にどんな願いを書きますか。

天（てん）	the heavens; the sky	怒る（おこる）	to get angry
神さま	God	連れて帰る	to bring (a person) back
娘（むすめ）	daughter	泣く（なく）	to cry
まじめ（な）	serious; sober; diligent	かわいそう（な）	pitiful
はたを織る（おる）	to weave	一年に一度	once a year
ある〜	one . . .（ある日　one day）	〜までに	by . . .
大人（おとな）	adult	願い（ねがい）	wish
見つける（みつける）	to find	かなう	to be realized
天の川（あまのがわ）	the Milky Way	私たち（わたしたち）	we
向こう（むこう）	the other side; over there	〜など	and so forth
牛	cow	たんざく	strip of fancy paper
畑（はたけ）	farm	人々	people

C. 質問に答えてください。

1. おりひめはどんな人ですか。

2. ひこぼしはどんな人ですか。

3. どうして神さまは怒りましたか。

4. 七月七日におりひめは何をしますか。

5. どうして私たちは七夕の日にたんざくに願いを書きますか。

6. 神さまはやさしい人だと思いますか。どうしてですか。

Ⅲ 書く練習

あなたの願いを五つ書いてください。どうしてその願いを書きましたか。理由 (reason) も書いてください。

巻末
かん　　まつ

Appendix

あいうえお　かきくけこ　さしすせそ　たちつてと　なにぬねの　はひふへほ　まみむめも　やゆよ　らりるれろ　わをん

いちねんせい　一年生　first-year student　会L1
いちねんにいちど　一年に一度　once a year　読L12-II
いちばん　一番　best　会L10
いちばんうしろ　一番後ろ　last car; tail end　会L10(e)
いちばんまえ　一番前　first car; front end　会L10(e)
いつ　when　会L3
いつか　五日　the fifth day of a month　会L4(e)
いっさい　一歳　one year old　会L1(e)
いっしょに　一緒に　together　会L5
いつつ　五つ　five　会L9
いってきます　I'll go and come back.　会G
いってらっしゃい　Please go and come back.　会G
いっぷん　一分　one minute　会L1(e)
いつも　always　読L6-III, 会L8
いぬ　犬　dog　会L4
いま　今　now　会L1
いみ　意味　meaning　会L11(e), 会L12
いもうと（さん）　妹（さん）　younger sister
　　　　　　　　　　　　　　　会L1, 会L7
いらっしゃいませ　Welcome (to our store).　会L2
いりぐち　入口　entrance　会L10(e)
いる　(a person) is in . . . ; stays at . . . [ru]　会L4
いる　to need [u]　会L8
いろ　色　color　会L9
いろいろ（な）　various　読L9-II

ううん　uh-uh; no　会L8
うえ　上　on　会L4
うし　牛　cow　読L12-II
うしろ　後ろ　back　会L4
うそをつく　to tell a lie [u]　会L11
うた　歌　song　会L7
うたう　歌う　to sing [u]　会L7
うち　home; house; my place　会L3
うちゅうひこうし　宇宙飛行士　astronaut　会L11
うみ　海　sea　会L5
うる　売る　to sell [u]　読L10-II
うん　uh-huh; yes　会L8
うんてんする　運転する　to drive [irr.]　会L8
うんどうする　運動する　to do physical exercises
　[irr.]　会L9

えいが　映画　movie　会L3
えいご　英語　English language　会L1

ええ　yes　会L1
えき　駅　station　読L6-I, 会L10
〜えん　〜円　. . . yen　会L2
えんぴつ　鉛筆　pencil　会L2, 会L2(e)

おいしい　delicious　会L2
おうふく　往復　round trip　会L10(e)
おおい　多い　there are many . . .　会L12
おおきい　大きい　large　会L5
オーストラリア　Australia　会L1, 会L11
おかあさん　お母さん　mother　会L1, 会L2
おかえり（なさい）　Welcome home.　会G
おかし　お菓子　snack; sweets　会L11
おかね　お金　money　会L6
おかねもち　お金持ち　rich person　会L10
おきる　起きる　to get up [ru]　会L3
おこる　怒る　to get angry [u]　読L12-II
おさけ　お酒　sake; alcohol　会L3
おじいさん　grandfather; old man　会L7
おしえる　教える　to teach; to instruct [ru]　会L6
おじぞうさん　guardian deity of children　読L10-II
おしょうがつ　お正月　New Year's　読L10-II, 会L11
おしり　buttocks　会L7(e)
おしろ　お城　castle　読L5-II
おそい　遅い　slow; late　会L10
おそく　遅く　(do something) late　読L4-III, 会L6
おそくなる　遅くなる　to be late [u]　会L8
おだいじに　お大事に　Get well soon.　会L12
おちゃ　お茶　green tea　会L3
おてあらい　お手洗い　restroom　会L12
おてら　お寺　temple　会L4
おとうさん　お父さん　father　会L1, 会L2
おとうと（さん）　弟（さん）　younger brother
　　　　　　　　　　　　　　　会L1, 会L7
おとこ　男　man　読L11-II
おとこのこ　男の子　boy　会L11
おとこのひと　男の人　man　会L7
おととい　the day before yesterday　会L4(e)
おととし　the year before last　会L4(e)
おとな　大人　adult　読L12-II
おどる　踊る　to dance [u]　会L9
おなか　stomach　会L7(e), 会L12
おなかがすく　to become hungry [u]　会L11
おにいさん　お兄さん　older brother　会L1, 会L7
おねえさん　お姉さん　older sister　会L1, 会L7

おねがいします（〜を）　. . . , please.　会L2

おばあさん　grandmother; old woman　会L7

おはよう　Good morning.　会G

おはようございます　Good morning. (polite)　会G

おふろ　お風呂　bath　会L6

おふろにはいる　お風呂に入る　to take a bath [u]　会L6

おへんじ　お返事　reply　読L11-II

おべんとう　お弁当　boxed lunch　会L9

おぼえる　覚える　to memorize [ru]　会L9

おまつり　お祭り　festival　会L11

おまんじゅう　sweet bun　読L4-III

おみやげ　お土産　souvenir　会L4

おもう　思う　to think [u]　会L8

おもしろい　面白い　interesting; funny　会L5

おもち　rice cake　読L10-II

おもちゃ　toy　会L11

おやすみ（なさい）　Good night.　会G

およぐ　泳ぐ　to swim [u]　会L5

おりる　降りる　to get off [ru]　会L6

おわる　終わる　(something) ends [u]　会L9

おんがく　音楽　music　会L3

おんせん　温泉　spa; hot spring　会L11

おんな　女　woman　読L11-II

おんなのこ　女の子　girl　会L11

おんなのひと　女の人　woman　会L7

か

〜か〜　or　会L10

〜が　. . . , but　読L5-II, 会L7

カーテン　curtain　会L2(e)

がいこく　外国　foreign country　会L11

かいさつ　改札　gate　会L10(e)

かいしゃ　会社　company　会L7

かいしゃいん　会社員　office worker　会L1, 会L8

かいすうけん　回数券　coupons　会L10(e)

かいだん　階段　stairs　会L10(e)

かいもの　買い物　shopping　会L4

かう　買う　to buy [u]　会L4

かう　飼う　to own (a pet) [u]　会L11

かえす　返す　to return (a thing) [u]　会L6

かえる　帰る　to go back; to return [u]　会L3

かお　顔　face　会L7(e), 会L10

かおがあおい　顔が青い　to look pale　会L9(e)

かがく　科学　science　会L1

かかる　to take (amount of time/money) [u]　会L10

かきとめ　書留　registered mail　会L5(e)

かく　書く　to write [u]　会L4

がくせい　学生　student　会L1

がくわり　学割　student discount　会L10(e)

〜かげつ　〜か月　for . . . months　会L10

かける（めがねを）　to put on (glasses) [ru]　会L7

かさ　bamboo hat　読L10-II

かさ　傘　umbrella　会L2

かし　菓子　snack; sweets　会L11

かしゅ　歌手　singer　会L11

かぜ　風邪　cold　会L12

かぜをひく　風邪をひく　to catch a cold [u]　会L12

かぞく　家族　family　会L7

かた　肩　shoulder　会L7(e)

かたいいいかた　かたい言い方　bookish expression　会L11(e)

かたみち　片道　one way　会L10(e)

かっこ　parenthesis　会L11(e)

かっこいい　good-looking　会L5

がっこう　学校　school　会L3

かど　角　corner　会L6(e)

かなう　to be realized [u]　読L12-II

かなしい　悲しい　sad　読L10-II

かね　金　money　会L6

かねもち　金持ち　rich person　会L10

かのじょ　彼女　girlfriend; she　読L11-II, 会L12

かばん　bag　会L2, 会L2(e)

かぶき　歌舞伎　Kabuki; traditional Japanese theatrical art　会L9

かぶせる　to put (a hat) on a person's head [ru]　読L10-II

かぶる　to put on (a hat) [u]　会L7

かみ　髪　hair　会L7, 会L7(e)

かみさま　神様　God　読L12-II

カメラ　camera　会L8

かようび　火曜日　Tuesday　会L4, 会L4(e)

〜から　because . . .　会L6

〜から　from . . .　読L7-II, 会L9

カラオケ　karaoke　会L8

からだにきをつける　体に気をつける　to take care of oneself [ru]　読L7-II

かりる　借りる　to borrow [ru]　会L6

かれ　彼　boyfriend; he　会L12

かわ　川　river　会L11

かわいい　cute　会L7

かわいそう（な）　pitiful　読L12-II

がんか 眼科 ophthalmologist 会L12(e)

かんこく 韓国 Korea 会L1, 会L2

かんごし 看護師 nurse 会L11

かんじ 漢字 kanji; Chinese character 会L6

かんたん（な） 簡単 easy; simple 会L10

かんぱい 乾杯 Cheers! (a toast) 会L8

き

きいろい 黄色い yellow 会L9(e)

きおん 気温 temperature (weather) 会L12

きく 聞く to ask [u] 会L5

きく 聞く to listen; to hear [u] 会L3

きせつ 季節 season 会L10

きた 北 north 会L6(e)

ギター guitar 会L9

きっさてん 喫茶店 cafe 会L2

きって 切手 postal stamps 会L5, 会L5(e)

きっぷ 切符 ticket 会L5

きっぷうりば 切符売り場 ticket vending area
　　　　　　会L10(e)

きのう 昨日 yesterday 会L4, 会L4(e)

きめる 決める to decide [ru] 会L10

きもの 着物 kimono; Japanese traditional dress
　　　　　　読L9-II

キャンプ camp 会L11

きゅうこう 急行 express 会L10(e)

きゅうさい 九歳 nine years old 会L1(e)

ぎゅうにゅう 牛乳 milk 会L10

きゅうふん 九分 nine minutes 会L1(e)

きょう 今日 today 会L3, 会L4(e)

きょうかしょ 教科書 textbook 会L6

きょうだい 兄弟 brothers and sisters 会L7

きょうみがある 興味がある to be interested (in)
　[u] 会L12

〜ぎょうめ 〜行目 line number . . . 会L11(e)

きょねん 去年 last year 会L4(e), 会L9

きらい（な） 嫌い disgusted with; to dislike 会L5

きる 切る to cut [u] 会L8

きる 着る to put on (clothes above your waist) [ru]
　　　　　　会L7

きれい（な） beautiful; clean 会L5

きんいろ 金色 gold 会L9(e)

ぎんいろ 銀色 silver 会L9(e)

きんえんしゃ 禁煙車 nonsmoking car 会L10(e)

ぎんこう 銀行 bank 会L2

きんじょ 近所 neighborhood 読L11-II

きんちょうする 緊張する to get nervous [irr.]
　　　　　　会L12

きんぱつ 金髪 blonde hair 会L9(e)

きんようび 金曜日 Friday 会L4, 会L4(e)

く

くうき 空気 air 会L8

くがつ 九月 September 会L4(e)

くじ 九時 nine o'clock 会L1(e)

くすり 薬 medicine 会L9

くすりをのむ 薬を飲む to take medicine [u] 会L9

くだけたいいかた くだけた言い方 colloquial
　expression 会L11(e)

ください（〜を） Please give me . . . 会L2

くち 口 mouth 会L7, 会L7(e)

くつ 靴 shoes 会L2

くに 国 country; place of origin 会L7

くび 首 neck 会L7(e)

くもり 曇り cloudy weather 会L12

〜ぐらい about (approximate measurement) 会L4

クラス class 会L4

グリーン green 会L9(e)

くる 来る to come [irr.] 会L3

くるま 車 car 会L7

グレー gray 会L9(e)

クレジットカード credit card 会L10

くろい 黒い black 会L9, 会L9(e)

け

けいざい 経済 economics 会L1, 会L2

けいさつかん 警察官 police officer 会L11

ケーキ cake 会L10

ゲーム game 会L7

けが injury 会L12(e)

げか 外科 surgeon 会L12(e)

けさ 今朝 this morning 会L8

けしゴム 消しゴム eraser 会L2(e)

けす 消す to turn off; to erase [u] 会L6

けっこうです 結構です That would be fine.; That
　wouldn't be necessary. 会L6

けっこんする 結婚する to get married [irr.] 会L7

げつようび 月曜日 Monday 会L4, 会L4(e)

けんかする to have a fight; to quarrel [irr.] 会L11

げんき（な） 元気 healthy; energetic 会L5

げんきがない 元気がない don't look well 会L12

~ご　~後　in . . . time; after . . .　会L10

~ご　~語　. . . language　会L1

こうえん　公園　park　会L4

こうくうびん　航空便　airmail　会L5(e)

こうこう　高校　high school　会L1

こうこうせい　高校生　high school student　会L1

こうせいぶっしつ　抗生物質　antibiotic　会L12(e)

こえ　声　voice　読L10-II

コーヒー　coffee　会L3

ゴールド　gold　会L9(e)

ごがつ　五月　May　会L4(e)

こくさいかんけい　国際関係　international relations　会L1

こくばん　黒板　blackboard　会L2(e), 会L8

ここ　here　会L2

ごご　午後　P.M.　会L1

ここのか　九日　the ninth day of a month　会L4(e)

ここのつ　九つ　nine　会L9

ごさい　五歳　five years old　会L1(e)

ごじ　五時　five o'clock　会L1(e)

ごぜん　午前　A.M.　会L1

ごぜんちゅう　午前中　in the morning　読L9-II

こたえ　答　answer　会L11(e)

こたえる　答える　to answer [ru]　読L8-II

ごちそう　excellent food　読L9-II

ごちそうさま（でした）　Thank you for the meal. (after eating)　会G

こちら　this person (polite)　会L11

こづつみ　小包　parcel　会L5(e)

こと　things; matters　読L11-II

ことし　今年　this year　会L4(e), 会L10

こども　子供　child　会L4

この　this . . .　会L2

このごろ　these days　会L10

ごはん　ご飯　rice; meal　会L4

ごふん　五分　five minutes　会L1(e)

ごめんなさい　I'm sorry.　会L4

これ　this one　会L2

これから　from now on　読L11-II

~ごろ　at about . . .　会L3

こわい　怖い　frightening　会L5

こんがっき　今学期　this semester　会L11

こんげつ　今月　this month　会L4(e), 会L8

コンサート　concert　会L9

こんしゅう　今週　this week　会L4(e), 会L6

こんど　今度　near future　会L9

こんにちは　Good afternoon.　会G

こんばん　今晩　tonight　会L3

こんばんは　Good evening.　会G

コンビニ　convenience store　会L7

コンピューター　computer　会L1, 会L2

サークル　club activity　会L7

サーフィン　surfing　会L5

~さい　~歳　. . . years old　会L1, 会L1(e)

さいごに　最後に　lastly　読L8-II

さいふ　財布　wallet　会L2

さかな　魚　fish　会L2

さくぶん　作文　essay; composition　会L9

さけ　酒　sake; alcohol　会L3

さっか　作家　writer　会L11

サッカー　soccer　会L10

ざっし　雑誌　magazine　会L3

さびしい　寂しい　lonely　会L9

サボる　to cut (classes) [u]　会L11

~さま　~様　Mr./Ms. . . .　読L5-II

さむい　寒い　cold (weather)　会L5

さようなら　Good-bye.　会G

さらいげつ　再来月　the month after next　会L4(e)

さらいしゅう　再来週　the week after next　会L4(e)

さらいねん　再来年　the year after next　会L4(e)

~さん　Mr./Ms. . . .　会L1

さんがつ　三月　March　会L4(e)

ざんぎょう　残業　overtime work　読L8-II

さんさい　三歳　three years old　会L1(e)

さんじ　三時　three o'clock　会L1(e)

さんじっぷん / さんじゅっぷん　三十分　thirty minutes　会L1(e)

ざんねん（ですね）　残念（ですね）　That's too bad.　会L8

さんふじんか　産婦人科　obstetrician and gynecologist　会L12(e)

さんぷん　三分　three minutes　会L1(e)

さんぽする　散歩する　to take a walk [irr.]　会L9

し

~じ　~時　o'clock　会L1

しあい　試合　match; game　会L12

しあわせ（な）　幸せ　happy　読L10-II

じんじゃ　神社　shrine　会L11
しんせつ（な）　親切　kind　会L7
しんぱいする　心配する　to worry [irr.]　会L12
しんぶん　新聞　newspaper　会L2
じんるいがく　人類学　anthropology　会L1

すいようび　水曜日　Wednesday　会L4, 会L4(e)
スウェーデン　Sweden　会L1
スーパー　supermarket　会L4
すき（な）　好き　fond of; to like　会L5
スキー　ski　会L9
すぐ　right away　会L6
すごく　extremely　会L5
すこし　少し　a little　読L7-II
すし　sushi　会L10
すずしい　涼しい　cool (weather)　会L10
すてき（な）　素敵　nice　会L12
すてる　捨てる　to throw away [ru]　会L8
ストレス　stress　読L8-II
スポーツ　sports　会L3
すみません　Excuse me.; I'm sorry.　会G
すむ　住む　to live [u]　会L7
する　to do [irr.]　会L3
すわる　座る　to sit down [u]　会L6

せいかつ　生活　life; living　会L10
せいけいげか　整形外科　orthopedic surgeon
　　　　　　　　　　　　　　会L12(e)
せいじ　政治　politics　会L1, 会L12
せいせき　成績　grade (on a test, etc.)　会L12
せかい　世界　world　会L10
せがたかい　背が高い　tall (stature)　会L7
せがひくい　背が低い　short (stature)　会L7
せき　cough　会L12
せきがでる　せきが出る　to cough [ru]　会L12
せなか　背中　back (body)　会L7(e)
ぜひ　是非　by all means　会L9
せまい　狭い　narrow; not spacious　会L12
せんげつ　先月　last month　会L4(e), 会L9
せんこう　専攻　major　会L1
せんしゅう　先週　last week　会L4, 会L4(e)
せんせい　先生　teacher; Professor . . .　会L1
ぜんぜん + negative　全然　not at all　会L3
せんたくする　洗濯する　to do laundry [irr.]　会L8

せんぱつ　先発　departing first　会L10(e)

そうじする　掃除する　to clean [irr.]　会L8
そうです　That's right.　会L1
そうですか　I see.; Is that so?　会L1
そうですね　That's right.; Let me see.　会L3
そくたつ　速達　special delivery　会L5(e)
そこ　there　会L2
そして　and then　読L9-II, 会L11
その　that . . .　会L2
それ　that one　会L2
それから　and then　会L5

ダイエットする　to go on a diet [irr.]　会L11
たいおんけい　体温計　thermometer　会L12(e)
だいがく　大学　college; university　会L1
だいがくいんせい　大学院生　graduate student　会L1
だいがくせい　大学生　college student　会L1, 会L8
だいきらい（な）　大嫌い　to hate　会L5
だいじょうぶ　大丈夫　It's okay.; Not to worry.;
　　Everything is under control.　会L5
だいすき（な）　大好き　very fond of; to love　会L5
たいてい　usually　会L3
だいとうりょう　大統領　president of a country　会L11
たいへん（な）　大変　tough (situation)　読L5-II, 会L6
たかい　高い　expensive; high　会L2
だから　so; therefore　会L4
たくさん　many; a lot　会L4
～だけ　just . . . ; only . . .　会L11
ただいま　I'm home.　会G
たつ　立つ　to stand up [u]　会L6
たとえば　例えば　for example　会L11(e)
たのしい　楽しい　fun　会L5
たのしみにする（～を）　楽しみにする　to look
　　forward (to) [irr.]　読L7-II
たばこをすう　たばこを吸う　to smoke [u]　会L6
たぶん　多分　probably; maybe　会L12
たべもの　食べ物　food　会L5
たべる　食べる　to eat [ru]　会L3
だれ　who　会L2
たんご　単語　word; vocabulary　会L9
たんざく　strip of fancy paper　読L12-II
たんじょうび　誕生日　birthday　会L5

ちいさい　小さい　small　会L5

ちかく　近く　near; nearby　会L4

ちかてつ　地下鉄　subway　会L10

ちこくする　遅刻する　to be late (for an
appointment) [irr.]　会L11

ちち　父　(my) father　会L7

ちゃ　茶　green tea　会L3

ちゃいろい　茶色い　brown　会L9(e)

ちゅうごく　中国　China　会L1, 会L2

ちゅうしゃ　注射　injection　会L12(e)

ちょっと　a little　会L3

ついたち　一日　the first day of a month　会L4(e)

つかう　使う　to use [u]　会L6

つかれている　疲れている　to be tired　読L8-II

つかれる　疲れる　to get tired [ru]　会L11

つぎ　次　next　会L6

つぎに　次に　secondly　読L8-II

つぎは〜　次は〜　next (stop), ...　会L10(e)

つくえ　机　desk　会L2(e), 会L4

つくる　作る　to make [u]　会L8

つける　to turn on [ru]　会L6

つごうがわるい　都合が悪い　inconvenient; to have
a scheduling conflict　会L12

つとめる　勤める　to work for [ru]　会L7

つまらない　boring　会L5

つめたい　冷たい　cold (things/people)　会L10

つり　fishing　会L11

つれてかえる　連れて帰る　to bring (a person) back
[u]　読L12-II

つれてくる　連れてくる　to bring (a person) [irr.]
　会L6

て　手　hand; arm　会L7(e)

〜で　by (means of transportation); with (a tool)　会L10

Tシャツ　T-shirt　会L2

DVD（ディーブイディー）　DVD　会L7

ていきけん　定期券　commuter's pass　会L10(e)

ていねいないいかた　ていねいな言い方　polite
expression　会L11(e)

デート　date (romantic, not calendar)　会L3

でかける　出かける　to go out [ru]　会L5

てがみ　手紙　letter　会L4

できるだけ　as much as possible　会L12

でぐち　出口　exit　会L10(e)

〜でしょう　probably; ..., right?　会L12

テスト　test　会L5

てつだう　手伝う　to help [u]　会L6

テニス　tennis　会L3

では、おげんきで　では、お元気で　Take care.
　読L5-II

デパート　department store　会L4

てぶくろ　手袋　gloves　会L10

でも　but　会L3

てら　寺　temple　会L4

でる　出る　to appear; to attend; to exit [ru]
　読L6-I; 会L9

テレビ　TV　会L3

てん　天　the heavens; the sky　読L12-II

〜てん　〜点　... points　会L11

てんき　天気　weather　会L5

でんき　電気　electricity　会L2(e); 会L6

てんきよほう　天気予報　weather forecast　会L8

でんしゃ　電車　train　会L6

てんぷら　天ぷら　tempura　会L10

でんわ　電話　telephone　会L1

でんわする　電話する　to call [irr.]　会L8

でんわをかける　電話をかける　to make a phone
call [ru]　会L6

と　戸　door　読L10-II

〜と　together with (a person)　会L4

〜ど　〜度　... degrees (temperature)　会L12

ドア　door　会L2(e)

トイレ　toilet, restroom　会L2

どうして　why　会L4

どうぞ　Please.; Here it is.　会L2

どうですか　How about ...?; How is ...?　会L3

どうも　Thank you.　会L2

どうやって　how; by what means　会L10

とお　十　ten　会L9

とおか　十日　the tenth day of a month　会L4(e)

とき　時　when ...; at the time of ...　会L4

ときどき　時々　sometimes　会L3

とけい　時計　watch; clock　会L2

どこ　where　会L2

とこや　床屋　barber's　会L10

ところ　所　place　会L8
ところで　by the way　会L9
とし　年　year　読L10-II
としょかん　図書館　library　会L2
どちら　which　会L10
とっきゅう　特急　super express　会L10(e)
どっち　which　会L10
とても　very　会L5
となり　隣　next　会L4
どの　which . . .　会L2
どのぐらい　how much; how long　会L10
トマト　tomato　会L8
とまる　泊まる　to stay (at a hotel, etc.) [u]　会L10
ともだち　友だち　friend　会L1
どようび　土曜日　Saturday　会L3; 会L4(e)
ドライブ　drive　会L11
とる　撮る　to take (a picture) [u]　会L4
とる　取る　to take (a class); to get (a grade) [u]
　　　　　　　　　　　　　読L7-II, 会L11
とる　to take off [u]　読L10-II
どれ　which one　会L2
とんかつ　pork cutlet　会L2
どんな　what kind of . . .　会L5

ないか　内科　physician　会L12(e)
なか　中　inside　会L4
ながい　長い　long　会L7
なく　泣く　to cry [u]　読L12-II
なくす　to lose [u]　会L12
なつ　夏　summer　会L8
〜など　and so forth　読L12-II
ななさい　七歳　seven years old　会L1(e)
ななつ　七つ　seven　会L9
ななふん　七分　seven minutes　会L1(e)
なにか　何か　something　会L8
なにも ＋ negative　何も　not . . . anything　会L7
なのか　七日　the seventh day of a month　会L4(e)
なまえ　名前　name　会L1
ならう　習う　to learn [u]　会L11
なる　to become [u]　会L10
なん / なに　何　what　会L1

にかげつまえ　二か月前　two months ago　会L4(e)
にがつ　二月　February　会L4(e)

にぎやか（な）　lively　会L5
にく　肉　meat　会L2
にさい　二歳　two years old　会L1(e)
にさんにち　二三日　for two to three days　会L12
にし　西　west　会L6(e)
にじ　二時　two o'clock　会L1(e)
にじっぷん　二十分　twenty minutes　会L1(e)
にじはん　二時半　half past two　会L1
にしゅうかんまえ　二週間前　two weeks ago
　　　　　　　　　　　　　　　　会L4(e)
にじゅうよっか　二十四日　the twenty-fourth day of
　a month　会L4(e)
にじゅっぷん　二十分　twenty minutes　会L1(e)
にちようび　日曜日　Sunday　会L3, 会L4(e)
〜について　about . . . ; concerning . . .　会L8
にっき　日記　diary　読L9-II
にふん　二分　two minutes　会L1(e)
にほん　日本　Japan　会L1
にほんご　日本語　Japanese language　会L1
にほんじん　日本人　Japanese people　会L1
にもつ　荷物　baggage　会L6
〜にん　〜人　[counter for people]　会L7
にんきがある　人気がある　to be popular [u]　会L9

ねがい　願い　wish　読L12-II
ねこ　猫　cat　会L4
ねつがある　熱がある　to have a fever [u]　会L12
ねむい　眠い　sleepy　会L10
ねる　寝る　to sleep; to go to sleep [ru]　会L3
〜ねん　〜年　. . . years　会L10
〜ねんせい　〜年生　. . . year student　会L1

ノート　notebook　会L2
〜ので　because . . .　会L12
のど　throat　会L12
のどがかわく　のどが渇く　to become thirsty [u]
　　　　　　　　　　　　　　　　会L12
のぼる　登る　to climb [u]　会L11
のみもの　飲み物　drink　会L5
のむ　飲む　to drink [u]　会L3
のりかえ　乗り換え　transfer　会L10(e)
のる　乗る　to ride; to board [u]　会L5

ふつかよい　二日酔い　hangover　会L12

ふとっています　太っています　to be on the heavy side　会L7

ふとる　太る　to gain weight [u]　会L7

ふなびん　船便　surface mail　会L5(e)

ふね　船　ship; boat　会L10

ふゆ　冬　winter　会L8

ふるい　古い　old (thing)　会L5

プレゼント　present　会L12

ふろ　風呂　bath　会L6

ふろにはいる　風呂に入る　to take a bath [u]　会L6

ぶんか　文化　culture　読L11-II

ぶんがく　文学　literature　会L1, 読L7-II

ぶんぽう　文法　grammar　会L11(e)

へ

へた（な）　下手　clumsy; poor at . . .　会L8

べつに＋negative　別に　nothing in particular　会L7

ページ　page　会L6

〜ページ　page number . . .　会L11(e)

へや　部屋　room　会L5

ペン　pen　会L2, 会L2(e)

べんきょうする　勉強する　to study [irr.]　会L3

べんごし　弁護士　lawyer　会L1

へんじ　返事　reply　読L11-II

べんとう　弁当　boxed lunch　会L9

べんり（な）　便利　convenient　会L7

ほ

ほうげん　方言　dialect　会L11(e)

ぼうし　帽子　hat; cap　会L2

〜ほうめん　〜方面　serving . . . areas　会L10(e)

ホーム　platform　会L10(e)

ホームシック　homesickness　会L12

ホームステイ　homestay; living with a local family　会L8

ほかに　anything else　会L11(e)

ぼく　僕　I (used by men)　会L5

ほけん　保険　insurance　会L5(e)

〜ぼしゅう　〜募集　looking for . . .　読L11-II

ホストファミリー　host family　読L9-II, 会L11

ホテル　hotel　会L4

ほん　本　book　会L2, 会L2(e)

ほんとうですか　本当ですか　Really?　会L6

ほんや　本屋　bookstore　会L4

ま

まあまあ　okay; so-so　会L11

〜まい　〜枚　[counter for flat objects]　会L5

まいしゅう　毎週　every week　会L8

マイナス　minus　会L12

まいにち　毎日　every day　会L3

まいばん　毎晩　every night　会L3

まえ　前　front　会L4

まがる　曲がる　to turn (right/left) [u]　会L6(e)

まじめ（な）　serious; sober; diligent　読L12-II

まず　first of all　読L8-II

また　again　読L5-II

まだ＋negative　not . . . yet　会L8

まち　町　town; city　会L4

まつ　待つ　to wait [u]　会L4

まっすぐ　straight　会L6(e), 読L6-I

まつり　祭り　festival　会L11

〜まで　to (a place); as far as (a place); till (a time)　会L5

〜までに　by (time/date)　読L12-II

まど　窓　window　会L2(e), 会L6

まどぐち　窓口　counter　会L5(e)

まる　○ (correct)　会L11(e)

まんがか　漫画家　cartoonist　会L11

まんじゅう　sweet bun　読L4-III

み

みぎ　右　right　会L4

みぎがわ　右側　right side　会L6(e)

みじかい　短い　short (length)　会L7

みず　水　water　会L3

みずいろ　水色　light blue　会L9(e)

みずうみ　湖　lake　会L11

みせ　店　shop; store　読L4-III

みっか　三日　the third day of a month　会L4(e)

みつける　見つける　to find [ru]　読L12-II

みっつ　三つ　three　会L9

みどり　緑　green　会L9(e)

みなさん　皆さん　everyone　読L6-III

みなみ　南　south　会L6(e)

みみ　耳　ear　会L7(e)

みやげ　土産　souvenir　会L4

みる　見る　to see; to look at; to watch [ru]　会L3

みんな　all　読L7-II, 会L9

みんなで　all (of the people) together　会L8

むいか　六日　the sixth day of a month　会L4(e)
むかしむかし　昔々　once upon a time　読L10-II
むこう　向こう　the other side; over there　読L12-II
むずかしい　難しい　difficult　会L5
むすめ　娘　daughter　読L12-II
むっつ　六つ　six　会L9
むね　胸　breast　会L7(e)
むらさき　紫　purple　会L9(e)

め　目　eye　会L7, 会L7(e)
メール　e-mail　会L4
めがね　眼鏡　glasses　会L7
メキシコ　Mexico　読L5-II
メニュー　menu　会L2

もう　already　会L9
もうすぐ　very soon; in a few moments/days　会L12
もくようび　木曜日　Thursday　会L4, 会L4(e)
もしもし　Hello? (used on the phone)　会L7
もち　rice cake　読L10-II
もちろん　of course　会L7
もつ　持つ　to carry; to hold [u]　会L6
もっていく　持っていく　to take (a thing) [u]　会L8
もってくる　持ってくる　to bring (a thing) [irr.]　会L6
もっと　more　会L11
もの　物　thing (concrete object)　会L12
もらう　to get (from somebody) [u]　会L9

やきゅう　野球　baseball　会L10
やきゅうせんしゅ　野球選手　baseball player　会L11
やさい　野菜　vegetable　会L2
やさしい　easy (problem); kind (person)　会L5
やすい　安い　inexpensive; cheap (thing)　会L5
やすみ　休み　holiday; day off; absence　会L5
やすむ　休む　to be absent (from); to rest [u]　会L6
やせています　to be thin　会L7
やせる　to lose weight [ru]　会L7
やっつ　八つ　eight　会L9
やま　山　mountain　読L5-II, 会L11
やまみち　山道　mountain road　読L10-II
やめる　to quit [ru]　会L11

やる　to do; to perform [u]　会L5

ゆうびんきょく　郵便局　post office　会L2
ゆうめい（な）　有名　famous　会L8
ゆうめいじん　有名人　celebrity　会L10
ゆき　雪　snow　読L10-II, 会L12
ゆっくり　slowly; leisurely; unhurriedly　会L6
ゆび　指　finger　会L7(e)
ゆめ　夢　dream　会L11

ようか　八日　the eighth day of a month　会L4(e)
ようじ　用事　business to take care of　会L12
よかったら　if you like　会L7
よく　often; much　会L3
よじ　四時　four o'clock　会L1(e)
よっか　四日　the fourth day of a month　会L4(e)
よっつ　四つ　four　会L9
よむ　読む　to read [u]　会L3
よやく　予約　reservation　会L10
よる　夜　night　読L5-II, 会L6
よろしくおねがいします　よろしくお願いします　Nice to meet you.　会G
よんさい　四歳　four years old　会L1(e)
よんぷん　四分　four minutes　会L1(e)

らいがっき　来学期　next semester　会L10
らいげつ　来月　next month　会L4(e), 会L8
らいしゅう　来週　next week　会L4(e), 会L6
らいねん　来年　next year　会L4(e), 会L6

りゅうがくする　留学する　to study abroad [irr.]　会L11
りゅうがくせい　留学生　international student　会L1
りょう　寮　dormitory　読L9-II
りょうり　料理　cooking; dish　読L6-III
りょうりする　料理する　to cook [irr.]　会L8
りょこう　旅行　travel　会L5
りょこうする　旅行する　to travel [irr.]　会L10
りんご　apple　会L10

ルームメート　roommate　会L11

あいうえお　かきくけこ　さしすせそ　たちつてと　なにぬねの　はひふへほ　まみむめも　やゆよ　らりる**れろ**　**わ**をん

れい　例　example　会L11(e)
れきし　歴史　history　会L1, 会L2
レストラン　restaurant　会L4
れんしゅう　練習　exercise　会L11(e)
れんしゅうする　練習する　to practice [irr.]　会L10
レントゲン　X-ray　会L12(e)

ろくがつ　六月　June　会L4(e)
ろくさい　六歳　six years old　会L1(e)
ろくじ　六時　six o'clock　会L1(e)
ろっぷん　六分　six minutes　会L1(e)

ワイン　wine　読L6-III
わかい　若い　young　会L9
わかる　to understand [u]　会L4
わかれる　別れる　to break up; to separate [ru]　会L12
わすれる　忘れる　to forget; to leave behind [ru]　会L6
わたし　私　I　会L1
わたしたち　私たち　we　読L12-II
わたる　渡る　to cross [u]　会L6(e)
わるい　悪い　bad　会L12

A B C D E F G H I J K L M N O P Q R S T U V W X Y Z

さくいん2　English-Japanese

会……会話・文法編
　　　(Conversation and Grammar section)
読……読み書き編
　　　(Reading and Writing section)
G……あいさつ (Greetings)
(e)……Useful Expressions
I・II・III……問題番号（読み書き編）
　　　(number of exercise in the
　　　Reading and Writing section)
[u] u-verb　[ru] ru-verb　[irr.] irregular verb

---

about (approximate measurement)　～ぐらい　会L4
about . . .　～について　会L8
absence　やすみ　休み　会L5
absent (from)　やすむ　休む [u]　会L6
actor　はいゆう　俳優　会L11
actress　はいゆう/じょゆう　俳優/女優　会L11
adult　おとな　大人　読L12-II
after . . .　～ご　～後　会L10
after (an event)　（～の）あと　（～の）後
　　　　　　　　　　　　　　　読L8-II, 会L11
again　また　読L5-II
air　くうき　空気　会L8
airmail　こうくうびん　航空便　会L5(e)
airplane　ひこうき　飛行機　会L5
alcohol　（お）さけ　（お）酒　会L3
all　みんな　読L7-II, 会L9
all (of the people) together　みんなで　会L8
alone　ひとりで　一人で　会L4
already　もう　会L9
always　いつも　読L6-III, 会L8
A.M.　ごぜん　午前　会L1
and so forth　～など　読L12-II
and then　そして　読L9-II, 会L11
and then　それから　会L5
(get) angry　おこる　怒る [u]　読L12-II
answer　こたえ　答　会L11(e)
answer　こたえる　答える [ru]　読L8-II
anthropology　じんるいがく　人類学　会L1
antibiotic　こうせいぶっしつ　抗生物質　会L12(e)
anything else　ほかに　会L11(e)
apartment　アパート　会L7
appear　でる　出る [ru]　会L9

apple　りんご　会L10
April　しがつ　四月　会L4(e)
arm　て　手　会L7(e)
art museum　びじゅつかん　美術館　会L11
as far as (a place)　～まで　会L5
as much as possible　できるだけ　会L12
Asian studies　アジアけんきゅう　アジア研究　会L1
ask　きく　聞く [u]　会L5
astronaut　うちゅうひこうし　宇宙飛行士　会L11
at about . . .　～ごろ　会L3
at the time of . . .　とき　時　会L4
attend　でる　出る [ru]　会L9
August　はちがつ　八月　会L4(e)
Australia　オーストラリア　会L1, 会L11

back　うしろ　後ろ　会L4
back (body)　せなか　背中　会L7(e)
bad　わるい　悪い　会L12
bag　かばん　会L2, 会L2(e)
baggage　にもつ　荷物　会L6
bamboo hat　かさ　読L10-II
band　バンド　読L11-II
bank　ぎんこう　銀行　会L2
barbecue　バーベキュー　会L8
barber's　とこや　床屋　会L10
baseball　やきゅう　野球　会L10
baseball player　やきゅうせんしゅ　野球選手　会L11
bath　（お）ふろ　（お）風呂　会L6
beautiful　きれい（な）　会L5
beauty parlor　びよういん　美容院　会L10
because . . .　～から　会L6
because . . .　～ので　会L12
become　なる [u]　会L10
beer　ビール　会L11
begin　はじめる　始める [ru]　会L8
(something) begins　はじまる　始まる [u]　会L9
best　いちばん　一番　会L10
between　あいだ　間　会L4
bicycle　じてんしゃ　自転車　会L2
birthday　たんじょうび　誕生日　会L5
black　くろい　黒い　会L9, 会L9(e)
black and white　しろくろ　白黒　会L9(e)
blackboard　こくばん　黒板　会L2(e), 会L8
blonde hair　きんぱつ　金髪　会L9(e)

blue　あおい　青い　会L9, 会L9(e)

board　のる　乗る [u]　会L5

boarding ticket　じょうしゃけん　乗車券　会L10(e)

boat　ふね　船　会L10

book　ほん　本　会L2, 会L2(e)

bookish expression　かたいいいかた　かたい言い方　会L11(e)

bookstore　ほんや　本屋　会L4

boring　つまらない　会L5

borrow　かりる　借りる [ru]　会L6

bound for . . .　～いき　～行き　会L10(e)

boxed lunch　（お）べんとう　（お）弁当　会L9

boy　おとこのこ　男の子　会L11

boyfriend　かれ　彼　会L12

bread　パン　会L4

break up　わかれる　別れる [ru]　会L12

breakfast　あさごはん　朝ご飯　会L3

breast　むね　胸　会L7(e)

bright　あたまがいい　頭がいい　会L7

bring (a person)　つれてくる　連れてくる [irr.]　会L6

bring (a person) back　つれてかえる　連れて帰る [u]　読L12-II

bring (a thing)　もってくる　持ってくる [irr.]　会L6

Britain　イギリス　会L1, 会L2

brothers and sisters　きょうだい　兄弟　会L7

brown　ちゃいろい　茶色い　会L9(e)

Bullet Train　しんかんせん　新幹線　会L10

bus　バス　会L5

bus stop　バスてい　バス停　会L4

business　ビジネス　会L1, 会L2

business to take care of　ようじ　用事　会L12

busy (people/days)　いそがしい　忙しい　会L5

but　でも　会L3

. . ., but　～が　読L5-II, 会L7

buttocks　（お）しり　会L7(e)

buy　かう　買う [u]　会L4

by (means of transportation)　～で　会L10

by (time/date)　～までに　読L12-II

by all means　ぜひ　是非　会L9

by the way　ところで　会L9

by what means　どうやって　会L10

Ⓒ

cafe　きっさてん　喫茶店　会L2

cafeteria　しょくどう　食堂　会L7

cake　ケーキ　会L10

call　でんわする　電話する [irr.]　会L8

camera　カメラ　会L8

camp　キャンプ　会L11

cap　ぼうし　帽子　会L2

car　くるま　車　会L7

Car No. 1　いちごうしゃ　一号車　会L10(e)

carry　もつ　持つ [u]　会L6

cartoonist　まんがか　漫画家　会L11

castle　（お）しろ　（お）城　読L5-II

cat　ねこ　猫　会L4

catch a cold　かぜをひく　風邪をひく [u]　会L12

CD　シーディー　CD　会L6

celebrity　ゆうめいじん　有名人　会L10

chair　いす　会L2(e), 会L4

cheap (thing)　やすい　安い　会L5

cheerful　あかるい　明るい　読L11-II

Cheers! (a toast)　かんぱい　乾杯　会L8

chef　シェフ　読L6-III

child　こども　子供　会L4

China　ちゅうごく　中国　会L1, 会L2

Chinese character　かんじ　漢字　会L6

chopsticks　はし　会L8

city　まち　町　会L4

class　クラス　会L4

class　じゅぎょう　授業　会L11

clean　きれい（な）　会L5

clean　そうじする　掃除する [irr.]　会L8

clever　あたまがいい　頭がいい　会L7

climb　のぼる　登る [u]　会L11

clock　とけい　時計　会L2

close (something)　しめる　閉める [ru]　会L6

clothes　ふく　服　会L12

cloudy weather　くもり　曇り　会L12

club activity　サークル　会L7

clumsy　へた（な）　下手　会L8

coffee　コーヒー　会L3

cold　かぜ　風邪　会L12

cold (things/people)　つめたい　冷たい　会L10

cold (weather)　さむい　寒い　会L5

college　だいがく　大学　会L1

college student　だいがくせい　大学生　会L1, 会L8

colloquial expression　くだけたいいかた　くだけた言い方　会L11(e)

color　いろ　色　会L9

come　くる　来る [irr.]　会L3

coming from　しゅっしん　出身　会L11

commuter's pass　ていきけん　定期券　会L10(e)

company　かいしゃ　会社　会L7

composition　さくぶん　作文　会L9

computer　コンピューター　会L1, 会L2

A B **C D E** F G H I J K L M N O P Q R S T U V W X Y Z

concerning . . . ～について 会L8
concert コンサート 会L9
convenience store コンビニ 会L7
convenient べんり（な） 便利 会L7
cook りょうりする 料理する [irr.] 会L8
cooking りょうり 料理 読L6-III
cool (weather) すずしい 涼しい 会L10
corner かど 角 会L6(e)
correct (○) まる 会L11(e)
cough せき 会L12
cough せきがでる せきが出る [ru] 会L12
counter まどぐち 窓口 会L5(e)
(counter for flat objects) ～まい ～枚 会L5
(counter for people) ～にん ～人 会L7
country くに 国 会L7
coupons かいすうけん 回数券 会L10(e)
cow うし 牛 読L12-II
cram school じゅく 塾 読L7-II
credit card クレジットカード 会L10
cross わたる 渡る [u] 会L6(e)
cry なく 泣く [u] 読L12-II
culture ぶんか 文化 読L11-II
curtain カーテン 会L2(e)
cut きる 切る [u] 会L8
cut (classes) サボる [u] 会L11
cute かわいい 会L7

D

dance おどる 踊る [u] 会L9
date (romantic) デート 会L3
daughter むすめ 娘 読L12-II
day after tomorrow, the あさって 会L4(e), 会L8
day before yesterday, the おととい 会L4(e)
day off やすみ 休み 会L5
deadline しめきり 締め切り 会L11(e)
December じゅうにがつ 十二月 会L4(e)
decide きめる 決める [ru] 会L10
. . . degrees (temperature) ～ど ～度 会L12
delicious おいしい 会L2
dentist しか 歯科 会L12(e)
departing first せんぱつ 先発 会L10(e)
departing second じはつ 次発 会L10(e)
department store デパート 会L4
dermatologist ひふか 皮膚科 会L12(e)
desk つくえ 机 会L2(e), 会L4
dialect ほうげん 方言 会L11(e)
diary にっき 日記 読L9-II
dictionary じしょ 辞書 会L2, 会L2(e)

die しぬ 死ぬ [u] 会L6
difficult むずかしい 難しい 会L5
diligent まじめ（な） 読L12-II
dining commons しょくどう 食堂 会L7
dinner ばんごはん 晩ご飯 会L3
disgusted with きらい（な） 嫌い 会L5
dish りょうり 料理 読L6-III
dislike きらい（な） 嫌い 会L5
do する [irr.] 会L3
do やる [u] 会L5
do laundry せんたくする 洗濯する [irr.] 会L8
do physical exercises うんどうする 運動する
    [irr.] 会L9
doctor いしゃ 医者 会L1, 会L10
dog いぬ 犬 会L4
don't look well げんきがない 元気がない 会L12
door と 戸 読L10-II
door ドア 会L2(e)
dormitory りょう 寮 読L9-II
dream ゆめ 夢 会L11
drink のみもの 飲み物 会L5
drink のむ 飲む [u] 会L3
drive うんてんする 運転する [irr.] 会L8
drive ドライブ 会L11
DVD ディーブイディー DVD 会L7

E

ear みみ 耳 会L7(e)
early はやい 早い 会L3
(do something) early はやく 早く/速く 会L10
east ひがし 東 会L6(e)
easy かんたん（な） 簡単 会L10
easy (problem) やさしい 会L5
eat たべる 食べる [ru] 会L3
economics けいざい 経済 会L1, 会L2
eight やっつ 八つ 会L9
eight minutes はっぷん/はちふん 八分 会L1(e)
eight o'clock はちじ 八時 会L1(e)
eight years old はっさい 八歳 会L1(e)
eighteen minutes じゅうはっぷん/じゅうはちふ
    ん 十八分 会L1(e)
eighth day of a month, the ようか 八日 会L4(e)
electricity でんき 電気 会L2(e), 会L6
eleven minutes じゅういっぷん 十一分 会L1(e)
eleven o'clock じゅういちじ 十一時 会L1(e)
eleven years old じゅういっさい 十一歳 会L1(e)
eleventh day of a month, the じゅういちにち
    十一日 会L4(e)

e-mail　メール　会L4

(something) ends　おわる　終わる [u]　会L9

energetic　げんき（な）　元気　会L5

English (language)　えいご　英語　会L1

ENT doctor　じびか　耳鼻科　会L12(e)

enter　はいる　入る [u]　会L6

entrance　いりぐち　入口　会L10(e)

erase　けす　消す [u]　会L6

eraser　けしゴム　消しゴム　会L2(e)

essay　さくぶん　作文　会L9

every day　まいにち　毎日　会L3

every night　まいばん　毎晩　会L3

every week　まいしゅう　毎週　会L8

everyone　みなさん　皆さん　読L6-III

Everything is under control.　だいじょうぶ　大丈夫　会L5

exam　しけん　試験　会L9

example　れい　例　会L11(e)

excellent food　ごちそう　読L9-II

Excuse me.　すみません　会G

exercise　れんしゅう　練習　会L11(e)

exit　でぐち　出口　会L10(e)

exit　でる　出る [ru]　読L6-I, 会L9

expensive　たかい　高い　会L2

express　きゅうこう　急行　会L10(e)

extremely　すごく　会L5

eye　め　目　会L7, 会L7(e)

=====（F）=====

face　かお　顔　会L7(e), 会L10

fall　あき　秋　会L10

family　かぞく　家族　会L7

famous　ゆうめい（な）　有名　会L8

farm　はたけ　畑　読L12-II

fast　はやい　速い　会L7

(do something) fast　はやく　早く / 速く　会L10

father　おとうさん　お父さん　会L1, 会L2

(my) father　ちち　父　会L7

February　にがつ　二月　会L4(e)

festival　（お）まつり　（お）祭り　会L11

fifteen minutes　じゅうごふん　十五分　会L1(e)

fifth day of a month, the　いつか　五日　会L4(e)

find　みつける　見つける　読L12-II

finger　ゆび　指　会L7(e)

firefighter　しょうぼうし　消防士　会L11

first　ひとつめ　一つ目　会L6(e)

first car　いちばんまえ　一番前　会L10(e)

first day of a month, the　ついたち　一日　会L4(e)

first of all　まず　読L8-II

first-year student　いちねんせい　一年生　会L1

fish　さかな　魚　会L2

fishing　つり　会L11

five　いつつ　五つ　会L9

five minutes　ごふん　五分　会L1(e)

five o'clock　ごじ　五時　会L1(e)

five years old　ごさい　五歳　会L1(e)

flight　びん　便　会L10

flower　はな　花　会L12

fond of　すき（な）　好き　会L5

food　たべもの　食べ物　会L5

foot　あし　足　会L7(e), 会L12

for example　たとえば　例えば　会L11(e)

for . . . months　〜かげつ　〜か月　会L10

for the first time　はじめて　初めて　会L12

for two to three days　にさんにち　二三日　会L12

for . . . weeks　〜しゅうかん　〜週間　会L10

foreign country　がいこく　外国　会L11

forget　わすれる　忘れる [ru]　会L6

four　よっつ　四つ　会L9

four minutes　よんぷん　四分　会L1(e)

four o'clock　よじ　四時　会L1(e)

four years old　よんさい　四歳　会L1(e)

fourteen minutes　じゅうよんぷん　十四分　会L1(e)

fourteenth day of a month, the　じゅうよっか　十四日　会L4(e)

fourth day of a month, the　よっか　四日　会L4(e)

Friday　きんようび　金曜日　会L4, 会L4(e)

friend　ともだち　友だち　会L1

frightening　こわい　怖い　会L5

from . . .　〜から　読L7-II, 会L9

from now on　これから　読L11-II

front　まえ　前　会L4

front end　いちばんまえ　一番前　会L10(e)

fun　たのしい　楽しい　会L5

funny　おもしろい　面白い　会L5

future　しょうらい　将来　会L11

==========

gain weight　ふとる　太る [u]　会L7

game　ゲーム　会L7

game　しあい　試合　会L12

gate　かいさつ　改札　会L10(e)

general admission seat　じゆうせき　自由席　会L10(e)

get (a grade)　とる　取る [u]　会L11

get (from somebody)　もらう [u]　会L9

A B C D E F **G H** I J K L M N O P Q R S T U V W X Y Z

get angry　おこる　怒る [u]　読L12-II
get off　おりる　降りる [ru]　会L6
get to know　しる　知る [u]　会L7
get up　おきる　起きる [ru]　会L3
Get well soon.　おだいじに　お大事に　会L12
girl　おんなのこ　女の子　会L11
girlfriend　かのじょ　彼女　読L11-II, 会L12
glasses　めがね　眼鏡　会L7
gloves　てぶくろ　手袋　会L10
go　いく　行く [u]　会L3
go back　かえる　帰る [u]　会L3
go on a diet　ダイエットする [irr.]　会L11
go out　でかける　出かける [ru]　会L5
go to sleep　ねる　寝る [ru]　会L3
God　かみさま　神様　読L12-II
gold　きんいろ　金色　会L9(e)
gold　ゴールド　会L9(e)
good　いい　会L3
Good afternoon.　こんにちは　会G
good at . . .　じょうず(な)　上手　会L8
good child　いいこ　いい子　会L9
good deed　いいこと　読L10-II
Good evening.　こんばんは　会G
Good morning.　おはよう/おはようございます　会G
Good night.　おやすみ(なさい)　会G
Good-bye.　さようなら　会G
good-looking　かっこいい　会L5
grade (on a test, etc.)　せいせき　成績　会L12
graduate student　だいがくいんせい　大学院生　会L1
grammar　ぶんぽう　文法　会L11(e)
grandfather　おじいさん　会L7
grandmother　おばあさん　会L7
gray　グレー　会L9(e)
gray　はいいろ　灰色　会L9(e)
green　グリーン　会L9(e)
green　みどり　緑　会L9(e)
green tea　(お)ちゃ　(お)茶　会L3
guardian deity of children　じぞう/おじぞうさん
　　　　　　　　　　　　　　　　読L10-II
guitar　ギター　会L9

hair　かみ　髪　会L7, 会L7(e)
half　はん　半　会L1
half past two　にじはん　二時半　会L1
hamburger　ハンバーガー　会L3
hand　て　手　会L7(e)
hangover　ふつかよい　二日酔い　会L12

happy　しあわせ(な)　幸せ　読L10-II
hat　ぼうし　帽子　会L2
hate　だいきらい(な)　大嫌い　会L5
have a fever　ねつがある　熱がある [u]　会L12
have a fight　けんかする [irr.]　会L11
have a lot of free time　ひま(な)　暇　会L5
have a scheduling conflict　つごうがわるい　都
　　合が悪い　会L12
have a talk　はなしをする　話をする [irr.]　読L9-II
he　かれ　彼　会L12
head　あたま　頭　会L7(e)
healthy　げんき(な)　元気　会L5
hear　きく　聞く [u]　会L3
heavens, the　てん　天　読L12-II
Hello? (used on the phone)　もしもし　会L7
help　てつだう　手伝う [u]　会L6
here　ここ　会L2
Here it is.　どうぞ　会L2
high　たかい　高い　会L2
high school　こうこう　高校　会L1
high school student　こうこうせい　高校生　会L1
history　れきし　歴史　会L1, 会L2
hobby　しゅみ　趣味　読L11-II
hold　もつ　持つ [u]　会L6
holiday　やすみ　休み　会L5
home　いえ　家　会L3
home　うち　会L3
homesickness　ホームシック　会L12
homestay　ホームステイ　会L8
homework　しゅくだい　宿題　会L5, 会L11(e)
hospital　びょういん　病院　会L4
host family　ホストファミリー　読L9-II, 会L11
hot (thing)　あつい　熱い　会L5
hot (weather)　あつい　暑い　会L5
hot spring　おんせん　温泉　会L11
hotel　ホテル　会L4
. . . hours　～じかん　～時間　会L4
house　いえ　家　会L3
house　うち　会L3
housewife　しゅふ　主婦　会L1
how　どうやって　会L10
How about . . . ?　どうですか　会L3
How do you do?　はじめまして　会G
How is . . . ?　どうですか　会L3
how long　どのぐらい　会L10
how much　いくら　会L2
how much　どのぐらい　会L10
(become) hungry　おなかがすく [u]　会L11

hurry　いそぐ　急ぐ [u]　会L6
hurt　いたい　痛い　会L12

I　わたし　私　会L1
I (used by men)　ぼく　僕　会L5
I do not know　しりません　知りません　会L7
I know　しっています　知っています　会L7
I see.　そうですか　会L1
ice cream　アイスクリーム　会L3
if that is the case, . . .　じゃあ　会L2
if you like　よかったら　会L7
I'll go and come back.　いってきます　会G
illness　びょうき　病気　会L9, 会L12(e)
I'm home.　ただいま　会G
I'm sorry.　ごめんなさい　会L4
I'm sorry.　すみません　会G
in a few moments/days　もうすぐ　会L12
in the morning　ごぜんちゅう　午前中　読L9-II
in . . . time　〜ご　〜後　会L10
inconvenient　つごうがわるい　都合が悪い　会L12
inexpensive　やすい　安い　会L5
injection　ちゅうしゃ　注射　会L12(e)
injury　けが　会L12(e)
inside　なか　中　会L4
instruct　おしえる　教える [ru]　会L6
insurance　ほけん　保険　会L5(e)
interested (in)　きょうみがある　興味がある [u]　会L12
interesting　おもしろい　面白い　会L5
international relations　こくさいかんけい　国際関
　係　会L1
international student　りゅうがくせい　留学生　会L1
introduce　しょうかいする　紹介する [irr.]　会L11
(a person) is in . . .　いる [ru]　会L4
Is that so?　そうですか　会L1
it has been a long time　ひさしぶり　久しぶり　会L11
Italy　イタリア　読L6-III
It's okay.　だいじょうぶ　大丈夫　会L5

J

January　いちがつ　一月　会L4(e)
Japan　にほん　日本　会L1
Japanese language　にほんご　日本語　会L1
Japanese people　にほんじん　日本人　会L1
Japanese traditional dress　きもの　着物　読L9-II
jeans　ジーンズ　会L2
job　しごと　仕事　会L1, 会L8
journalist　ジャーナリスト　会L11

juice　ジュース　会L12
July　しちがつ　七月　会L4(e)
June　ろくがつ　六月　会L4(e)
just . . .　〜だけ　会L11

K

Kabuki　かぶき　歌舞伎　会L9
kanji　かんじ　漢字　会L6
karaoke　カラオケ　会L8
kimono　きもの　着物　読L9-II
kind　しんせつ（な）　親切　会L7
kind (person)　やさしい　会L5
(get to) know　しる　知る [u]　会L7
Korea　かんこく　韓国　会L1, 会L2

L

lake　みずうみ　湖　会L11
. . . language　〜ご　〜語　会L1
large　おおきい　大きい　会L5
last car　いちばんうしろ　一番後ろ　会L10(e)
last month　せんげつ　先月　会L4(e), 会L9
last train　しゅうでん　終電　会L10(e)
last week　せんしゅう　先週　会L4, 会L4(e)
last year　きょねん　去年　会L4(e), 会L9
lastly　さいごに　最後に　読L8-II
late　おそい　遅い　会L10
(do something) late　おそく　遅く　読L4-III, 会L6
late (for)　おそくなる　遅くなる [u]　会L8
late (for an appointment)　ちこくする　遅刻する
　[irr.]　会L11
later on　あとで　後で　会L6
lawyer　べんごし　弁護士　会L1
learn　ならう　習う [u]　会L11
leave behind　わすれる　忘れる [ru]　会L6
left　ひだり　左　会L4
left side　ひだりがわ　左側　会L6(e)
leg　あし　足　会L7(e), 会L12
leisurely　ゆっくり　会L6
Let me see.　そうですね　会L3
letter　てがみ　手紙　会L4
library　としょかん　図書館　会L2
life　せいかつ　生活　会L10
light blue　みずいろ　水色　会L9(e)
like　すき（な）　好き　会L5
line number . . .　〜ぎょうめ　〜行目　会L11(e)
listen　きく　聞く [u]　会L3
literature　ぶんがく　文学　会L1, 読L7-II
little, a　すこし　少し　読L7-II

little, a　ちょっと　会L3

live　すむ　住む [u]　会L7

lively　にぎやか（な）　会L5

living　せいかつ　生活　会L10

living with a local family　ホームステイ　会L8

local (train)　ふつう　普通　会L10(e)

lonely　さびしい　寂しい　会L9

long　ながい　長い　会L7

look at　みる　見る [ru]　会L3

look forward (to)　（〜を）たのしみにする　楽しみにする [irr.]　読L7-II

look pale　かおがあおい　顔が青い　会L9(e)

looking for . . .　〜ぼしゅう　〜募集　読L11-II

lose　なくす [u]　会L12

lose weight　やせる [ru]　会L7

lot, a　たくさん　会L4

love　だいすき（な）　大好き　会L5

lunch　ひるごはん　昼ご飯　会L3

—Ⓜ—

magazine　ざっし　雑誌　会L3

major　せんこう　専攻　会L1

make　つくる　作る [u]　会L8

make a phone call　でんわをかける　電話をかける [ru]　会L6

man　おとこ　男　読L11-II

man　おとこのひと　男の人　会L7

many　たくさん　会L4

March　さんがつ　三月　会L4(e)

(get) married　けっこんする　結婚する [irr.]　会L7

match　しあい　試合　会L12

matters　こと　読L11-II

May　ごがつ　五月　会L4(e)

maybe　たぶん　多分　会L12

meal　ごはん　ご飯　会L4

mean-spirited　いじわる（な）　意地悪　会L9

meaning　いみ　意味　会L11(e), 会L12

meat　にく　肉　会L2

medicine　くすり　薬　会L9

meet　あう　会う [u]　会L4

memorize　おぼえる　覚える [ru]　会L9

menu　メニュー　会L2

Mexico　メキシコ　読L5-II

milk　ぎゅうにゅう　牛乳　会L10

Milky Way, the　あまのがわ　天の川　読L12-II

minus　マイナス　会L12

Monday　げつようび　月曜日　会L4, 会L4(e)

money　（お）かね　（お）金　会L6

month after next, the　さらいげつ　再来月　会L4(e)

more　もっと　会L11

morning　あさ　朝　会L3

mother　おかあさん　お母さん　会L1, 会L2

(my) mother　はは　母　会L7

mountain　やま　山　読L5-II, 会L11

mountain road　やまみち　山道　読L10-II

mouth　くち　口　会L7, 会L7(e)

movie　えいが　映画　会L3

Mr./Ms. . . .　〜さま　〜様　読L5-II

Mr./Ms. . . .　〜さん　会L1

much　よく　会L3

municipal hospital　しみんびょういん　市民病院　会L6

music　おんがく　音楽　会L3

my place　うち　会L3

—Ⓝ—

name　なまえ　名前　会L1

narrow　せまい　狭い　会L12

near　ちかく　近く　会L4

near future　こんど　今度　会L9

nearby　ちかく　近く　会L4

neck　くび　首　会L7(e)

need　いる [u]　会L8

neighborhood　きんじょ　近所　読L11-II

(get) nervous　きんちょうする　緊張する [irr.]　会L12

new　あたらしい　新しい　会L5

New Year's　（お）しょうがつ　（お）正月　読L10-II, 会L11

newspaper　しんぶん　新聞　会L2

next　つぎ　次　会L6

next　となり　隣　会L4

next (stop), . . .　つぎは〜　次は〜　会L10(e)

next month　らいげつ　来月　会L4(e), 会L8

next semester　らいがっき　来学期　会L10

next week　らいしゅう　来週　会L4(e), 会L6

next year　らいねん　来年　会L4(e), 会L6

nice　すてき（な）　素敵　会L12

Nice to meet you.　よろしくおねがいします　よろしくお願いします　会G

night　よる　夜　読L5-II, 会L6

nine　ここのつ　九つ　会L9

nine minutes　きゅうふん　九分　会L1(e)

nine o'clock　くじ　九時　会L1(e)

nine years old　きゅうさい　九歳　会L1(e)

nineteen minutes　じゅうきゅうふん　十九分　会L1(e)

ninth day of a month, the　ここのか　九日　会L4(e)

no　ううん　会L8

No.　いいえ　会G

nonsmoking car　きんえんしゃ　禁煙車　会L10(e)

noon　ひる　昼　読L9-II

north　きた　北　会L6(e)

nose　はな　鼻　会L7(e)

not . . . anything　なにも＋negative　何も　会L7

not at all　ぜんぜん＋negative　全然　会L3

Not at all.　いいえ　会G

not busy　ひま(な)　暇　会L5

not much　あまり＋negative　会L3

not spacious　せまい　狭い　会L12

Not to worry.　だいじょうぶ　大丈夫　会L5

not . . . yet　まだ＋negative　会L8

notebook　ノート　会L2

nothing in particular　べつに＋negative　別に
　会L7

November　じゅういちがつ　十一月　会L4(e)

now　いま　今　会L1

number　ばんごう　番号　会L1

number . . .　～ばん　～番　会L11(e)

nurse　かんごし　看護師　会L11

===== O =====

obstetrician and gynecologist　さんふじんか
　産婦人科　会L12(e)

occupation　しごと　仕事　会L1, 会L8

o'clock　～じ　～時　会L1

October　じゅうがつ　十月　会L4(e)

of course　もちろん　会L7

office worker　かいしゃいん　会社員　会L1, 会L8

often　よく　会L3

okay　まあまあ　会L11

old (thing)　ふるい　古い　会L5

old man　おじいさん　会L7

old woman　おばあさん　会L7

older brother　おにいさん　お兄さん　会L1, 会L7

older sister　おねえさん　お姉さん　会L1, 会L7

(my) older sister　あね　姉　会L7

on　うえ　上　会L4

on foot　あるいて　歩いて　会L10

(be) on the heavy side　ふとっています　太ってい
　ます　会L7

once a year　いちねんにいちど　一年に一度　読L12-II

once upon a time　むかしむかし　昔々　読L10-II

one　ひとつ　一つ　会L9

one . . .　ある～　読L12-II

one hour　いちじかん　一時間　会L4

one minute　いっぷん　一分　会L1(e)

one o'clock　いちじ　一時　会L1, 会L1(e)

one person　ひとり　一人　会L7

one way　かたみち　片道　会L10(e)

one year old　いっさい　一歳　会L1(e)

oneself　じぶん　自分　読L10-II

only . . .　～だけ　会L11

open (something)　あける　開ける [ru]　会L6

operation　しゅじゅつ　手術　会L12(e)

ophthalmologist　がんか　眼科　会L12(e)

or　～か～　会L10

orthopedic surgeon　せいけいげか　整形外科
　会L12(e)

other side, the　むこう　向こう　読L12-II

otorhinolaryngologist　じびか　耳鼻科　会L12(e)

outdoor activities　アウトドア　読L11-II

over there　あそこ　会L2

over there　むこう　向こう　読L12-II

overtime work　ざんぎょう　残業　読L8-II

own (a pet)　かう　飼う [u]　会L11

===== P =====

page　ページ　会L6

page number . . .　～ページ　会L11(e)

painful　いたい　痛い　会L12

pants　パンツ　会L10

parcel　こづつみ　小包　会L5(e)

parenthesis　かっこ　会L11(e)

park　こうえん　公園　会L4

part-time job　アルバイト　会L4

party　パーティー　会L8

pay　はらう　払う [u]　会L10

pen　ペン　会L2, 会L2(e)

pencil　えんぴつ　鉛筆　会L2, 会L2(e)

people　ひとびと　人々　読L12-II

. . . people　～じん　～人　会L1

perform　やる [u]　会L5

person　ひと　人　会L4

personal computer　パソコン　会L6

photograph　しゃしん　写真　会L4

physician　ないか　内科　会L12(e)

piano　ピアノ　会L9

picture　しゃしん　写真　会L4

pink　ピンク　会L9(e)

pitiful　かわいそう(な)　読L12-II

pizza　ピザ　読L6-III, 会L9

place　ところ　所　会L8

place of origin　くに　国　会L7

A B C D E F G H I J K L M N O **P Q R S** T U V W X Y Z

seven minutes　ななふん　七分　会L1(e)

seven o'clock　しちじ　七時　会L1(e)

seven years old　ななさい　七歳　会L1(e)

seventeen minutes　じゅうななふん　十七分　会L1(e)

seventh day of a month, the　なのか　七日　会L4(e)

she　かのじょ　彼女　会L12

Shinkansen　しんかんせん　新幹線　会L10

ship　ふね　船　会L10

shirt　シャツ　会L10

shoes　くつ　靴　会L2

shop　ばいてん　売店　会L10(e)

shop　みせ　店　読L4-III

shopping　かいもの　買い物　会L4

short (length)　みじかい　短い　会L7

short (stature)　せがひくい　背が低い　会L7

shoulder　かた　肩　会L7(e)

show (someone) around　あんないする　案内する [irr.]　読L9-II

shower　シャワー　会L6

shrine　じんじゃ　神社　会L11

sickness　びょうき　病気　会L9, 会L12(e)

silver　ぎんいろ　銀色　会L9(e)

silver　シルバー　会L9(e)

simple　かんたん（な）　簡単　会L10

sing　うたう　歌う [u]　会L7

singer　かしゅ　歌手　会L11

sit down　すわる　座る [u]　会L6

six　むっつ　六つ　会L9

six minutes　ろっぷん　六分　会L1(e)

six o'clock　ろくじ　六時　会L1(e)

six years old　ろくさい　六歳　会L1(e)

sixteen minutes　じゅうろっぷん　十六分　会L1(e)

sixth day of a month, the　むいか　六日　会L4(e)

ski　スキー　会L9

skillful　じょうず（な）　上手　会L8

sky, the　てん　天　読L12-II

sleep　ねる　寝る [ru]　会L3

sleepy　ねむい　眠い　会L10

slow　おそい　遅い　会L10

slowly　ゆっくり　会L6

small　ちいさい　小さい　会L5

smart　あたまがいい　頭がいい　会L7

smoke　たばこをすう　たばこを吸う [u]　会L6

snack　（お）かし　（お）菓子　会L11

snow　ゆき　雪　読L10-II, 会L12

so　だから　会L4

sober　まじめ（な）　読L12-II

soccer　サッカー　会L10

something　なにか　何か　会L8

sometimes　ときどき　時々　会L3

song　うた　歌　会L7

so-so　まあまあ　会L11

south　みなみ　南　会L6(e)

souvenir　（お）みやげ　（お）土産　会L4

spa　おんせん　温泉　会L11

speak　はなす　話す [u]　会L3

special delivery　そくたつ　速達　会L5(e)

spend time pleasantly　あそぶ　遊ぶ [u]　会L6

sports　スポーツ　会L3

spring　はる　春　会L10

stairs　かいだん　階段　会L10(e)

stand　ばいてん　売店　会L10(e)

stand up　たつ　立つ [u]　会L6

standard Japanese　ひょうじゅんご　標準語　会L11(e)

stare (at)　じろじろみる　じろじろ見る [ru]　会L8

station　えき　駅　読L6-I, 会L10

stay (at a hotel, etc.)　とまる　泊まる [u]　会L10

stays at . . .　いる [ru]　会L4

stomach　おなか　会L7(e), 会L12

store　みせ　店　読L4-III

straight　まっすぐ　会L6(e), 読L6-I

stress　ストレス　読L8-II

strip of fancy paper　たんざく　読L12-II

student　がくせい　学生　会L1

student discount　がくわり　学割　会L10(e)

study　べんきょうする　勉強する [irr.]　会L3

study abroad　りゅうがくする　留学する [irr.]　会L11

subway　ちかてつ　地下鉄　会L10

summer　なつ　夏　会L8

Sunday　にちようび　日曜日　会L3, 会L4(e)

sunny weather　はれ　晴れ　会L12

super express　とっきゅう　特急　会L10(e)

supermarket　スーパー　会L4

surface mail　ふなびん　船便　会L5(e)

surfing　サーフィン　会L5

surgeon　げか　外科　会L12(e)

(be) surprised　びっくりする [irr.]　読L10-II

sushi　すし　会L10

Sweden　スウェーデン　会L1

sweet　あまい　甘い　会L12

sweet bun　（お）まんじゅう　読L4-III

sweets　（お）かし　（お）菓子　会L11

swim　およぐ　泳ぐ [u]　会L5

tail end　いちばんうしろ　一番後ろ　会L10(e)

take (a class)　とる　取る [u]　読L7-II, 会L11

take (a picture)　とる　撮る [u]　会L4

take (a thing)　もっていく　持っていく [u]　会L8

take (amount of time/money)　かかる [u]　会L10

take a bath　（お）ふろにはいる　（お）風呂に入る [u]
　　　　　　会L6

take a shower　シャワーをあびる　シャワーを浴び
　る [ru]　会L6

take a walk　さんぽする　散歩する [irr.]　会L9

Take care.　では、おげんきで　では、お元気で
　　　　　　読L5-II

take care of oneself　からだにきをつける　体に気
　をつける [ru]　読L7-II

take medicine　くすりをのむ　薬を飲む [u]　会L9

take off　とる [u]　読L10-II

talk　はなす　話す [u]　会L3

tall (stature)　せがたかい　背が高い　会L7

teach　おしえる　教える [ru]　会L6

teacher　せんせい　先生　会L1

telephone　でんわ　電話　会L1

tell a lie　うそをつく [u]　会L11

temperature (weather)　きおん　気温　会L12

temple　（お）てら　（お）寺　会L4

tempura　てんぷら　天ぷら　会L10

ten　とお　十　会L9

ten minutes　じゅっぷん／じっぷん　十分　会L1(e)

ten o'clock　じゅうじ　十時　会L1(e)

ten years old　じゅっさい／じっさい　十歳　会L1(e)

tennis　テニス　会L3

tenth day of a month, the　とおか　十日　会L4(e)

test　テスト　会L5

textbook　きょうかしょ　教科書　会L6

Thank you.　ありがとう／ありがとうございます　会G

Thank you.　どうも　会L2

Thank you for the meal. (after eating)　ごちそう
　さま（でした）　会G

Thank you for the meal. (before eating)　いただ
　きます　会G

that . . .　その　会L2

that . . . (over there)　あの　会L2

that one　それ　会L2

that one (over there)　あれ　会L2

That would be fine.　けっこうです　結構です　会L6

That wouldn't be necessary.　けっこうです　結
　構です　会L6

That's right.　そうです　会L1

That's right.　そうですね　会L3

That's too bad.　ざんねん（ですね）　残念（ですね）
　　　　　　会L8

then . . .　じゃあ　会L2

there　そこ　会L2

there are many . . .　おおい　多い　会L12

there is . . .　ある [u]　会L4

therefore　だから　会L4

thermometer　たいおんけい　体温計　会L12(e)

these days　このごろ　会L10

thin　やせています　会L7

thing (concrete object)　もの　物　会L12

things　こと　読L11-II

think　おもう　思う [u]　会L8

third day of a month, the　みっか　三日　会L4(e)

(become) thirsty　のどがかわく　のどが渇く [u]
　　　　　　会L12

thirteen minutes　じゅうさんぷん　十三分　会L1(e)

thirty minutes　さんじゅっぷん／さんじっぷん
　三十分　会L1(e)

this . . .　この　会L2

this month　こんげつ　今月　会L4(e), 会L8

this morning　けさ　今朝　会L8

this one　これ　会L2

this person (polite)　こちら　会L11

this semester　こんがっき　今学期　会L11

this week　こんしゅう　今週　会L4(e), 会L6

this year　ことし　今年　会L4(e), 会L10

three　みっつ　三つ　会L9

three minutes　さんぷん　三分　会L1(e)

three o'clock　さんじ　三時　会L1(e)

three years old　さんさい　三歳　会L1(e)

throat　のど　会L12

throw away　すてる　捨てる [ru]　会L8

Thursday　もくようび　木曜日　会L4, 会L4(e)

ticket　きっぷ　切符　会L5

(boarding) ticket　じょうしゃけん　乗車券　会L10(e)

ticket vending area　きっぷうりば　切符売り場
　　　　　　会L10(e)

till (a time)　～まで　会L5

(be) tired　つかれている　疲れている　読L8-II

(get) tired　つかれる　疲れる [ru]　会L11

to (a place)　～まで　会L5

today　きょう　今日　会L3, 会L4(e)

together　いっしょに　一緒に　会L5

together with (a person)　～と　会L4

toilet　トイレ　会L2

A B C D E F G H I J K L M N O P Q R S T U V **W X Y** Z

with (a tool)　〜で　会L10
woman　おんな　女　読L11-II
woman　おんなのひと　女の人　会L7
word　たんご　単語　会L9
work　しごと　仕事　会L1, 会L8
work　はたらく　働く [u]　会L11
work for　つとめる　勤める [ru]　会L7
world　せかい　世界　会L10
worry　しんぱいする　心配する [irr.]　会L12
write　かく　書く [u]　会L4
writer　さっか　作家　会L11
wrong（✕）　ばつ　会L11(e)

X-ray　レントゲン　会L12(e)

Y

year　とし　年　読L10-II

year after next, the　さらいねん　再来年　会L4(e)
year before last, the　おととし　会L4(e)
. . . year student　〜ねんせい　〜年生　会L1
. . . years　〜ねん　〜年　会L10
. . . years old　〜さい　〜歳　会L1, 会L1(e)
yellow　きいろい　黄色い　会L9(e)
. . . yen　〜えん　〜円　会L2
yes　うん　会L8
yes　ええ　会L1
yes　はい　会L1
yesterday　きのう　昨日　会L4, 会L4(e)
you　あなた　会L4
young　わかい　若い　会L9
younger brother　おとうと（さん）　弟（さん）
　　　　　　　　　　　　　　　　会L1, 会L7
younger sister　いもうと（さん）　妹（さん）
　　　　　　　　　　　　　　　　会L1, 会L7

日本地図
にほんちず

Map of Japan

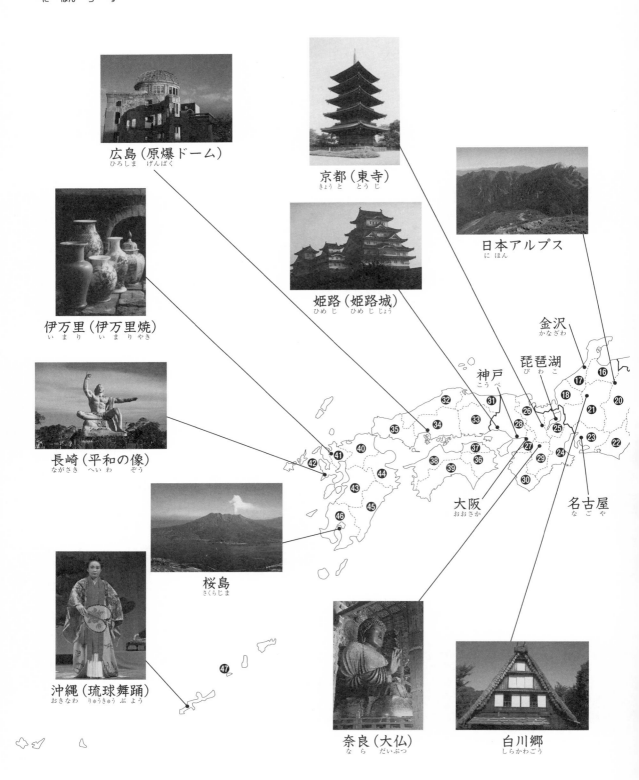

広島（原爆ドーム）
ひろしま　げんばく

京都（東寺）
きょうと　とうじ

日本アルプス
にほん

姫路（姫路城）
ひめじ　ひめじじょう

伊万里（伊万里焼）
いまり　いまりやき

金沢
かなざわ

琵琶湖
びわこ

神戸
こうべ

長崎（平和の像）
ながさき　へいわ　ぞう

大阪
おおさか

名古屋
なごや

桜島
さくらじま

沖縄（琉球舞踊）
おきなわ　りゅうきゅうぶよう

奈良（大仏）
なら　だいぶつ

白川郷
しらかわごう

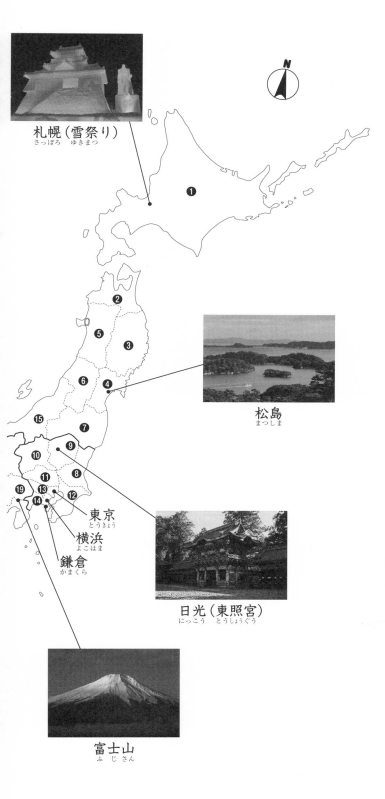

札幌（雪祭り）
さっぽろ　ゆきまつ

松島
まつしま

日光（東照宮）
にっこう　とうしょうぐう

富士山
ふじさん

東京
とうきょう

横浜
よこはま

鎌倉
かまくら

北海道地方
ほっかいどう　ち　ほう
❶ 北海道
　ほっかいどう

東北地方
とうほく　ち　ほう
❷ 青森県
　あおもりけん
❸ 岩手県
　いわ　て　けん
❹ 宮城県
　みや　ぎ　けん
❺ 秋田県
　あき　た　けん
❻ 山形県
　やまがたけん
❼ 福島県
　ふくしまけん

関東地方
かんとう　ち　ほう
❽ 茨城県
　いばら　き　けん
❾ 栃木県
　とち　ぎ　けん
❿ 群馬県
　ぐん　ま　けん
⓫ 埼玉県
　さいたまけん
⓬ 千葉県
　ち　ば　けん
⓭ 東京都
　とうきょう　と
⓮ 神奈川県
　か　な　がわけん

中部地方
ちゅうぶ　ち　ほう
⓯ 新潟県
　にいがたけん
⓰ 富山県
　とやまけん
⓱ 石川県
　いしかわけん
⓲ 福井県
　ふく　い　けん
⓳ 山梨県
　やまなしけん
⓴ 長野県
　なが　の　けん
㉑ 岐阜県
　ぎ　ふ　けん
㉒ 静岡県
　しずおかけん
㉓ 愛知県
　あい　ち　けん

近畿地方
きんき　ち　ほう
㉔ 三重県
　み　え　けん
㉕ 滋賀県
　し　が　けん
㉖ 京都府
　きょう　と　ふ
㉗ 大阪府
　おおさか　ふ
㉘ 兵庫県
　ひょう　ご　けん
㉙ 奈良県
　な　ら　けん
㉚ 和歌山県
　わ　か　やまけん

中国地方
ちゅうごく　ち　ほう
㉛ 鳥取県
　とっとりけん
㉜ 島根県
　しま　ね　けん
㉝ 岡山県
　おかやまけん
㉞ 広島県
　ひろしまけん
㉟ 山口県
　やまぐちけん

四国地方
し　こく　ち　ほう
㊱ 徳島県
　とくしまけん
㊲ 香川県
　か　がわけん
㊳ 愛媛県
　え　ひめけん
㊴ 高知県
　こう　ち　けん

九州地方
きゅうしゅう　ち　ほう
㊵ 福岡県
　ふくおかけん
㊶ 佐賀県
　さ　が　けん
㊷ 長崎県
　ながさきけん
㊸ 熊本県
　くまもとけん
㊹ 大分県
　おおいたけん
㊺ 宮崎県
　みやざきけん
㊻ 鹿児島県
　か　ご　しまけん
㊼ 沖縄県
　おきなわけん

写真提供・協力：東寺／東大寺(撮影：矢野建彦)／奈良市観光協会／伊万里市観光課

数 Numbers
かず

	regular				h→p	h→p/b	p	k
1	いち				いっp	いっp	(いっ)	いっ
2	に							
3	さん				p	b		
4	よん	し	よ	よ	p			
5	ご							
6	ろく				ろっp	ろっp	(ろっ)	ろっ
7	なな	しち	しち					
8	はち				(はっp)	はっp	(はっ)	はっ
9	きゅう	く	く					
10	じゅう				じゅっp じっp	じゅっp じっp	じゅっ じっ	じゅっ じっ
how many	なん				p	b		

regular				h→p	h→p/b	p	k
～ドル *dollars* ～円 えん *yen* ～枚 まい *sheets* ～度 ど *degrees* ～十 じゅう *ten* ～万 まん *ten thousand*	～月 がっ *month*	～時 じ *o'clock* ～時間 じ かん *hours*	～年 ねん *year* ～年間 ねんかん *years* ～人 にん *people*	～分 ふん *minute* ～分間 ふんかん *minutes*	～本 ほん *sticks* ～杯 はい *cups* ～匹 ひき *animals* ～百 ひゃく *hundred*	～ページ *page* ～ポンド *pounds*	～か月 げっ *months* ～課 か *lesson* ～回 かい *times* ～個 こ *small items*

This chart shows how sounds in numbers (1-10) and counters change according to their combination.
1. *Hiragana* indicate the sound changes in numbers, and alphabets show the changes in the initial consonant of counters.
2. ( ) means that the change is optional.
3. An empty box means no sound change occurs.

k→g	s	s→z	t	special vocabulary for numbers			
いっ	いっ	いっ	いっ	ひとつ	ついたち	ひとり	1
				ふたつ	ふつか	ふたり	2
g		z		みっつ	みっか		3
				よっつ	よっか		4
				いつつ	いつか		5
ろっ				むっつ	むいか		6
				ななつ	なのか		7
はっ	はっ	はっ	はっ	やっつ	ようか		8
				ここのつ	ここのか		9
じゅっ じっ	じゅっ じっ	じゅっ じっ	じゅっ じっ	とお	とおか		10
g		z		いくつ			how many
～階 *kai* floor ～軒 *ken* houses	～セント *cents* ～週間 *shūkan* weeks ～冊 *satsu* books ～歳 *sai* years of age	～足 *soku* shoes ～千 *sen* thousand	～通 *tsū* letters ～丁目 *chōme* street address	*small items years of age* cf. はたち (20 years old)	*date* cf. じゅうよっか (14) はつか (20) にじゅうよっか (24) なんにち (how many)	*people* cf. ～人 *nin* (three or more people)	

活用表 Conjugation Chart
かつ よう ひょう

verb types	dictionary forms	long forms (*masu*) (L.3)	*te*-forms (L.6)	short past (L.9)	short present neg. (L.8)	short past neg. (L.9)
irr.	する	します	して	した	しない	しなかった
irr.	くる	きます	きて	きた	こない	こなかった
ru	たべる	～ます	～て	～た	～ない	～なかった
u	かう	～います	～って	～った	～わない	～わなかった
u	まつ	～ちます	～って	～った	～たない	～たなかった
u	とる	～ります	～って	～った	～らない	～らなかった
u	ある	～ります	～って	～った	*ない	*なかった
u	よむ	～みます	～んで	～んだ	～まない	～まなかった
u	あそぶ	～びます	～んで	～んだ	～ばない	～ばなかった
u	しぬ	～にます	～んで	～んだ	～なない	～ななかった
u	かく	～きます	～いて	～いた	～かない	～かなかった
u	いく	～きます	*～って	*～った	～かない	～かなかった
u	いそぐ	～ぎます	～いで	～いだ	～がない	～がなかった
u	はなす	～します	～して	～した	～さない	～さなかった

The forms with * are exceptions.